Knitting With Daisy

By

Ron Craig

ISBN: 0615472850
ISBN-13: 9780615472850

Table of Contents

Introduction

I guess the first question a lot people have is why did you write a book? It actually started out as my mom's book, I was going to help her put all her notes together and see what it looked like, unfortunately that never happened. Also through the years of telling these stories to friends over a drink, co-workers at the water cooler or to total strangers as we killed time on a long airline flight, the consensus has been "you should write a book." I must add this disclaimer, I am not an English Major and other than some minor editing help I did want to keep true to my writing style and voice. Out of respect for other's privacy some names have been changed.

My mom did state in her notes one of her reasons for writing was she wanted her children to know her life story. She had a ton of information jotted down, it was unorganized, but I was able to put the story together. For her younger years I had to rely on her notes for a lot of it although I do recall hearing many of these stories throughout the years. I also want to thank her older brother and only sibling, my Uncle Herb, for sharing his recollections which helped add clarity to those early days. As for her later years, I was able to add a lot to those stories based on being part of them. While I read her notes I realized her life was a story of strength, survival and hope, my wish is I make her as proud of me as I was proud and blessed to have a mother like Daisy.

There are many people who have directly or indirectly motivated and inspired me in many different ways. The main people I want to thank are my loving siblings, brothers Rob, Steve and my sister Michele. I also would like to thank my daily inspiration, my loving wife Carol who has been supportive of just about every crazy idea I have had and there has been a bunch. I love you, Carol. We have two wonderful sons who equally inspire me, Marcus and Lucas, they continue to prove how little I know and how much more I have to learn before I become somewhat knowledgeable of what is really going on in the world today. Boys, I'm trying, I hope I make you proud and I love you both very much.

I would like to thank Charlie Strother for taking my vision for the book cover and creating a beautiful portrait and in addition express thanks his wonderful wife Nan who has been a friend and great motivator during this process. Kudos also goes to my talented nephew John (aka Johnboy) for his technical help not only on this project but for our entire families tech issues throughout the years.

I dedicate this book to my niece Sabrina who inspired me more than I ever realized. Even at such a young age she taught me so much; to be who you are regardless of what others may think, don't be afraid of experiencing something new, if you want to know something ask a question and be sure to dance every day.

Finally, I want to thank the person who showed me a different view of life than I would have experienced because I saw her taking chances her whole life. She was never afraid of anything, if you don't like your current situation or where you are in life just pick up and try something or someplace new. She was a true cavalier spirit who refused to be knocked down by the bad hand that some people thought she may have been dealt. She never saw it that way, she saw it as "some may have it better but some definitely have it worse." I would have never had the guts to put the first word of this book down on paper without my biggest supporter, greatest source of encouragement and someone who thought I could never do any wrong, my beautiful mother, Daisy, thank you, Mom I love you and I miss you more than words can say.

Chapter 1:

Daisy's Early Years

I have to start by telling you it's a miracle that Daisy, my mother, or the rest of us are even here to tell this story. You'll see throughout this book where if several events were to happen just a little differently most of us wouldn't be around. It was evident early and throughout our life God would have his hand on us.

Born to Jewish parents, Frieda and George it all began for Daisy on May 8, 1932 in Vienna, Austria. Being Jewish was not a problem in 1932 but a few years later when this crazy man named Adolf Hitler came into power it became a BIG problem.

The first few years offered a pretty typical upbringing for low to middle class Europeans. Most people lived in an apartment building where several families shared a hall bathroom, although the kids bathed in a metal tub that was kept in the kitchen. Their apartment was right across the street from an army base which fascinated Daisy; she would stare out the window for hours watching the soldiers march. They had very nice neighbors, in time Daisy and her older brother Herb became best friends with the brother and sister down the hall.

By 1938 that close friendship would be tested now that Hitler was in power and the environment became very tense. It got to a point where their friends, who were not Jewish but German, were no longer allowed to play with Daisy and Herb. They did not know how serious things were getting so the neighbor kids would sneak over and play anyway. One day their friend's father came looking for them but Daisy didn't want them to leave so she hid them in the closet. The father became very upset and convinced Daisy the children must come with him. They assumed that would be the last they would see of their friends. Their father forbade them to ever come over again as it was now becoming very dangerous to be a Jew or associate with someone who was Jewish.

A few short days later there was a knock on their apartment door and there stood a young soldier, maybe 17 years old, and he instructed Frieda "get your husband, grab a pail, a brush and follow me." Daisy spoke of seeing the SS on his armband, which means he was a Nazi, he had orders to follow and they were under his command. Daisy and Herb nervously waited all day for their parents to return and finally several hours later they returned dripping wet with sweat, Frieda had blood running down her legs from working on her hands and knees like an animal and was crying in pain. They had just been ordered to scrub the sidewalks because there were Jewish stars on them and the Nazis didn't want them to been seen anymore.

They rounded up all the Jews in the neighborhood, this became a daily ritual until all the sidewalks was clean and had no sign of the Star of David. A few days later they received another knock on their door and to their shock it was Herb's friend from down the hall. This young boy of about 12 years of age was now a soldier and had his SS armband on. They were all very scared wondering what was happening. The young boy said, "As a friend I must tell you that you have to leave here tonight, if you don't you will all be put in a camp by tomorrow." That's all Frieda and George had to hear, as soon as the boy left they began putting on layers of clothes, as much as they could wear. They put on layer upon layer because that's all they would leave with; they were forced to leave their apartment with everything in it. They had just recently bought new furniture before this uprising and now they would have to leave it behind. With the help from some sympathetic German border guards, they crossed the German-French border illegally. With some luck they made it through the woods eventually taking a bus and arriving in Paris, France mid September 1938. Once there they stayed with George's brother Max and his family who preceded them there.

Shortly thereafter the French government did not want Paris flooded with refugees and mandated they relocated to the provinces. This took George, Frieda, Herb and Daisy to Lyon, France. Lyon is situated in the eastern middle of France, about halfway between Paris and Marseille The first place they found to live was not great, they actually had to share a room with another family. It was old and dirty, the roof leaked so badly that Daisy and Herb actually slept with an umbrella over them to keep them dry. Luckily they would not stay there long; in time they found their own room to rent where they at least had some privacy.

Daisy and Herb got checked into school but during this time the Jews were not allowed to work. Luckily for Frieda this would not be a problem, she had a master certificate as a seamstress (the trade equivalent of a Ph.D.). Frieda built up a nice clientele for whom she made custom garments, among them were the Deputy Mayor's wife and other well to do people.

It was great that she was making all this under-the-table cash, the problem was money didn't mean much at that time because everything was rationed. There was not much food to be had, you had to have ration coupons which were very closely watched and not easy to get. This is where Daisy started a lifelong attribute of being a go-getter and a survivor.

She made friends with the girl whose father owned the bakery down the street so she could get bread from them on a daily basis. They had a neighbor, Madame Margeron, who happened to be a big fan of wine. One day Daisy was in Madame's apartment and noticed a big box under her couch. Being a little nosey, Daisy looked in the box and saw it was full of potatoes. Back then, that was like hitting the jackpot. Daisy asked if she could take a couple home for her mom to cook but Madame quickly replied with an emphatic "NO!" Daisy quickly thought if she had some wine to trade Madame's answer might be different.

Always thinking of ways to get ahead, Daisy went home and asked her mother for a bottle of wine to which Frieda responded, "Why do you need a bottle of wine?" She told her about the idea of wine for potatoes so Frieda gave her a bottle that was about a third full but that didn't matter to Daisy, you see the bottles were made of dark glass, she filled the rest of the bottle up with water and it still had a red tint to it. Madame was half drunk all the time and Daisy figured she wouldn't notice.

This worked to perfection as Daisy continued this trading until she had gotten all her potatoes. Now the next venture would be how to get more eggs. You would only get one coupon per person per month, so four people in the house only got four eggs for the month. That would not work for Daisy since she liked eggs too much. So she went down to the market with her coupons for her four eggs, once she had them she would then get back in line. While waiting she would start to cry and as the adults would come up to her to see what was wrong she would tell them she lost her coupons and if she went home without her four eggs she would get the beating of her life. The man who ran the egg stand felt sorry for her and gave her four more eggs. She continued this piece of drama throughout the market at the other egg stands and eventually went home with almost two-dozen eggs. Her mother used to say, "If you want anything just ask Daisy, she'll get it."

Time came when George volunteered for the army to fight against the Germans, that left only Daisy, Herb and Frieda. As the war raged on every night sirens would go off, forcing all the people to run to the shelters realizing they only had a few minutes before the bombs would come. The shelters would close shortly after the sirens sounded and would not open again until the all-clear siren. One time during a run to the shelter Daisy, Herb and Frieda didn't make it in time and were locked out. They ran to try to hide under some stairs and while running Frieda slipped and broke her leg, after the all clear siren they went to the hospital to get Frieda's leg taken care of.

They struggled for a while as Frieda mended her broken leg. After some time had passed and Frieda's leg had healed the most important thing was to find George. He had been off fighting the war and nobody had heard from him in quite some time. They made posters and hung them around town on a type of kiosk or round advertisement stands.

They were having no luck in finding him; they even called the Red Cross to no avail. Then one day Frieda ran into a friend who said he had heard someone say they saw George in Marseilles, as soon as she got home she told Daisy and Herb they were going on a train ride to find their father. Frieda knew this would be very dangerous for her and the children but she was desperate to be reunited with her loving husband.

They didn't have any trouble getting train tickets because they were in the north of France which was considered "non-occupied" and the Nazis were invading the south which was "occupied". A couple days into their journey another train was stopped at a station and someone threw a loaf of bread into their train, one of the passengers yelled that the Nazis were coming and they didn't want them to get their bread. Luckily their train took off before they got there but about an hour later the train stopped and everyone was told to get off the train. They heard the Nazis were only a few kilometers away so everybody ran for their life. I remember my mom telling me how horrified she was, seeing all the people running, luggage left right there in the middle of the road. She told me it was a haunting memory that never left her; it was the first time she really feared for her life.

They ran until they got to a bridge where they stopped for a moment to catch their breath. At that time they all had to wear gas masks which Daisy hated, they had that cheap rubber smell. She decided this was a good time to get rid of it and tossed it into the river while nobody was looking. A few moments later a young boy came up to her and handed her the mask stating "I guess you dropped this in the river and I just wanted to get it back to you." She thanked him and although she didn't want that thing around her neck anymore she did put it back on.

Now they needed to find a place to stay and hide until the Nazis cleared out. They went knocking on doors offering money, luckily Frieda still had plenty of cash from her sewing jobs. They finally found a French woman willing to let them hide in her basement, it would be costly but worth it. She took them down to a small hidden bathroom in the basement and let them stay there for what Daisy said seemed like an eternity but was about a week. Herb was the tallest so he got to sleep in the bathtub, Frieda and Daisy slept on the floor. The lady would slip food into a crack in the wall because she had the door barricaded to make it look like it was not useable.

The French woman came down one morning and told them the Nazis had knocked on her door the previous day looking for

Jews, she convinced them she had not seen anybody in weeks. She told them the Nazis finally left and they should be far enough away for them to leave. With that information they went back and caught the train heading south toward Marseille with hope of finding George. After a couple of days on the train they were stopped by French soldiers and all the Jews were transported to a camp supervised by the French army. They knew in time the Nazis would be coming and the French wanted to keep them out of harm's way. They were put in barracks with double deck beds made of straw and hay, the soldiers took all their papers (ID) and without that you could not travel anywhere.

They were able to go outside the camp but had to be back when the gates closed at 8:00 PM sharp. After being in the camp for a few weeks they walked to the railroad to check if the trains were running again. Daisy was not sure what Frieda was thinking because without their papers she knew they could not leave. When they saw the trains were indeed running Frieda told them they were going to catch the train in the morning.

Sure enough they headed to the train the next day and snuck on without the conductor seeing them. Every time the conductor would come to collect the tickets they would all go hide in the bathroom until he went to the next train. They would keep doing this until they eventually made it to Marseille.

When they finally got there they began looking for George but could not find him anywhere. They ran into someone they knew and were told George caught a train back to Lyon to find them. This forced them to go sneaking back onto the train hoping to catch George in Lyon, after a few days of the same hiding routine they finally arrived. While walking around the train station to see if anyone had seen or heard from George, Frieda remembered what George always told her, if she was ever lost in a crowd to whistle a certain song and he would be able to find her. After some time, looking around the station she began her whistling and in a few short moments who comes walking up, Papa, as they called him. It was a great reunion full of hugs and kisses, it was obvious that all the time, effort and risk to find George were well worth it.

They went back to their apartment in Lyon and things went back to normal for a while with Frieda doing her sewing, Daisy and Herb back in school and George working at the market for bread, butter and other foods. George would take some of the excess food and give it to some of the neighbors who were in need. Unfortunately I don't remember my grandfather but from what my mom had told me he was a very caring, giving and special man.

One of the men George had helped knocked on the door and told him about this guide he heard about. The guide could help them get to Switzerland, which meant freedom. It would cost a bunch of money if they were interested, George told him to arrange the meeting. During this meeting George liked what he heard and gave the guide some money to start the process.

The next part of the story is something that makes me think of that fine line between life and death. Before they began the journey they took Daisy to a convent to be looked over by the nuns. She was treated great there as Frieda and George put their escape plan together. Herb was old enough that he did not require supervision and was actually helping with the details. Daisy was told they would come for her soon and within a couple of days they brought her to a French woman. She was instructed to take Daisy on the train and meet up with Frieda, George and Herb a day or two later at a hotel. They did not want Daisy to be involved with the first part of the journey due to the danger it involved.

To meet back up with Daisy they had to be transported in the back of a furniture truck. George, Frieda, Herb and 14 others hid in the front section of the truck, the rest of the truck, separated by a fake partition, was packed with furniture so if they were stopped by the Nazis they would only see the furniture. Sure enough the truck was stopped and the Nazis opened the back door and saw nothing but furniture, instead of just closing the door they took swords and poked them through the canvas in the front of the truck narrowly missing anybody in the truck.

They eventually made it to the hotel but the Nazis were patrolling there as well. Through the guide George had everyone paid off, including the hotel manager, who hid them on the roof of the hotel until the Nazis cleared out. They met up with the French woman who was taking care of Daisy and now the four of them were once again reunited. The plan from there was they would all meet in a café and get further instructions on their escape. They were told they could not carry suitcases or bags, nothing extra, everything must be on their person. So they started emptying their suitcases and putting on layers of clothes, sweater on top of sweater, pants on top of pants, multiple layers of skirts and underwear as well. I've heard the saying "I have nothing but the clothes on my back." That's exactly what they had and nothing more.

They were told where to meet the following morning and there would be two buses waiting to pick them up, a couple of families on each bus. As they reached their meeting place early the next morning they loaded up the two buses and took off in opposite directions only to meet up again at the next stop. After driving for a few hours the bus stopped in what seemed like the middle of nowhere, they were told this was where they stop and were instructed to wait for the families from the other bus. They waited for a while but the other bus did not show up. So the two families began walking down a desolate road on a cool fall day and after walking for a while they heard a voice from the woods. They saw a man walking out toward them wearing a French beret so they knew he was friendly. He told them he was their next guide and to follow him quietly to the next point. When they inquired about the other bus he told them he heard the Nazis stopped them, the other families would not be joining them, they were executed.

The two families walked closely behind him until reaching an old abandoned wagon. He told them to wait there as he would go ahead and make sure the coast was clear. He had to wait for the Nazis to make their rounds and then they would be able to continue. After a couple of hours the guide came back and lead them a little while longer to a farm house where the guide had arranged some food and water for them. They all ate and then they rested for a while until it was time to go again. It was late at night, the guide went out first to chase all the cows and at that moment he told them to quickly run out into the field. The noise from the cows and their cowbells ringing would muffle the sound of them running over the dried leaves on the ground. Luckily it was a full moon so it was easy to follow the path. After walking for a few hours the guide said "This is as far as I go." George was furious as the guide was paid very well, the deal was to get them to the Swiss border and if they died he would die with them. After arguing a bit he agreed to lead a little while longer. After walking about another hour the guide stopped again and said, "This is it, I'm done, you just need to go straight ahead and you will hit the border." Nobody argued this time as they felt like they were close to Switzerland. The guide slipped off back into the woods and the two families proceeded on their own.

As they walked they saw a light up ahead that was getting closer and closer. They decided not to take a chance so they all walked down into the creek beside the road. This was not fun for Daisy, tracking through this mucky water, which was made more difficult with their multi-layer of clothes and fear of who knows what type of creatures were floating in there. As they continued in the creek for a little while, the light eventually went away and then they made their way back onto the road. They felt they should be hitting the border by now according to what the guide had said but saw nothing.

They continued straight ahead as the guide instructed them to until they hit a fork in the road, this was not what they wanted to see. The other family immediately said they are going left. George stated emphatically, "I'm not a communist I'm going right." Well that's when they parted ways. It was now just George, Frieda, Herb and Daisy walking in the light of the moon for a good while until they heard a man's voice, "Who goes there?" From what my mom told me that about put them all into cardiac arrest. It was a soldier with a gun, again with a loud voice, "Are there any more people with you?" They didn't know if he was a Nazi, French or Swiss, he did speak in French so that put them at ease for a moment. George told them it was just the four of them and the soldier said words that would change the history of our family, "WELCOME TO SWITZERLAND!"

Always worrying about other people George asked if another family had hit the border before them. The soldier said he had not seen anybody else for days, when George told them the direction they were heading he said "Unfortunately that would have taken them directly back into one of the Nazi camps and they were surely dead."

Chapter 2:

Freedom

The four of them arrived in Geneva, Switzerland September 9, 1942 and were taken to a house where it was nice and warm; they were fed and were allowed to clean up. After that they were shuttled by bus to another location where they took all their money, jewelry and anything of value. They were told it would be given back but they could not carry it around at this time. Anybody that knows their history also knows none of Jews got their valuables back. (As a side note, nearly 65 years later, through a herculean effort from my Uncle Herb, the family actually received a small amount of money back from the Swiss Government.) They weren't allowed to work in Switzerland, there were very few jobs and they wanted all the Swiss to get the jobs not foreigners. For the next three years George was able to find work at an orphanage where they gave him just enough money for food which was their main expense as the refugees lived for free during this time. Frieda also made some money as she began sewing again for locals while Daisy and Herb went to school in Geneva.

After a while the Swiss government decided to put all the refugees in camps and no longer allow them to live for free. George and Frieda did not want their kids living in camps so they found two families to take in Daisy and Herb. Daisy went to live with a single lady named Ms. Levy; she was very nice and took good care of her. Herb went to live with a family named the Millsteins, they owned a men's clothing shop and also took very good care of Herb.

Daisy and Herb would see their parents on weekends but then things would change. George and Frieda heard there was a chance they could be sent to a camp, as soon as they heard that was a possibility they decided to get the kids go to where many Jews were going and that was Palestine which would later become Israel. In order to get there they would have to make their way about 800 kilometers to Barcelona Spain where they boarded a small crowded freightliner which included livestock on the aft deck. That began a long indirect journey on some very rough seas that included stops in Algier, Malta and Naples before finally reaching Haifa, Palestine.

After having to spend several weeks in a camp before determining they were legal immigrants they contacted a cousin of Frieda and stayed with her for a while until they found another place to stay. Rooms were tough to come by, it was now 1945 and Palestine was under British rule. They eventually found a room in a four-bedroom apartment to be shared by three other families. They had one of the bedrooms and shared the kitchen and bathroom with the other three families.

Daisy was approaching her 13th birthday and wanted to pursue her passion of becoming a hairdresser so she went to work as an apprentice at a local beauty shop. She worked from 8:00 a.m. to 12:00 p.m., went home for an hour lunch and then worked from 1:00 p.m. until 7:00 p.m. She would have dinner and then go to night school from 8:00 p.m. to 10:00 p.m., Sunday through Friday, no school or work on Saturdays. George was working as a chef, Frieda did her sewing and Herb worked at a bakery.

Daisy had some interesting experiences as a hairdresser. She worked for a big tough Russian lady named Mrs. Stengel. For the first couple of months she would only let Daisy clean up around the shop, make soap and other chores. Then one day Mrs. Stengel left telling Daisy she would be back soon. No sooner does she leave that a woman comes in for a haircut. Daisy was nervous but figured how tough could it be to cut her hair, she had watched for a while now so she gave it a try. As soon as the lady sat down she took off her wig and had short hair underneath. Daisy didn't know what to do now, did she want the wig styled or her real hair cut. Back then the real religious Jews all had to wear wigs and had their own hair cut very short. After getting over the shock of this lady pulling off the wig she went ahead and starting cutting the woman's hair.

As she started to cut the lady's hair the lady asked for it to be cut very short. As Daisy starts cutting it, one side then the other and after cutting for a while she realizes her scissors are stuck and won't cut through the lady's hair. The real problem was she was trying to cut through her ear lobe and as she pulled her scissors away the blood began gushing out. The crazy part of it is the lady never moved or said a word. As Daisy tried to stop the blood with a towel Mrs. Stengel returned and used one of those septic sticks to stop the bleeding and had to finish the cut as Daisy was way too upset to continue. The lady got up paid full price and left without saying a word. Mrs. Stengel assured Daisy it was fine, part of the business was having apprentice cut hair and mishaps just went along with the territory, customers had no say in the matter. Being so young Daisy just didn't understand.

The next episode would involve giving a customer a permanent wave. The machine she used was this large contraption with long electric cords hanging down with clamps and silver papers on the end. Mrs. Stengel started the perm and asked Daisy to check on her to see how it was coming along. When she took one of the clamps off she noticed there was no hair there and told

Mrs. Stengel. After a puzzled look, Mrs. Stengel came over to check herself and took another clamp off and saw there was no hair there either. It turns out the clamps were on too long and burned off the lady's hair. She walked out unfazed, totally calm and totally bald, quite the start to Daisy's hairdressing career.

The British had an 8:00 PM curfew which was strictly enforced; if you were caught on the street you could be shot. All the stores would be robbed at night and nothing was being done, in that environment Daisy could no longer go to night school. George and Frieda had wanted to go to the United States for a long time and now was the time to make it happen. George's oldest brother, Sigi (pronounced Ziggi but his real name was Siegfried) came to the U.S. in 1936 and lived in New York. George asked Sigi to get visas set up for them. The U.S. sponsor had to submit a record of earnings and assets to the State Department with which to guarantee the U.S. government that the sponsored new immigrants would not become a burden to the States for five years. The five year limit assumed in that time period the immigrant would be integrated into society, become a citizen and earn a living.

Sigi's financials were not a problem, when he first arrived in the States he worked with at his brother's very successful furrier business and shared the profits. Just a couple years later his brother became seriously ill and passed away leaving the business to him.

Sigi originally left Austria in 1939 for the U.S. to continue his pursuit of being a doctor as he did in Austria. When he found out he would have to go back to school and start over as well as learn to speak English he decided against it. His furrier business was very successful but also involved 12 to 14 hour work days and a six to seven day work.

Frieda was born in London and she was allowed in the U.S. on an English quota which was around 65,000 per year and very underutilized. Daisy and Herb being under 21 they were allowed in with her under her visa. That was good news, the bad news was they had a problem with George, he was Austrian born and that quota was closed. It was a tough decision but they would have to come to the U.S. without George, they would need to wait for one of them to become a citizen, this would allow them to bring George over.

Chapter 3:

Welcome To The United States

They made their arrangements for the big trip, it was now time for Frieda, Herb and Daisy to say their very difficult and tearful goodbyes to George. There were many hugs and kisses as they were hopeful a reunion would happen soon but there were no guarantees.

They took a ship to the U.S., a U.S. Army ship named The SS Marine Carp, it would be a three week journey by sea. During that time things got worse in Israel and George decided it was time to leave. He went back to live in Paris and wait for his chance to rejoin his family in the U.S.

It was December 1, 1947 and the ship was arriving in New York, my mom said it was one of the most thrilling days of her life. The emotions she was feeling as they passed the Statue of Liberty and what that meant to her, freedom at last. No more war, no more hiding, no more running, pure freedom. We have all heard many stories of immigrants saying the same thing as they saw the Statue of Liberty. To really think about what it must have felt like, something most of us couldn't even imagine. This is something my generation takes for granted, our freedom. No matter how many years went by my mom's face always had a special glow when she told that story. My praise and gratitude goes out to all our brave men and woman of the U.S. Armed Forces who continue to fight to preserve that same freedom for me and my family.

Sigi picked them up and drove them to his apartment in Manhattan, they all marveled at the huge buildings and the wonderful scenery. He lived in a beautiful building at 89th Street and Broadway. When they walked in the apartment it was like a palace compared to where they had been living the last several years, they had a doorman and even a man to run the elevator.

For Daisy, Herb and Frieda the transition to the U.S. had its ups and downs with the language barrier being the toughest part. The food, culture and just general way of life were very different from what they were used to in Europe. After a short while they started to settle in with Daisy going to school and learning to speak English. Herb got a job as a jeweler apprentice and also worked as an usher at Loews Movie Theater on 45th and Broadway, it was obvious early on Herb was not afraid of hard work. Frieda took a job working at a sewing factory in the garment district on 38th street.

Frieda's sewing talent became evident very quickly and she went to work for the famous dressmaker Haute Couture and made dresses for several celebrities including Ingrid Bergman as well as Mrs. Gimbels of the Gimbels department stores. Daisy had a big advantage in school with her advanced European education and after quickly learning English she actually skipped a couple years of school to graduate early. She then went to beauty school to fulfill her dream of becoming a licensed beautician.

Chapter 4:

Here's Sammy

It was now 1948 and things would take an interesting turn when one day the phone rang and it was a young man asking for Daisy. She was surprised that someone was calling for her; after all she was only 16 years old. He said his name was Sam and he wanted know if she would go out with him. She was curious to how he got her number or even knew her. He said he would tell her if she agreed to go out with him, after thinking about it for a moment, she agreed to the date.

A few days later they met outside the beauty shop where she worked. Daisy and her friends were smiling as Sam walked up, he was a handsome man with thick black hair, big smile and tanned skin. After a brief introduction they went for a long walk, from 42nd Street all the way to Daisy's apartment on 87th Street. When Daisy asked how he got her number he told her that he worked for the VA. While he was a assisting a gentleman the man pulled out his wallet for his VA ID card and Sam saw this picture of two pretty women. It was a picture of Daisy and her friend Marion. He asked for the phone number of the blonde woman but the gentleman said "I'm friends with Marion but I don't know the other woman." Sam told the man he could make things easier for him at the VA if he could manage to get that number, a few days later he gave Sam the number.

They had a very nice conversation during their long walk and Daisy found Sam to be a perfect gentleman. Daisy was saying goodbye and Sam wanted to know if he could see her again. She told him yes but he would have to meet her mother first. He called the next day (there was a phone in the lobby that several families shared) and wanted to take her to the movies. Daisy agreed but he would have to come over to get approval from her mother.

The next day he came over to meet Frieda, she approved due to the fact that he worked for the government given the lofty status of government workers in Europe. Frieda later admitted to Daisy she also had a strange feeling about Sam, she wasn't sure what it was but something just wasn't right. Sam and Daisy took the subway to Radio City Music Hall and saw a movie called Blue Sky. After the movie they walked and talked for quite a while, before they knew it they walked all the way back to Daisy's apartment. Daisy found him to be very nice but more in a friend way than a romantic way. She remembered something just wasn't right but couldn't put her finger on it. He gave her a nice kiss on the cheek and sheepishly walked away.

When Daisy went inside her mother asked if she had a good time and admitted she did but no real sparks flew. Frieda looked at Daisy and said, "That is the man you will end up marrying," which had Daisy saying "NO WAY."

Sam kept calling day after day, they continued to date and Daisy starting liking him more and more. Before long, Daisy had fallen in love with him even though he had many odd ways about him. One thing that stood out was as they began dating it was still wintertime in New York and Sam would show up with only a sweater. Daisy asked one night, "Aren't you cold, don't you have a heavy jacket?" Sam said, "Yes I do but it's a very nice one and I don't want to wear it outside."

As they got closer they exchanged stories of their childhood. Sam told Daisy he was raised in an all boys New York orphanage due to his parents being very poor. His parents came to the U.S. from Salonika, Greece (they were Turkish, Spanish-Greek Jews) and struggled to make ends meet. They had six children and after giving birth for the sixth time Sam's mother had a nervous breakdown, was sent to a mental hospital and would stay there for the next 15 years. With the mother in an institution and the father battling poverty, all the children were eventually sent away. Sam and his twin brother, Gabriel, were sent to a Jewish orphanage, the other brother Abraham, and three sisters, Adel, Rachael, and Ester were sent there as well but would eventually go to foster homes.

Sam and Gabriel were seven years old when they were sent to the orphanage where their father would come to visit every once in a while but not often. Most of the other children got to go home on weekends with their parents but not Sam and Gabriel. Years later Sam had told me how lonely and sad he and Gabriel felt those weekends. Abraham was taken in by a nice family who also took in the sisters; although they were all separated they tried to keep in touch. At that time in 1931, still in the depths of the Great Depression, with very tough economic times getting adopted or taken in by a family was not easy.

Gabriel eventually moved in with a family after a few years at the orphanage but Sam ended up staying there until he was 18. His upbringing was very rough because they kept the kids sheltered from the real world. They didn't let them interact with girls, all the kids there were Jewish (Sam would later say he didn't know there were other religions, he thought everyone was Jewish). He also admitted he had never seen a person of color until getting out into society. The orphanage did the best they could under the circumstances but it wasn't a very loving environment; it was more of a survival situation for all of the kids.

Not long after coming out of the orphanage in the early 1940s Sam and Gabriel both went into the U.S. Army. Here were two young men who had grown up very sheltered and now were heading overseas to fight in a war. This would be a learning experience for both of them as they began their military duty. Sam ended up in the Philippines where he would actually meet General Macarthur; Gabriel went over and saw combat, combat that would take a psychological toll on him for the rest of his life.

Sam's sisters had a tough life as well. Rachel was engaged to a man, and had all the plans for the wedding complete, invitations sent out, everything was ready to go. Two days before the wedding her fiancé told her he could not marry her; he was already married and had two children. He walked away never to be seen again. Rachel went into deep depression and seclusion for quite some time; she would end up living her life alone and never marrying. Many years later Gabriel and Sam tried calling her but couldn't get her on the phone, they went to her apartment but nobody answered the door. They got the superintendent to open the door only to find her dead lying on the couch. Years later, I had a random conversation with a New York City police officer who told me with the number of elderly people who lived alone in the city it was not uncommon for this to happen. After a few days, sometimes weeks, when a loved one or friend have not spoken or seen them they send someone to their apartment to check on them and make the grim discovery.

Sam's other sister Esther married a French sailor, she got pregnant shortly after getting married, when her husband found out he left her. She did the best she could raising the boy by herself, unfortunately the boy found trouble with drugs and died of an overdose at age 18. She lived a very quiet life by herself, her brothers and sisters would visit her every now and then but she preferred being alone. They would eventually lose contact with her; last they knew she was living in Florida.

Adele, Sam's other sister was married to a nice man in the Navy. She got pregnant prior to him going to sea; unfortunately he died in some type of submarine accident never having a chance to see his son. The other brother Abraham was distant from the siblings and they lost touch with him years ago not knowing if he was dead or alive.

Sam's twin brother Gabriel was a very quiet man, a loner who never had any friends. He was very intelligent and great with numbers; he ending up going to work for the IRS after coming back from the service. He worked there for years before retiring disabled; I'll talk more about my Uncle Gabe later.

In a way I think Daisy felt sorry for Sam even though her upbringing was full of love she could still relate because her childhood was difficult as well. The dating continued and after a while they decided it was time to get married. Before this could happen she would need the blessing of her Uncle Sigi, with her father still in Paris his brother would be the one who would approve or disapprove.

Sigi looked Sam up one side and down the other and drilled him with questions about what he did for a living to what his plans for the future were. Even though Sigi wasn't overly impressed and Sam was 25 with Daisy only being 17, he did give his approval. George would have to go to the American Consulate in Paris to sign all kinds of paperwork because Daisy was only 17 and she needed this to get married.

Herb and Frieda both tried to talk Daisy out of doing it but that was a lost cause, when Daisy made up her mind to do something that was it. She even threatened to elope and never speak to them again if they would not approve. Daisy mentioned many years later how she regretted saying those words.

They had their small little wedding and also had their first of many arguments on the way to their honeymoon. My mom's notes are a little fuzzy about the honeymoon but what I got from it was they were both very innocent and it was pretty much a nightmare, as she puts it 'this was the beginning of a very big mistake."

They had a one-room apartment for the first year of their marriage as they tried to work out their personal issues. They would have a few good days but most of them were full of arguing. They moved to a bigger apartment uptown but overall they led a simple life. If they weren't arguing they did find some commonality, they both liked dancing (Sam was a very good dancer), long walks in Central Park and going to the movies.

By now Herb had also moved out and was on his own, Frieda then moved into the same building where Daisy and Sam lived. She was on the third floor and Daisy and Sam were right above on the fourth floor. This was not good for their relationship. They continued to argue over everything which would cause Daisy go stay in her mother's apartment for a few days and then go back to Sam. This went on for some time until Frieda finally told Daisy, "You either leave him or you stay with him but you can't keep going back and forth."

After realizing the marriage was not going to work Daisy decided to leave and went to Miami for a divorce. Back then getting a divorce in Florida was much easier than in New York, it would only take three months and for Daisy the sooner the better. She was very relaxed and was enjoying her time alone in Florida. While she was there she had a couple chance meetings that turned into a casual dinner date with Tony Bennett; she also went on a date with Caesar Romero. For us dedicated Batman fans he was the Joker in the 1960's TV series. Years later when my mom had told me she actually had dinner with the Joker I knew she was a cool woman.

After about two months in Florida Daisy got a phone call from one of Sam's sisters saying she needed to come home right away. Sam was very depressed, had a nervous breakdown and if anything happened to him it would be her fault. Feeling a large dose of guilt she quickly jumped on a train and went back to New York.

Upon arriving back to her apartment she found Sam a wreck. He was lost without her and pleaded for a chance to work things out. Daisy, being a softie, decided to try again and rekindled the relationship with Sam. They did what a lot of married couples do when marriages struggle, they figured if they have a baby it would be a good way to strengthen their relationship. There was a problem; they weren't sure Daisy could get pregnant.

Chapter 5:

Bring On the Kids

About a year earlier on one of their walks Daisy doubled over in extreme pain and Sam rushed her to the hospital. After a quick exam they said she was fine and sent her home, but the harsh pain did not go away. She called her Aunt Gene (Sigi's wife) and asked what she should do about this pain. Gene called her doctor and got Daisy an appointment, after seeing the doctor's the recommendation was to go to the hospital right away. Daisy was rushed into surgery, when she woke up she was heavily bandaged on her mid section. The doctor came in and told her she was lucky to be alive; her ovaries had burst and he had to remove one and a half of them leaving her with just a half of an ovary.

Of course that left one big question, could she have children? The doctor said it was not impossible but it would be tough. Surprisingly, as soon as they tried Daisy did get pregnant. One day while at work in the beauty parlor she felt a sharp pain in her stomach. Back then the chairs the customers would sit in were very heavy and not easy to maneuver. While working on one of her customers she tried to move the chair and that's when she knew something was wrong. Within a day or so she would lose the baby three months into the pregnancy.

After losing the baby the doctor said to rest for a few days and then she could go back to work. Unfortunately Daisy was still in severe pain for a few days and called the doctor, he advised her to meet him at the hospital where she was admitted right away for a bad infection. They had to do a procedure called a DNC. After recouping for a few days she was fine physically, emotionally it took a bit of a toll on her. She really felt this would have helped her marriage get back on track but it was not to be, not yet.

They tried to get pregnant again and for a few months it just wouldn't happen until one day she felt different and knew she was pregnant. Sure enough they did a test with the doctor and he confirmed the pregnancy. This time there were no complications and nine months later on August 19th, 1953 Rob was born. Surprisingly Sam was a very good father with Rob and enjoyed the experience; unfortunately that passion for parenting would not last.

With Daisy becoming an official citizen of the U.S. they could start the proceedings to get her father into the States. His first visa request was rejected by the immigration board due to having a black spot on his lung that showed up in an old x-ray.

An interesting fact about Daisy, English was now the fifth language (German, French, Hebrew and Arabic were the other four) she became fluent with and even though she had only been in the U.S. a short time she quickly lost her European accent. As the years went on you would be hard pressed to guess she was not born in the states, the only give away was when she would said the word "three", for some reason she pronounced it with a European flair and it sounded like "tree". It would bring us many laughs throughout the years.

Sam knew how much getting her father in the country meant to Daisy so he was going to do everything he could to help. Daisy was amazed as she now saw another side of Sam she didn't know existed. He went to the library and started doing all kinds of research to see how to get this law overturned. He was there day and night writing letters to Congressmen and even the President of the United States. After months of working nonstop, getting rejected time and again, he finally did it. He had a special bill passed in the 82nd Session of Congress and in a short period of time George would be reunited with his family. We never knew the details of the bill or how Sam got it done, but we knew it was Sam's shining moment as far as Daisy was concerned.

Herb had also written numerous letters and feels he had a hand in getting his father into the states. I don't know who ultimately was responsible for getting my grandfather in the U.S. but I know it made everyone very happy.

By this time Herb had met his wife Eleanor. Daisy really liked her, she was a spirited woman with a great sense of humor. She was from a large coal mining family in Pennsylvania. Herb was a real go-getter; he was not afraid to work and always put in a lot of hours. He tried many different jobs trying to make money and get his new family on firm ground. After some time he and Eleanor bought a house in Southern New Jersey where Daisy, Sam, Frieda and George would go and visit. He would eventually get a great job offer in Ohio and moved his family there. They would have a daughter Gail and a few years later a son named Bruce. They eventually ended up in Southern California where he went to work for a large Fortune 500 company and worked his way up the ladder while traveling mostly internationally. He would leave on Sunday night or Monday morning and return Friday night, he did this for years, and while it was tough on the family he made a very good living.

As the years went on unfortunately Daisy and Herb never really stayed in contact on a consistent basis. I think the fact that Daisy was spoiled by Frieda (as much as she could be based on what they had growing up) did not sit well with Herb. He definitely was not spoiled he worked very hard from day one. A Jewish mother and son relationship is much different than the mother and daughter relationship, the bond between a Jewish mother and daughter is very tight.

Daisy only had a few other family members here in the States; most were killed by the Nazis during the war. The specifics for which of the family members were killed was not something Daisy talked about. Her feelings were, "That is the past, I can't live in the past I have to live for today." I know that's something her and Herb differed on as well. Daisy always tried to focus on the positive in life, looking back at the Holocaust was not something she wanted to do.

George had his brother Sigi and Frieda had two brothers, Sigo and Kurt. Sigo was sick for many years with Multiple Sclerosis and it eventually killed him. Kurt had a very successful medical practice before retiring in Colorado, living a very nice life and peacefully pasted on of old age in the last couple of years. One of his sons, Daisy's cousin, Mark Heisler, became a very well respected sports journalist for the Los Angeles Times and has written numerous books.

George's youngest brother had stayed in France and during World War ll was out traveling for business. When he returned home his wife and three daughters were gone, he found out the Nazis had come through his town and taken all the Jews to prison camps including his family. He told George he was going to find them, but George warned him against it. Needless to say he, his wife and children were never heard from again. The assumption was they were all gassed to their death in Auschwitz.

Sam and Daisy were getting on with their life together even though the arguing never stopped. Rob was a little over two when

Daisy found out she was pregnant again. She was not happy about this as they were having a hard enough time financially and emotionally handling one child; two would make it that much tougher. The good news was Rob was a great baby; all he wanted to do was sleep and eat. He would sleep for 12 to 15 hours at a time, Daisy would have to wake him up just to feed him and he would go right back to sleep.

Daisy went into labor on July 30th, 1956. Sam said he couldn't leave work so Daisy went by herself in a taxi to the hospital. After a brief labor another bouncing baby boy is born, my brother Steve. On the ride back when it was time to take baby Steve home from the hospital, Rob looked at Steve, took his toy gun and said "I'm going to shoot that five-cent baby, I won't get any more toys or money now that there he's here." This would be the beginning of a very competitive and jealous relationship that would last for years.

Life moved on as Sam worked at the VA and Daisy continued being a hairdresser. The fighting and arguing continued on as well, Sam would leave for hours upon hours, Daisy later found out he was either at the library reading about history or going to the movies alone. Sam loved the movies; it was his escape. He didn't like all the noise of having young children at home and when he did finally come home the boys had to be in bed.

Move the calendar a few years and Daisy found she was pregnant again. She for sure was not happy about this as her relationship with Sam had deteriorated as he began to exhibit strange behavior and the last thing they needed was another child. Not to get the wrong message about Daisy and kids, she loved children; she just didn't like the idea of having them with Sam. In her notes she would state, "My children are my life." This time on May 9th, 1960 a beautiful baby girl named Michele arrived, only one day from Daisy's birthday of May 8th. Daisy and her mother were in heaven as a little girl was added to the family and another lifelong bond was started.

Having three young children was not making things easy on Sam, with Frieda living just downstairs. She wanted to stay close to Daisy and the kids and would visit often, this did not make Sam a happy man. He would come home from work or the movies (he would regularly skip work in favor of a good movie) and again the kids would have to be in bed, he would take his dinner, go straight into the bathroom and sit on the toilet and eat. He would stay in there for a while, Daisy would check on him and he would be looking out the window talking to the moon. Daisy didn't know how much longer this would last before Sam lost his mind altogether. When he came home from work the first thing he would do is touch the television, he would be upset if it was warm, that meant Daisy was watching and he did not like her watching too much TV.

One day the apartment superintendent knocked on the door and when Daisy answered the door he handed her a big bag. After asking what was in the bag the super said "It's all your husband's underwear." You see when Sam went into the bathroom every night to eat his dinner, when he was done he would take off all his clothes and use his underwear to clean the bathroom floor, sink as well as the tub and then throw them out the window into the courtyard of the apartment building. In his younger years Sam was a clean freak, everything, including himself had to spotless. The super told Daisy he was tired of seeing the underwear out there and thought he may want them back. He also asked if he would stop clogging the toilets as the people on the lower floors were complaining. Sam was not a big fan of my mom's cooking and most nights he would flush the food down the toilet, meat bones, chicken bones and all. He used to call her cooking "European shit."

For two people that fought a lot they sure stayed intimate to each other or were very fertile people because within a few months of Michele being born Daisy was pregnant again and on August 22, 1961 came the last of their children. With two boys and one girl Daisy was hoping for another girl but instead she got me, Ron.

Chapter 6:

There Goes Sammy

Daisy did not have to worry about getting pregnant again from Sam. Within a few hours of the day I came home from the hospital Sam said it was way too noisy and picked up and left. He came back after a few days but by the time I was three months old he had enough. His sister Adele called one night and said Sam was going to stay with her for a couple of months, as all the babies crying and noise was not good for his nerves.

I have won many games of "Can You Top This," when someone says "I had it tough my dad left when I was 10 years old or something like that." I always come back with, "Wow that is tough, my dad left the first time when I was three days old and for good when I was three months old." It usually shuts them up when they realize there is always someone that has it tougher than they did.

Sam actually stayed with his sister for three months without ever sending a penny to Daisy for her or us kids. If not for Daisy parents there would have been no way for her to pay the rent or feed us on just what she made working as a hairdresser. Frieda always went shopping on the weekends to buy us clothes, we had no needs and we were all well taken care of.

Sam was very smart, of course spending all that time at the library didn't hurt; when he was younger they had checked his IQ and it was off the charts. The problem was he was not smart to ways of the world: growing up behind the walls of the orphanage was his biggest disadvantage.

The fighting between Daisy and Sam not only ended their marriage but it had also taken a toll on Frieda's health, remember that bond between a Jewish mother and her daughter is very tight and if Daisy hurt Frieda hurt. One night when George and Frieda were out for a rare dinner at a restaurant Frieda experienced chest pains and passed out. They rushed her to the hospital and found out she had a heart attack.

When Daisy arrived at the hospital she was horrified at what she saw. Frieda was lying in a hospital bed covered in this big tent with all kinds of tubes, things hanging off her and she looked very sickly and weak. Daisy knew the heartache she had caused from her failing marriage directly resulted in her mother's heart attack. On the way out of the hospital she looked at her father and said "Take me to a lawyer tomorrow; I'm filing for a divorce, we need this man out of our life permanently." Her father was ecstatic and said, "We'll go first thing in the morning."

At that time in New York you first had to have a legal separation before getting divorced, so that is what she got. That night Sam wanted to come home and talk with Daisy but she wouldn't let him in. After banging on the door for a while he went out to the street and came back with a police officer. The officer knocked on the door and asked what the problem was and Daisy quickly showed him the legal separation papers. The officer then told Sam he must leave the property, as he was no longer allowed there. Sam was furious and asked for all his stuff, Daisy told the officer he could come back tomorrow and she would have it for him. He came back the next day and all his stuff was thrown in the hallway, the neighbors were walking all over it to get to their apartments. Sam was having a cow to say the least.

Chapter 7:

You're From Jersey, What Exit?

As a side note, I actually have never been asked by anyone who was from New Jersey what exit I lived off of. That is just a saying that has turned into this myth over the years.

Daisy was relieved her bad marriage was done with and she just wanted to get the divorce to make it official. She heard it might be easier to get a divorce in New Jersey and a friend of hers named Joe, who owned the local hardware store, told her he had a customer that had a house in Teaneck, NJ. It was an old farmhouse, they lived upstairs and they wanted to rent out the lower level. Daisy went to look at it and loved it, four bedrooms, a nice kitchen and family room, so she decided to take it.

It was not uncommon for men to want to help my mom out; she was quite the looker, before she met Sam she had won the "Miss Manhattan" Beauty Pageant.

The divorce part turned out to be not so easy. Every time the lawyer sent documents to Sam he wouldn't sign them; he still loved his wife and didn't want a divorce. This went on for months and months. They went to court to handle the alimony and child support issue and the judge awarded my mom $42.50 a week. Sam said, "Before I pay you any money I will retire!"

He did send the money but only for two weeks, right after that he was admitted to the psyche ward of the VA hospital and was eventually diagnosed with schizophrenia and depression. Back in the early 1960's the treatment for these diseases were barbaric at best. He had received shock treatment as well what equated to horse tranquilizers. He stayed in the hospital for quite some time and after coming out he retired from the VA on disability at the age of 38. They went back to court to get the alimony and child support worked out, but once the judge realized he was retired, disabled and on a fixed income he told Daisy "Sorry but you can't get blood from a stone," and that was the end of that, no money, very different times than today.

All of Daisy's friends told her to put us in foster homes; there was no way she could do it financially with four of us. That was not an option for her; she loved us and would do whatever it took to survive. A quote from my mom's notes, "That would never happen; if I have to work day and night my children would always be with me no matter what!"

Daisy didn't believe in any public assistance, she had the children and she would figure out a way to support them. She got a full time job at a beauty parlor in Leonia, NJ only 10 minutes from the house. Frieda watched us for two weeks and then told Daisy she had enough. She said, "I don't want to be mean, but I raised my children and you now must raise yours." I think that was her version of tough love.

Things all happen for a reason and per her notes "God was looking out for me." She went to work at the beauty parlor and as she was explaining her dilemma to her boss, a client overheard the conversation and told her she might be able to help. She had a housekeeper whose mother was in need of a job, Daisy immediately asked to send her over. The lady came to meet us the next day, her name was Tanny. Tanny was from Belize, British Honduras, a heavyset woman in her mid 50's who spoke with a heavy accent. Even though I was very young I do remember her being with us. She turned out to be a savior for our family, she cooked, cleaned, did laundry, loved all us kids and we loved her as well. She took one of the bedrooms and lived with us for over three years. When Daisy got home from work Tanny would go to her room and read the Bible, she never missed a night. Robbie (nickname for Rob) would love to go in there and listen to her read. What would seem like a rough time for our family was anything but, in discussions over the years with my older siblings they had fond memories of those years and I give credit to my mom positive attitude and the blessing that was Tanny!

Mom got a second job to make ends meet; she went to work at a diner in Tenafly, NJ. When filling out her job application she stated she had a lot of experience as a waitress, which was a bit of a white lie, she had none, but still got the job. She would work all day in the beauty parlor, come home to see us, have dinner together (she always wanted the family together at dinner), she would then take a nap until about 10:00 PM and then go to work the nightshift at the diner.

Her first night as a waitress was quite an experience. She showed up, was very nervous and the short order cook could tell. He introduced himself, Vinnie was his name, and said "Why are you so nervous?" Daisy confessed she had never been a waitress before, to put her at ease he told her that he was a dishwasher for 20 years and this was his first night as a cook. As the night got started Daisy watched Vinnie work the kitchen like an old pro and as she placed the orders he cooked them up. That was very comforting for Daisy, she figured if he could cook without any experience surely I could take the orders and brings the dishes out.

Things started to get a little busy; a gentleman came in and ordered a steak dinner. That was not for the short order cook that was for the chef in the main kitchen. So Daisy brought the order in and within 15 minutes the steak was ready. It was in the middle of winter and the kitchen floor was covered in sawdust so the delivery people coming in and out of the back door would not slip.

As Daisy went to grab the dish off the shelf she slipped, the steak went flying in the air and landed right in the sawdust on the floor. She was panicked and asked the chef to make another steak; in his very broken English (he was Greek) he said, "You give me $4.00." Daisy said "If I had the $4.00 to spare I wouldn't be working here." He told Daisy to hold the plate and he took his pointy shoes and stuck his right shoe under the steak and flipped it right onto the plate. Daisy walked toward the sink to rinse it off and the chef said "No, take it like that." She said "It has sawdust on it." "Not problem, bring like that" he barked. Daisy looked at him in shock and said, "You have to be kidding." "Take him dinner" he replied. She knew she had no choice; she didn't want to get fired on her first night so she did as she was told.

Out she came with the steak and almost dropped the plate in front of the man as she quickly ran back to the kitchen and began crying her eyes out. After a few minutes one of the other waitresses came back to the kitchen and told Daisy the man with the steak wanted to see her. This almost caused a panic attack but she had to go face the music. She walked out with her head down and approached the table. The man said "I don't know what type of seasoning you use here but that was one of the best steaks I've ever had." Needless to say Daisy was a little surprised and to make things even stranger he left a two-dollar tip. With an hourly wage of 32 cents, two dollars was a big deal and Daisy's waitress career was off and running.

With Daisy working two jobs the schedule was exhausting, although after a while it became a routine. It helped with her and Vinnie becoming good friends and after a while they actually began dating. By the way, Vinnie had 20 years experience as a cook and lied that first night just to make Daisy feel better.

The dating got serious but could not go any further even though Vinnie was divorced. The problem with the relationship was Sam who would still not grant Daisy a divorce. Vinnie had four daughters from his first marriage that he would see on weekends. As for his first wife, the story was his wife left him for another man. During this time Daisy's father became very sick, he needed a gall-bladder operation. He was not strong enough for the surgery so the doctor sent him home to rest for a week, regain his strength and then they would do the surgery. That first night home Frieda called Daisy and said "Papa is in great pain, please come right away." Daisy jumped in her car and drove to Manhattan, picked them up and drove to the hospital to get George's pain checked out. He was admitted and put in a room with 11 other patients, Daisy had asked for a semi-private room but none were available. The nurse said if one came open he would be moved. Before Daisy and Frieda, left George asked Daisy to find out what the horrible pain in his chest was. She gave him a hug and a kiss and said she would talk to the doctor in the morning.

Early the next morning the phone rang and Daisy answered the phone. It was the nurse at the hospital; she was expecting the call regarding her father's new room number. Instead she said, "I'm so sorry but your father passed away at about 3:00 ." Daisy was stunned and very sad, but quickly realized she needed to regain her composure, she needed to drive to Manhattan to break the news to her mother. Tanny said, "I will pray for you, Daisy" and prayer is what she needed because telling her mother was not going to be easy.

Frieda thought she was there to take her to the hospital to see George but then told her the bad news. Frieda did not take it well as they sat there and cried together reflecting on what a great man George was. He was so giving, loving and a gentle man. They had been married for 38 years and had been through a lot, surviving the Holocaust, separated for years while awaiting his approved visa and the whole Sam and Daisy episode. They made it through all that but a simple gallbladder problem is what killed him. He developed a stone that punctured a hole and the internal bleeding drowned his heart. It was something that was totally preventable if it had been diagnosed properly, instead he was gone.

Life did go on although they missed Papa very much, Frieda was very down and lonely. One day on the way to visit Frieda, Daisy ran into an old neighbor, Hugo. He told her how he lost his wife from cancer about a year ago. Well the light bulb went off in her head and said "Why don't I introduce you to my mother." Daisy set up the meeting and to her surprise they hit it off and became involved.

It was just under a year since George had died and Frieda asked Daisy what she thought of her marrying Hugo. She told Daisy she was very lonely and Hugo filled that void even though she still was not over missing George. Even though it seemed very quick Daisy said "If that would make you happy I'm all for it." So when they got married on the same date Frieda married George, she knew it would be good luck.

They were married a couple of months when Frieda started coming over Daisy's house and would stay all weekend; she complained that "Hugo was nothing like Papa." George worshiped the ground she walked on, he gave her everything and she realized nobody could ever replace him. They tried to work it out. Hugo was a nice man but just very different than George. Daisy told her, "Hugo doesn't have a lot of money to buy you things but he's doing the best he can." But that wasn't it, he just wasn't George. They were married about six months and one night Hugo was not feeling well so he went to bed early. The next morning Frieda could not wake him up so she called an ambulance and had him taken to the hospital. He ran a very high fever and fell into a coma: two days later he passed away.

When they finalized his estate it turned out Hugo did have some money. The law back then was if you were married at least six months you were entitled to half of the estate. This did not sit well with Hugo's family but there was nothing they could do about it. This left Frieda in a good spot financially and also put her in a better position to help Daisy and us kids.

Frieda went back to living alone, she knew there would not be another man for her and she was OK with that now. She and Daisy would go visit Papa's grave often and spend as much time together as they could. Daisy was getting very serious with Vinnie but still waited for the divorce from Sam to be finalized. To make things more formal Vinnie took Daisy back to his house to meet his mother; he had moved back in with her after separating from his wife. She lived in a big house in Hackensack, New Jersey. It had four apartments attached to it, which she rented out and generated a good income for her.

Daisy and Vinnie's mother, Rose, did not get along very well right from the start, she was nothing like Daisy's family, and she was a bit of an old spinster. When Vinnie first moved in with her he did not have much money, most of it was spent in the divorce. Rose kept notes on a calendar of the weeks he did not pay her rent and when he got back on his feet he would have to pay her back.

Vinnie wanted Daisy to quit her night job and spend more time with him and the kids; he told her they would somehow figure it out financially once he recovered from the divorce. It had been

28 months of that hectic schedule for Daisy, with working two jobs, but she did not want to take his money.

Frieda called Daisy late one night in a bit of a panic, she was sick and wanted to go to the hospital. It turned out she needed her gallbladder taken out. With what happened to her father Daisy was very nervous. Luckily the surgery went all right and she came to stay at our house after a week in the hospital. That first night she screamed in pain all night long. The next morning Daisy called the surgeon but he had left to go out of town so she called our family doctor who she liked a lot, he said to bring her right in. After doing some initial tests he felt she needed to go back to the hospital due to possibly suffering from internal bleeding.

Once they reached the hospital they took her in for more tests as Daisy nervously waited for the results. After waiting for hours the doctors came out to tell Daisy the news, they were sorry to say but Frieda had lung cancer. Daisy didn't know what to do, she had just lost her father and now her mother was deathly ill. She also didn't understand how she could have lung cancer, she never smoked a day in her life. They told her everyone has cancer cells and sometimes when you have a surgery the cells are exposed to air and they can multiply very quickly they think that's what happened after the gallbladder surgery. Today we know many of the old sewing factories like the one Frieda worked in had asbestos in the walls and ceilings.

Vinnie now insisted he move in with Daisy, she quit her night job and let him help with the bills. Daisy had no choice but to agree. Frieda was staying at Holy Name Hospital in Teaneck and was being very well taken care of by the nuns there. Daisy constantly got calls at work and her boss at the beauty parlor, Ralph, was great about it. She had worked for him for almost three years and he saw her through all her ups and downs and never docked her pay for the hours she missed.

Frieda was getting delirious from all the morphine she was taking for pain and would be screaming at the nuns. They would call Daisy and tell her she was asking for all kinds of crazy food. Daisy would go to the hospital late at night with her strange requests and when she got there Frieda would say, "Why the hell did you bring me that, who eats that junk 12 o'clock at night?" She would tell Daisy she was happy that Vinnie and Papa were working together as her delusions from all the drugs got worse.

While Frieda was battling her illness my brother Steve was having his own medical issues as well, bad stomach pains. He had been to the doctor for numerous tests but they couldn't find anything wrong with him. This was very difficult on my mom as not only was her mother dying but also now one of her kids was very sick.

When Frieda was staying with us before going to the hospital she would sleep on the couch and we would all see her there, most times moaning in pain. She would tell us "I'm going to die on this couch." Although Michele and I were too young to understand that wasn't the case for Steve and Rob. This bothered Steve so much that even after Frieda (we called her Nanny) went to the hospital he wouldn't go near that couch.

The doctor told Daisy to bring Steve to the hospital for more tests and the area of the hospital where the tests were to be done was just past where Frieda's room was. As they walked by the room and peeked in to see how Frieda was doing Steve doubled over in pain then ran to the bathroom and threw up.

The doctors were getting very concerned at this point with his continuing pain and vomiting. They convinced Daisy they needed to do some exploratory surgery to find out what was wrong, but before they did that surgery they wanted Steve to see another doctor, a psychiatrist.

After a brief visit with the psychiatrist he came out and told Daisy Steve would be better real soon and no surgery was needed. Daisy did not understand but at this point she was close to needing a psychiatrist herself and did not question it. Two days later, Daisy received a phone call from the hospital, the head nun wanted to meet with her regarding Frieda. During this meeting the nun explained how Holy Name Hospital was a Catholic hospital and they had rules. Daisy was stunned when she thought they would not treat Frieda any longer because they found out she was Jewish but the Nun said that was not it. She said "Your mother tried to kill herself; not only is that a sin in our religion but we are not equipped to handle these types of patients." Frieda had taken a drinking glass, broke it and cut both of her wrists.

Daisy immediately went to see her mother and was shocked when she walked in. She saw Frieda all bandaged up with her arms and legs tied to the bed. Now she was in a real bind, she knew she couldn't bring her mother home in that condition having four young children in the house. One of the nuns came in and told Daisy she had called a nursing home right down the street. They had a room available and could handle someone in the Frieda's condition.

Upon arriving at the nursing home Daisy went to get Frieda checked in. The head of the nursing home asked if this was the woman coming from Holy Name Hospital, which Daisy replied "Yes." She went on to tell Daisy that after thinking more about it they would not be able to care for a woman in that condition. Daisy was at a loss for words and was begging for help. The woman said she might be able to work something out if Daisy was willing to hire a nurse 24/7 to watch her. The insurance would cover the nursing home but not the private nurse. Daisy was delighted just to have a place for her mother knowing she could not bring her home.

As soon as Daisy got home Steve wanted to know how Nanny was doing. Daisy assured him she was doing much better which was a big lie. That put a smile on Steve's face and within a couple of days he was going back to school after being out for almost two months with his stomach disorder. Luckily for Steve it only took him a week to catch up on all the old assignments, he definitely got the brains in the family. After another quick visit to the psychiatrist he said Steve was doing much better and would be just fine real soon.

A few days later Daisy received a phone call from her lawyer stating they were going to court tomorrow and finally get that divorce from Sam. She couldn't believe it; she had to run over to give the good news to her mother. Frieda was ecstatic and it was the first time Daisy saw her mother smile in quite some time. Frieda went on to tell Daisy that's what she was waiting for and now Daisy could get on with her life. Daisy did not know what she really meant but she would find out real soon.

Later that night Frieda peacefully passed away, now that the stress of the marriage to Sam was over she was as peace with the fact that Daisy could move on with her life and marry Vinnie. Daisy had been praying for God to ease her mother's pain and take her to heaven as Frieda suffered so much near the end, her prayers were answered. Daisy missed her mother but was glad the suffering was over.

After a few days of handling all the details of Frieda's passing it was time to take Steve back to the psychiatrist for a follow up. After another brief visit the doctor assured Steve he was fine and told Daisy he was being released from his care. Daisy was more than a little curious at this point and asked the doctor how he cured Steve. He went on to explain that all Steve's pains were sympathy pains for his grandmother, so every time he saw her in pain it would affect his pain. Now that she has passed, so did all of his symptoms. Daisy was very pleased, confused, but very pleased.

Even though we all missed Nanny a lot we did try to get back to a normal life. I was very young (not quiet 5) when my grandmother died, yet I still have very vivid fond memories of her. She loved her grandchildren and we all loved her. Daisy was now working Saturdays at the beauty shop and Monday through Friday as a waitress. She waited three months for the divorce to finally settle and then she and Vinnie got married.

The interesting part about the divorce was how quick it was finalized after fighting for it for so many years. What happened was Sam had been writing all kinds of crazy letters to the judge about all these conspiracies and how the government was taking away his family. He explained how his marriage was a government project and Daisy was paid by the government for marrying him and the kicker was that she was lesbian and not good for his children. After reviewing those letters and many more just like them the judge decided to put an end to the madness and ordered the divorce final.

Chapter 8:

What Is A Hackensack?

Now it was time to get a house for our new family. Vinnie actually had built a house several years earlier in a town just outside of New York City, a place called Hackensack, New Jersey. Unfortunately when he was divorced from his first wife he could not afford it. His mother took over the house, she gave Vinnie $5000 for it with the agreement that when he had the money he would pay back the $5000 and then he could have the house back. His mother rented the house out for a couple of years and now Vinnie wanted all of us to move in.

They didn't expect a problem with the renter moving out as they were on a month-to-month deal anyway. Daisy had inherited some money when Frieda passed away so they went to Vinnie's mother to pay her back the $5000 which would allow all of us to move into the house. Small problem: Rose told them she liked getting the monthly rent and didn't want to give that up. Cut to the chase on this and the bottom line is Vinnie's own mother made him pay her $10000 instead of the previously agreed amount of $5000. They were of course extremely upset but paid the money. That was all Daisy needed to see from Rose, after that she told Vinnie she wanted nothing to do with his mother and Vinnie felt the same way.

Now they just needed to get the renters out and move all of us in. Vinnie went to the house with Daisy to give her the tour and when they got there the renter was not so welcoming. They made it to the kitchen but when Vinnie went to walk through the rest of the house the tenant said, "You can't see any more of the house." They thought he was joking and just kept walking until the tenant told them if they walked any further he would kill them. Vinnie replied by saying, "If he put a hand on either one of us I will kill you." This went on for a few minutes until they thought it was just best to leave. As Vinnie and Daisy are getting into their car and trying to back out of the driveway a police car pulls up behind them and blocks them in. To their surprise during the argument the wife went and called the police. The police officer walks up and abruptly places Vinnie under arrest, handcuffs him and puts him in the back of the police car. The renter's wife had told the police Vinnie threatened their life.

After spending a few hours in jail Daisy posted bail for him and a few days later they were in court. When the judge asked where his lawyer was he told him he didn't think he needed one. The judge told Vinnie he should re-think that as this was a major offense, he could see real jail time for threatening someone's life. They were caught off guard by the severity of the situation and did indeed hire an attorney.

The tenant wanted Vinnie in jail because he figured he could then stay in the house longer. The two attorneys got together and negotiated a deal, the tenant could stay in the house for an extra two months with no rent (worth $600 @ $300 a month) and be paid $100 for his trouble. This was a decent amount of money for 1966 but Vinnie and Daisy just wanted this over and done with. They agreed to it and in a couple of months we were in our new house.

We were all excited as this was our first house that we actually owned. It was on Washington Avenue in Hackensack, New Jersey, a suburb about 20 minutes outside of New York City. After we all settled in Daisy and Vinnie thought with both of them being in and around the food business they figured getting their own restaurant would be a great idea. They found this old restaurant for sale pretty cheap next to a lumber yard. The man who owned it wanted to retire so they struck a deal. They paid $5000 for the place and opened up in the beginning of December, 1966. As they finalized everything they had one problem, the insurance policy would not kick in until January 1st. It was a quirk with the insurance company but they figured no big deal, it's only one month.

The first month's business was pretty good and they were enjoying the American dream, they owned their own business. We celebrated a fun Christmas, even though we were Jewish we celebrated both Hanukah and Christmas, for a kid this was the best of both worlds. My mom always showered us with dozens of toys, nothing real expensive but fun little things. Mom always said, "I'm going to spend it on my children while I'm here to watch them enjoy it, no sense in leaving it to them when I'm dead." This is something that never changed throughout her entire life. She was a very giving person, she never came first, she always thought of the four kids long before she thought of herself; she didn't want or need much for herself. I think this had a lot to do with where she came from, since she never expected to survive the Nazis, life itself was a gift.

As the holiday season came to an end they were home preparing to watch the ball drop from Times Square on TV. At 11:30 p.m. they got a call from Vinnie's mother, she told them they better go check on their restaurant, she heard on the news the lumber yard right next to it was on fire. They raced down to the restaurant only to see their dream burning up in flames. Daisy was so upset but Vinnie said not to worry that they would build another one. Of course the insurance company would inform them the fire officially started at 11:05 p.m. and their policy didn't kick in until 12:00 a.m., so based on the fire starting 55 minutes too soon the whole thing was a total loss.

After licking their wounds they decided to go back to work for someone else, they both got jobs at the Holiday Inn in Little Ferry, New Jersey, Vinnie as a cook and Daisy as a waitress. They were settling into their life together and Vinnie's children from his previous marriage became friendly with our family. I remember visiting one of his daughter's apartment numerous times. She would do my mom's hair while Michele and I would play with her kids. In the meantime Tanny, our great childcare provider, maid, cook, handy woman around the house and all things to all of us had to leave. I guess her visa had expired quite a while back and she was being deported. We were all very surprised and upset not only for Tanny but for us; she had become part of the family. She had helped Daisy get through so much especially when Frieda was dying, but the law was the law and Tanny was forced to leave.

Daisy still needed someone to help with us kids and stuff around the house. She called an agency to see if they could find someone like Tanny for us, although we all knew there would never be another Tanny. The first girl didn't last long: after she used the iron to do her hair and most of her hair ended up in our food, she was fired!!!!

The next lady they sent was a bit older and she didn't like kids. She would chase us around the house with a hanger threatening to beat us, fired!!!! The next one they sent over was an interesting woman. Within the first week of being hired she waited for Daisy to leave for work. For some reason Daisy had an uneasy feeling that day and decided to hang around. Thinking she left the woman picked up the phone to make a call. Being a bit suspicious Daisy picked up the phone in another room to listen in on the conversation which turned out to be her boyfriend. But they weren't making dinner plans or anything like that, they were putting together a plan to steal all our stuff; they were going to come while Daisy was at work and clean us out. After hanging up the phone Daisy walked out into the kitchen and almost gave the lady a heart attack. The woman quickly said "I thought you left for work"? Daisy told her to leave now before she called the police and within 60 seconds the woman was gone, fired!!!.

Daisy figured let's try this one more time. The agency sent over another woman and after a few days she seemed to be doing a good job, Daisy thought we finally have someone that will stick. During a conversation with the woman she asked Daisy if she could have a break and take a walk while she was there to watch the kids. Daisy saw no problem with that and the woman left. My mom's famous quote was "She must not be tired of walking yet because as of today she still hasn't come back from her walk." The woman vanished, us or the agency never heard from her again.

Daisy decided with all the kids in school now she really didn't need anyone else, didn't need to spend the money and decided to go on without any help. Our house was in a great neighborhood full with kids of all ages. The four of us would start to develop our own little personalities, groups of friends and hobbies, and not all of that turned out to be good.

Rob being the oldest was the first to get into a little trouble. He had the worst habit of being late for dinner. Mom didn't have many rules, but one she was adamant about was for us being home on time so we can eat dinner together. It never failed, when the last dish was washed Rob would walk in ready to eat. This happened time after time, Daisy would scream at him and tell him if he ever did it again he would not get to eat.

One day sure enough we are sitting down to eat and Rob was nowhere to be found. Just as we starting eating the phone rings; it's the hospital telling Daisy Rob had an accident and to come down right away. She and Vinnie rushed to the hospital and found Rob with a big cut on his head crying like crazy. The cut wasn't what was making him cry, he wanted to know even though he was late for dinner could he still eat? He got a few stitches and went home for his dinner.

A few months later Daisy got another call, it's the police again, Rob is at the police station. She tells the officer on the phone, "There must be some mistake Rob is at school." The person tells her, "No, he's here at the police station, under arrest and you need to come bail him out." Down to the station she went to see what happened. It turns out Rob and one of his friends was walking to school and saw a big 18 wheeler truck with the door open. They jumped in it and found the keys in the ignition. They decided to take it for a joy ride and got arrested for grand theft, based on being minors they both were released to their parents with stern warning.

Rob just seemed to find the trouble; he was the ultimate follower as a teenager. If one of his buddies said, "Let's jump off the bridge," he was right there with them. He meant no harm to anyone but himself. He wasn't what you called a great student in school either. Daisy would get calls all the time from the high school Vice Principal telling her Rob would have to stay after school for his bad behavior.

Once he locked the teacher in the closet on a dare from another student. He also shut off the main electric switch leaving the entire school in the dark. Then he pulled the pin cushion trick on one of his teachers leading her to jump up from her seat screaming. In yet another episode he put a pile of chewed up gum on a teacher's seat which had him in trouble again. It was nothing real serious but it was annoying to Daisy and Vinnie who just wanted a normal life of peace and quiet. There would be many more wild stories about Rob and some major life changes as he got older which I'll share later.

Chapter 9:

Tragedy Strikes Again

After being married to Daisy for a little over a year Vinnie came home one day in such pain he could hardly make it up the front stairs to get in the house. Daisy immediately took him right to the doctor to see what was wrong. They said they weren't sure what it was so the doctor referred him to a specialist in New York City. After getting the appointment the next day Daisy would receive some devastating news, Vinnie had a tumor in his pancreas. They told Daisy without immediate surgery he would die within six months, with the surgery he might live two years.

Daisy was distraught to say the least but she didn't want to tell Vinnie the severity of the illness. She finally had the life she wanted,, a nice house and a man who loves her and her children, but it was not to be. Vinnie did have the surgery in New York and after coming out into the recovery room he was in horrible pain. Daisy tried to assure him he would be fine, it would just take some time. She hired a private nurse to stay with Vinnie so she could go home and check on the kids then quickly rush back to the hospital.

After some time in the hospital Daisy was told by the doctors there was nothing else they could do, it was time for him to go home and be as comfortable as possible for the time he had left. He was under the impression he was coming home to recoup and then go back to work, Daisy knew differently. It turned out the doctor never removed the tumor, it was the size of a large grapefruit and if he tried to remove it he feared he would have died right on the operating table.

Vinnie's mom Rose would come over to visit every day to see how her son was doing. She would bring over soup for him to eat that she made from her garden vegetables. As soon as she would leave he would tell Daisy to flush it down the toilet. He would say "She's trying to kill me, all her cats pissed in her garden and she wants me to eat that, no way." He did not want Daisy to let her in after a while. He really didn't like his mother, she was not such a nice person, and I'm being kind.

I would pass Rose on the street all the time and she would be nice to me but I was just a kid. I was very close with my step cousin Tommy; he was Vinnie's nephew who lived right down the street. Daisy was not close with Vinnie's sister (Tommy's mother) but I was over there all the time, eating dinner, they even drove me school in later years when we both went to junior high. We were all functionally dysfunctional.

A little bit of time passed and obviously Vinnie was not getting any better. A lady who worked with Daisy told her she knew someone that could heal Vinnie. Desperate for anything she inquired how. She told her they would need some type of garment that belonged to Vinnie and she would need to bring it over the house. Vinnie knew nothing about this, for one he didn't know how sick he was and two he would have never agreed to it.

Daisy didn't know what she was about to get into but if it would help Vinnie she was all for it. She went to her co-workers house where the lady's mother and aunt were waiting for them. They sat around the kitchen table, almost like a séance, her mother was feeling Vinnie's shirt when all of a sudden she started shaking and her face began to change colors. Her aunt screamed out, "Oh my God," and then the mother ran from the table to vomit in the sink. When she came back she told Daisy someone close to Vinnie had put the Maloik on him, this was a term for an Italian curse. If he could confront the person who did it he would be healed.

Again, desperate for him to feel better Daisy wanted to believe this and went home to tell Vinnie what she had learned. Daisy thought his mother must have put a curse on him, Vinnie said he would talk to her about it but I don't think that ever happened. A couple weeks passed and Vinnie actually started to feel a little better, Daisy thought maybe this little spell had actually been lifted. I believe in her heart of hearts she knew there was no spell but she was desperate for his survival and like many of us would do, wanted believe it. One day when she came home from work she noticed Vinnie's car was not in the driveway. She ran into the house but he wasn't there. While Daisy panicked for a few minutes Vinnie walked in and said that he felt so good he decided to go for a drive. They were very excited that he was on the road to recovery. Unfortunately the next day reality set back in when Vinnie awoke to horrible pain and could not get out of bed.

I don't have many memories of Vinnie, but I do remember always coming in the house and he would be sitting in the big recliner we had in the living room. He didn't want to lie in bed so he stayed in that chair all day. Things started to get worse, Vinnie was giving up, he wouldn't eat or drink much and began to lose a bunch of weight. His mother came for a visit and realizing Vinnie was not doing well, she asked Daisy what she would do when he passes away. Daisy told her she had not thought that far ahead. Rose said, "He would not be able to be buried next to his father at St. Joseph's." When Daisy asked why Rose said, "That cemetery is only for Catholics." Daisy quickly replied back stating, "He is Catholic." Rose told her, "Now that he has married a Jewish woman the church does not see him as Catholic anymore." Daisy said, "Not to worry, I'll have him buried in my Jewish cemetery."

A few days later Rose came back and told Daisy it was all cleared up, her daughter got the OK to have Vinnie buried in their cemetery. Daisy said, "It's good to know you can negotiate with your God to get things worked out." This obviously was not helping the relationship with her mother in-law.

Vinnie was going downhill fast; he had lost more weight and was extremely weak. Because he would not eat Daisy took him back to the hospital to get him an IV of fluids. He had weighed 235 pounds when he was healthy but now he was down to 85 pounds, he was basically just skin and bones. Daisy would put sheep's cloth under him to lay on for an extra cushion to keep the pressure off his bones.

Vinnie would ask Daisy, "Why am I not getting any better?" Daisy continued to make excuses telling him he had a rare disease and it would take a while to get better. After much suffering, Daisy was there holding Vinnie in her arms when he finally passed away at the young age of 47. The priest came in to talk with Daisy and she was ready for him based on what Rose had told her. He cleared up all the confusion and said it would not be a problem having him buried at St. Joseph's.

Daisy prepared a bunch of food for all the family and friends to come over the house after the funeral. After most of the people had left, Rose showed up at the front door asking if she was still welcome now that her son had passed. Daisy told her she would always be welcome; Daisy was always a forgiving person.

My last memory of that day was when we were driving back from the funeral, my mom, Michele, Steve and Rob were crying and I asked "Why is everyone crying?" They tried to explain to me that Vinnie had died but at age six I just didn't understand.

Daisy would somehow have to survive another life tragedy. She missed Vinnie a lot, even though they were together just short time it was her first real love. Daisy was still young woman of 34 and again was left alone to raise her four children. It turned out Rob would miss Vinnie a lot as well; he was so good to all of us and really liked Rob even though he was a bit of a problem child. Being 14 years old he had made a big impact in Rob's life and he missed his fatherly influence. Rob had switched high schools and the cemetery where Vinnie was buried was right across the street. He went to visit the grave site every day for the first six months after his death.

Chapter 10:

You're a Real Hockey Puck

After a few weeks of grieving Daisy's brother Herb urged Daisy to bring the entire family on a trip to trip to California. This was very surprising because Daisy and Herb weren't that close. They would speak maybe a couple times a year at the most. Before going that far from home Daisy wanted to make sure we were all healthy so all the kids went for routine checkups at the doctor. It turned out our trip would have to be delayed a while because I had a hernia and needed surgery right away. The plans were postponed and arrangements made for a quick surgery. It was actually fun, all the nurses pampered me and the other kids in the children's ward of the hospital. We got to eat a bunch of ice cream and had wheelchair races in the halls.

The first day home from the hospital I almost gave my mom a heart attack when she saw me jumping into our pool. She called the doctor right away and told him what I was doing. He said, "Is he complaining about pain?" She said, "No." He responded by saying, "So why are you worried?" A few days later I would get my stitches out and the California trip was back on.

My uncle's house was beautiful, up on a hill in Fullerton, California, just outside of Los Angeles. Everything was meticulous in the house and we had to make sure we didn't break anything or spill our drinks. It was the first time I remember meeting my Uncle Herb, Aunt Eleanor (we called her Aunt El), and my cousins Bruce and Gail.

We all got along real well although my uncle was very strict, we weren't used to it but while there we would have to abide by his house rules. That's how we were raised, respect your elders and if we were in someone's home we obeyed their rules. He surprised Daisy by making reservations for her to go to Las Vegas for a quick getaway while my aunt and uncle took care of the kids.

While in Las Vegas Daisy went to see a comedian and was lucky enough to sit in the front row, so she thought until the comedian began to pick on her. Back then my mom was a pretty big woman with bleached blonde hair so she stood out in a crowd. Daisy always had a good sense of humor about her weight and did not mind the ribbing. The comedian asked if she was married and she told him she was widowed. The comedian responded by saying, "Well sure, you probably smothered him." He got a bunch of laughs and Daisy laughed right along with them. He kept picking on her and many others in the crowd throughout the show. At the end of the show, while the audience was finishing their dinner, the comedian came down to speak to Daisy and said, "I hope you didn't take it personal, it's just my act." She said, "Not at all" and they laughed about it. He thanked her for being a good sport and told her he would be picking up her tab for being such a good sport. He also took her over to another table to introduce her to his wife and fellow comedian, Jackie Mason. The comedian was none other than the GREAT Don Rickels.

Throughout the years I heard my mom tell this story numerous times and every time she would smile and laugh, it was easy to see how much fun she had that night during what was such a tough time in her life. Throughout the years as I would see Don Rickels on TV I would always think of that story and from then on he was my favorite comic. Years later as an adult, on a trip to Las Vegas my wife, Carol and I would get to see his live show and we really enjoyed it. If I ever have a chance to meet him I would like to shake his hand and thank him for what he did for my mom. Just recently I found out something very interesting about Don Rickels, his birthday is May 8th, just like Daisy's.

Chapter 11:

Daisy's First Diner

After taking some time off Daisy decided it was time to go back to work. There was not an immediate need for money as she still has some left in reserve. She went to visit her former boss Bob. He and a partner owned a small luncheonette on Main Street in Hackensack. She walked in during the lunch hour and they were very busy, she saw that they needed help at the cash register so Daisy jumped in. She told Bob she was not working and would love to help out. Bob said he could use the help but he could not afford to pay her right away. Daisy felt that Bob let her take so much time off when Vinnie was sick and never said a word so she thought it would be a good way to repay the favor. This went on for a few weeks when one day Bob said they would be closing the doors that day; they were out of cash. He didn't have any more money to put in and neither did his partner.

Daisy thought she would help out by offering a loan. Bob said it would take $5000 to pay off the food distributors and get them back on their feet. This was a good chunk of money for 1968 but she did it. Part of that money was also to buy out the other partner, this made Bob and Daisy equal partners. Daisy did what she did best, the cooking. They had two other waitresses who worked the tables with Bob and Daisy handling the customers at the counter. My brother Steve would come in before and after school and work for a few hours, he was about 12 or 13 and was already working the grill like a pro. He liked making some extra cash, it seemed like he was always looking for ways to make money, the complete opposite of my other brother Rob, he didn't want anything to do with work.

Business seemed to be going pretty good, Daisy saw all the receipts and the money was coming in. Bob would take care of all the money and make all the deposits to the bank. Bob lived pretty far away and had complained about the commute. We had a nice finished basement which had a complete kitchen, living room, bedroom and bathroom. Daisy offered for him to move in and he jumped on the offer, I'm not completely sure but knowing my mom my guess is she let him live there for free.

Daisy decided it was time for a new car; she went out and bought a brand new Oldsmobile 98 convertible, green with white leather interior. The car was a thing of beauty. Bob convinced Daisy that new cars were a great investment and told her she should buy a new Lincoln Continental as well. Daisy was not an investment guru by any stretch of the imagination. She liked the idea and she went out and got it, a black four door. That was the model where the front doors and back doors opened opposite to each other; it was pretty cool thing from a boy only seven years old.

Conveniently Bob said he would drive the Lincoln until she decided she was ready to cash in on her profit. Looking back I thought Bob and my mom were dating but they weren't. That and the fact I think he was actually gay, "Not that there is anything wrong with that," quoting the famous line from a classic Seinfeld episode. At the time there was a guy, Vern that kept coming into the diner and would bug Daisy about going out to dinner until, after numerous attempts Daisy finally gave in and went out with him. They dated for while and things pretty quickly got serious and the rumbles of marriage started. I don't have much memories of Vern other than I hated his name, although one thing does stick in my head.

One night I was getting ready for bed, I gave my mom a kiss good night and went to give Vern a hug and he just stood there not knowing what to do. My mom finally told him I was looking for a hug good night, so he begrudgingly gave me one. Being seven years old I was at a point that I really wanted and needed a father figure but I went to bed that night hoping my mom would not marry this jerk. He was not the father I wanted.

Well they did set a date but it was not going to be a big formal affair after all this would be Daisy's third marriage. About a week before the wedding day one of Daisy's co-workers asked her if she wanted to have her horoscope read. With one week before her wedding day she thought it would be a good idea. She got her chart done and when the lady handed it back to her Daisy said, "The timing is good, I'm getting married this Saturday." The lady responded, "No way, you are not getting married Saturday." Daisy thought she was nuts and replied, "Of course I am." The lady assured her that she would not get married that weekend and asked her to call her on Monday and let her know what happened over the weekend.

That Friday night before the wedding day Daisy and Vern were out to dinner and an argument erupted, one thing led to another and it turned into some tremendous fight which, as predicted by the horoscope lady, forced their wedding to be called off. Very late that night after their big fight, for good measure Vern drove his car over our front lawn, killing all the bushes and left our house looking like a tornado hit it. My mom was upset but like with most things in her life she would say, "What are you gonna do?"

Now back to her little restaurant business. Her accountant had called her and said they would need to discuss the current business status. Daisy was a little concerned when she showed up for the meeting and for a good reason. The meeting started with the accountant wanting to know why all the checks were bouncing. Daisy assured him that was not possible; she gave Bob all the money to deposit. He then inquired about where all the deposit slips were, Daisy told him that Bob must have them.

Daisy went in the next day and asked Bob what the deal was with the money. He was insulted and hurt that she didn't trust him, he basically told Daisy a bunch of lies to hold her off for a couple of days. He came up with stories about borrowing money from the wrong people and he had to take money out of the business to pay them back. He said he would get the money from his family and put it back in the business but that never happened.

Things got worse when the food deliveries now became COD, there would be no credit based on the last few checks bouncing. In order to pay off some of the debt Daisy told Bob she would sell the Lincoln he was driving, cash in on the profit he talked about. Then as now, cars lose their value as soon as they are driven off of the lot, but she needed the money and had no choice but to take the loss and sell the car.

After a few more weeks of trying to catch up on all the lies, cheating and bills piling up Bob decided to do Daisy a big favor, he gave her his half of the business. He walked out of the restaurant, went back and cleaned out his stuff from our basement, even conveniently took some of our furniture and we never saw him again. When all the dust settled there were a lot more unpaid bills that Daisy didn't know about. After clearing up all the mess Bob left behind his former partner showed up wondering if he could buy the place back. Daisy jumped at the chance to get out and made a payment arrangement where he could pay $200 a week until the purchase price was paid in full. This lasted a few weeks, the payments stopped and a few weeks later the door closed for good. A very expensive lesson for Daisy, most of the money she had inherited was gone. Daisy will survive: she still had a nice house, a nice car and four healthy kids.

Chapter 12:

The Woman of The Fort Lee Diner

Daisy had continued working off and on as a hairdresser; she was very loyal to her boss Ralph whom she had worked with for years. He would always hold a spot open for her through her tough times when her parents were dying and with Vinnie passing as well. Ralph had several girls quit at the same time over some type of dispute, when the girls asked Daisy why she wasn't quitting she reminded them how good Ralph was to her and she couldn't leave him hanging. They eventually hired some new girls and Ralph told Daisy once he built the business back up he would sell it. She promised to stay until he sold but after that all bets were off.

Ralph did find a buyer, an Arab man who was not so nice, especially to woman. Daisy said she would stay on for two weeks after the sale and then that would be it. The first day under the new owner went smooth; when they closed for the day he paid Daisy and she was ready to leave. He asked her "Where are you going?" Daisy said "Home." He told her she had to clean the shop before leaving, she reminded him that she did that on Saturdays and it would cost him an additional $25. He told her she would do it now and there would be no extra pay. That was it. Daisy quit on the spot and after many years of enjoying the business that would be the end of her hairdressing career.

Daisy found a new job working as a waitress at the Fort Lee Diner. Fort Lee New Jersey is just over the George Washington Bridge just out of New York City. During her time at the diner is where she would meet her new best friend and fellow Jewish woman named Toby. Daisy now had a companion that would share in some of her bizarre stories; they would find themselves in the strangest situations. They were like Lucy and Ethel, Lavern and Shirley or any other kind of comedy team, plain and simple, they were crazy.

One of the first stories from their friendship was when a young woman was sitting at the counter at the diner and seemed very nervous. While sitting there for a while she asked Daisy "Do you need some furniture?" This caught her off guard but suspecting this might be interesting she said, "Maybe." The lady told her she was moving and needed to sell most of her stuff. Daisy told the woman she might be interested and quickly told Toby as well. The lady told them she would have her chauffer pick them up if they needed a ride, which really had them curious now. The lady gave them the address and said for them to come over when their shift was done. They recognized the address; it was an expensive high rise down the street and they drove there right after their shift ended. They went up to the 12th floor and went into this beautifully furnished apartment. The problem was neither Daisy nor Toby had much money; they had their tip money from the day but that's it.

The lady said, "Everything is for sale, just make an offer." After looking over the furnishings Toby and Daisy had picked out some things they wanted, the dining room chairs, a blue velvet couch, a black leather couch, box spring and mattress as well as a TV console. When Toby asked the lady how much she wanted the woman went on to explain how she needed money real bad for a doctor's appointment, "How about $150 each?" Both ladies knew that was a steal, all this furniture was very expensive. The problem was the lady wanted cash which neither of them had. Daisy told the woman that she could go to the bank and cash a check; the lady jumped at that option and sent Daisy on to the bank. When they got back with the cash the lady grabbed it and ran out the door telling them to go ahead and take their stuff. This had Daisy and Toby totally confused but took what they could fit in their cars but would need to come back with a truck. When they returned the next day to get the rest the woman's husband was there. They saw a beautiful statue of an older distinguished man with diamonds for eyes, as they began to look closer at it the man quickly said, "The statue was not for sale, if I sold that statue I would be in big trouble, I'm holding it for somebody."

It turns out the man's name ended in a vowel , probably had some very interesting friends and his wife's urgent medical need was for drugs she was buying off the street. The husband explained the whole story of the problems he was having with his wife, after that Daisy and Toby wanted nothing else to do with this woman, which was of course after they came and picked up their furniture, a deal was a deal.

My favorite Toby story was a classic told by my mother. Toby needed to go to the DMV for some car tag issue she was having but wanted to call first to see what time the closed. So she took a break from work and went out to the lobby to use the pay phone. A moment later the diner phone rang and Daisy answered "Fort Lee Diner." The voice on the other end inquired "is this the DMV?' Daisy answered " No." Then Toby asked "Daisy is that you?" Daisy responded "Yes, who is this?" Toby quipped back "it's Toby, what are you doing at the DMV?' Daisy laughing answered "I'm not you idiot you dialed the wrong number." They had a huge laugh about that one, classic Toby!

One of the other ladies who worked with my mom and Toby was Virginia. The easiest way to describe Virginia is to give you her measurements, 62"-19"-32". I know it sounds hard to believe but very true and this was before breast implants were the norm. Stealing a line from another classic Seinfeld episode, "They're real and they're spectacular!"

She was in her late 30's and was a very strange woman. There was talk of an ex-husband and possibly a daughter but I don't think Daisy or Toby ever met them. Virginia was a very generous person; any time the three of them went out she would always want to pick up the tab. When they were at work it was a complete different story, if someone would work one of her tables while she was on break or in the restroom she would kill you for that dollar tip. Needless to say a lot of people would want to sit in her area just for the viewing pleasure.

Virginia had an apartment about a mile down the road from us in Hackensack and she would call our house at random times. She had a huge sweet tooth, and she would ask me to pick up two frozen Milky Way Bars or Frozen Snickers and deliver them to her apartment. She would usually give me a five dollar tip for the delivery which I was ecstatic over, that was a lot of money to a kid in those days.

One last note on The Fort Lee Diner, because it was just outside of New York City many of the New York Yankees would come in there to eat. My mom got me autographs from Bobby Mercer, Felipe Alou, Thurman Munson and Roy White to name a few. Only a true Yankees fan, which I am, can appreciate that.

Chapter 13:

Hanging Out

The year was now 1972, I was now 11 years old and us four kids starting making roots in Hackensack. We really were enjoying our childhood, even through all the turmoil because Daisy rolled with the punches we learned to do the same. Rob had a bunch of friends; some of them were up to no good. Steve was busy working and trying to meet girls. Michele and I were making friends in our neighborhood and some of the friends would end up being lifelong ones. A few years earlier I met a kid name Peter that lived around the corner. Peter was a year younger than me even though he looked older because he was about a foot taller than me. He had three older brothers and an older sister and they were all very tall. He was like me, a surprise last child. Once we started hanging out together we became best of friends and did everything together, even though he went to private school and I went to the local public school. There was a bunch of us that hung out together; Jeff, Carlo and Tommy (my step cousin) were the immediate group.

The big place to go was the park, Pulaski Park. This was right down the street from our house and was the center of our universe, if anything happened it started at the park. The group (gang) that hung out there was called the Owls, the Pulaski Park Owls; to be honest I'm not real sure how that name came about. There were the older Owls which my brother Rob and Pete's older brother's Paul and Donnie were part of. Pete and I were part of the young Owls along with many others, Danny, Rob, Ray, Peter, Tim, and Jerry to name a few. Even though the other guys were older than us by about four or five years we were all part of the younger Owls.

Basically we were a bunch of street kids and trouble would never be far from us. There were gang fights when kids from other towns tried to invade our park, I witnessed a few of these (hiding in the bushes) with the older group and it was ugly. Just like what you would see in a movie, these guys kicking the crap out of each other and at some point the guys from out of town would run to their cars and speed off.

The older Owls had some tough son of a guns including three Italian brothers, Stash, John and Frank, who may have been the toughest guys I ever knew. John was as big as a house and nobody wanted to mess with him. Yet, away from the fights he was a gentle giant. I remember one day I was walking down the street, he was getting in his car and he made a point to acknowledge me. "Hey, Ron, how you doing?" He wouldn't leave until I would respond, "Hey, John, I'm doing good." John and Frank were best friends with my brother Rob and one of the reasons they were cool to me. As a side note regarding Rob and the fighting, that was not his forte, he was not a violent guy at all and was more of a spectator when it came to the gang fights, in all honesty these guys didn't need his help.

Our group didn't have the gang fight issues, by the time we took over the park the fights were pretty much over. Within our group of young Owls, the older guys would make us play tackle football against them. If we said no they would just kick our butts anyway so we took our chances of trying to outrun them which didn't work either. When you are 11 or 12 years old and play football against guys that are 15 and 16 you can imagine the outcome. There were a few times where there were broken bones like when Dave broke his thumb, I almost threw up when I saw him come screaming out of the pile of bodies with his thumb bent in a way that was not normal unless you were quadruple jointed.

The other thing the older guys made us do was box each other. One Christmas one of the guys got boxing gloves as a gift from his parents and he brought them down the park. We took those old wooden police barricades and used them to make a boxing ring out of them. Let the fights begin! This lasted for several months until we all got tired of getting our faces punched in, so we went back to football to unleash our aggression.

The nicknames were the best for some of the Owls, like Boobie, Weirdsville, Anti, Rollee, Whitey, Bones, JJ, Smitty, Pig, Crazy Jerry, Pigeon, Klinker, Fishman, Garo, Smiley and Bogart (that was Rob's) were some of the good ones.

The older Owls were guys who were born in the early to mid 1950's. So as the crazy late 1960's came into play these guys were in their mid to late teens and having a ball. Drugs were a big part of life for some of them; surprisingly some didn't let it get control of their life. Unfortunately several of Rob's friends died because of it. One of the girls, Gail, who hung out with the group was one who didn't make it. She got sick after a night of heavy partying and while throwing up she actually choked to death.

One of Rob's best friends, Smitty, was a big drug user. One day his father walked in their house and found him lying dead on the couch with a needle sticking out of his arm. One of the guys who lived the down the street, kind of an outsider, sold him the drugs. Once the police did their work and found out it was him who was the dealer he was sent to prison. I'm not sure of the details but within a few months he was found dead in his jail cell from an apparent suicide.

A lot of crazy and sad things happened back in those days. One of the saddest was when John, one of the Italian brothers I mentioned earlier, was cruising in upstate New York one day with his friend Joe when he suddenly lost control of his car and tragically died from his injuries. Joe suffered serious head injuries and would take years to fully recover. Where I didn't know the others that well I was truly upset when John died, he was such a great guy who everyone liked (unless you were fighting him). He was engaged to Pam, whom lived around the corner from us. She was Sal's youngest daughter, I'll tell you more about Sal a little later. Needless to say Pam was devastated, she would admit today she never got over it and his death altered her life more than she could have ever imagined.

Those are just a few of the stories from the older Owls. My brother Rob would always find trouble mainly because he continued to be the ultimate follower. Rob was a smart guy, not book smart and surely not interested in school but he loved cars, motorcycles which would become a lifelong passion.

By the way while all this was going on Michele and I were watching most of this happen as 11 and 12 year old kids, talk about growing up fast. Steve was not interested in the park and the goings on there. He was too busy doing his own thing, hanging out with a completely different crowd. With his group there was no fighting, no gangs, just some smart kids that had no time for that lifestyle. They still managed to find trouble but most times they never got caught and it never happened close to home. It was very clear even at my young age that my two brothers were VERY different.

Rob's first car was a 1961 limousine which barely ran, it looked great but was a clunker at best. The car would eventually blow up because he didn't know to put oil in the engine. The car was sitting in our driveway and Rob asked me and Michele if we could help him with something fun. It was freezing outside and it had just snowed about six inches. Rob decided with the limo having a blown engine why not fill it with snow. So Rob, Michele and I filled inside of the car all the way up to the roof in snow, it was a blast. Once my mom found out the car was dead she asked Rob to get it towed to the junk yard for scrap.

On the other hand Steve's first car was an Aston Martin, an older one that didn't cost him a bunch of money but it was in great condition and was a very cool car. He looked like James Bond driving that thing around town. Rob's second car was an old hearse, yes the type of car used to transport dead people. At least this one was in a little better shape than his first car, it actually lasted him for a while. Never the normal kid, Rob took me, Michele and a buddy of his to this big public park in the hearse. We were just hanging out in the parking area which was very crowded, I was wondering what we were doing. Rob looked at this buddy and said "Let's do it." I had no idea what he was up to but it would be a classic. His buddy pulled out a fake gun which sure looked real; it just made a lot of noise. So Rob told us what he wanted to do, he wanted to fake a shooting and conveniently take the dead body away in the hearse. So we planned it out, his buddy shot me, I hit the ground; Michele screamed while Rob and his buddy carried me into the back of the car and then quickly drove off. You could hear people screaming as we flew out of there. Yes we were juvenile delinquents.

His next car was an old Pontiac which he name Uncle Albert. This car didn't last long either as the engine blew up on this one too. Before letting this one go to the junkyard Rob and his buddies decided they wanted to paint the car. Their version of a paint job was to get some old unused paint cans from everyone's garage and just start throwing the paint on the car covering the windshield and all. It was quite a site, about 10 different colors of paint just poured all over the car, a few days later it was off to the junkyard. Yes, I would realize at a very young age my two brothers were very different. Steve was all about the finer things, I remember my mom telling a story where she had taken Steve shopping for school clothes and he saw a shirt that was $40. This was the early 1970's where $40 for a shirt was unheard of, which is exactly what my mom told Steve. He said "Not to worry, I will work to make that money and buy that shirt." And he did. He was not afraid to work, he knew he had expensive tastes and it was something the family couldn't afford. The only way he could fulfill his taste was to buy it himself. Rob on the other hand would have a job long enough to buy something he wanted then quit and enjoy his new car, stereo or whatever it was that he bought. At an early age it was pretty easy to see which brother's path I needed to follow. I began to look up to my brother Steve and knew I needed to be more like him than Rob.

Chapter 14:

Rob's In Trouble

Again, Rob wasn't a bad kid just a misguided follower. Interestingly, this would be the complete opposite of what he would become later in life. But in his youth there was trouble which included experimenting with drugs. By now he had quit high school and would go from job to job trying to make money for his new project, a Harley Davidson Chopper. After many months of saving some money he got with a local motorcycle shop and with his design they built a custom metallic green and chrome Harley Davidson Chopper, like something right out of the movie *Easy Rider.* That was his pride and joy, he cruised it everywhere. Unfortunately after a few months he crashed it, and I remember him being pretty scratched up but no major injuries other than his pride.

The motorcycles and cars did not keep him busy enough to stay out of trouble. Things got so bad with his abuse of drugs and getting into trouble that my mom had him put away in a youth detention center called Bergen Pines. He did not like Daisy very much at this point in his life, he didn't think he needed to be put in a rehab center but Daisy did. Rob stayed in there for a few weeks and when he got out he didn't want to live with us anymore, so he went to live with the aunt of one of his best friends. It was a mile or so down the road but we didn't see him much although

I remember one day he was walking by the house and I ran up to him to say hi because I hadn't seen him in a while and I missed him. He just ignored me. I thought he was stoned or something because he had a strange look on his face, almost in a trance. At the time it really bothered me. As a young boy I just couldn't understand why he didn't speak to me, I never did anything wrong to him. Years later, as adults, I asked him about this and he swore he didn't remember it ever happening. I did.

Daisy was hoping for a normal life after Vinnie had died; Rob's constant episodes were not allowing that to happen. Rob and mom had a tough relationship, the real problem was the fact that Rob was a spitting image of our father Sam, in looks, mannerisms, habits and the reminders of their relationship just made things worse for him and Daisy.

Speaking of my father, we would see him periodically, maybe once or twice a year. My mom had always told us "the problems I had with your father were our problems but he is still your father and you will respect him." These would be words that I would play back in my head my entire life. Because of his mental issues the visits had to be supervised and at this point it was just Michele and I that visited him. Rob and Steve had their visits on their own. Daisy would drop us off at a local orphanage and we would visit with him for a few hours and that was pretty much it. This went on for a few years and then when Michele and I were a little older we would actually visit him in New York City. He lived in Queens, NY and would meet us at Grand Central Station. We would go to the movies, have lunch and a couple times even spend the night at his sister's apartment but never at his.

One classic story that will give you a better idea of Sam's problems was when I went to visit him by myself many years later. We went to the movies and saw the movie "Endless Love" with Brooke Shields. If you know the movie it's about a girl who falls in love with a young troubled boy and eventually breaks it off and breaks his heart at the same time. We are in a very large theater that is half full at best so if you said anything your voice carried throughout the theater. During some of the scenes where Brooke's character refuses the give the boy another chance Sam decided to add some additional background for the audience and would blurt out "that bitch!" The first time he did it I looked over at him and he just smiled. A few people gave us a dirty look as I scooted down in my seat a few inches to try to hide. A few minutes later during another similar scene he blurts out a little louder this time "just like all women." A few more dirty looks and few more inches down in my seat. After this happened for the eighth time and the dirty looks turned into people yelling "shut up you jackass", after all this was New York and they will tell you how they feel, I was almost under my seat and couldn't wait for the movie to end. After it was over we walked out and Sam looked at me and calmly said "that was a good movie, did you like it?' My reply? "Yeah, it was great."

Back to Rob, he wanted to see more of life and left New Jersey for a cross country trip to California. He had a few dollars in his pocket and stuck his thumb out and hitchhiked all the way out there. He was gone for several months and told me years later that he had a blast, just lots of partying. That was Rob in a nut shell, he didn't want any responsibility, just live for the day. He eventually got homesick and also ran out of money so he had to make his way back to Hackensack. When he returned he showed up on our front steps, rang the door bell, Daisy answered the door saying, "Can I help you?" Rob replied by saying, "Mom, it's me, Rob." The issue was Rob now had a head of thick curly hair down to his shoulders, a full beard and an earring in each ear. Daisy told him no son of hers looked like that and if he wanted to come in he would have to get cleaned up then slammed the door in his face. With no place to go he came back a couple hours later with a shave, a haircut and moved into the apartment we had in our basement. This would be the first of many times Rob moved away and then came running home for shelter and a warm meal.

A few days later Daisy was leaving early for work and she came back into the house screaming. We all ran to the front door to see what the commotion was about and saw what looked to be a homeless man sleeping in our front yard. We all knew this had to have something to do with Rob and when he finally came to the door Rob told us "There is nothing to worry about; that's just Jiggs." Daisy asked, "What is a Jiggs?" Rob said, "That is my friend who I met on the train we jumped on coming back from California." To which Daisy said, "OK, but why is he sleeping in our front yard?" Rob said "I knew you wouldn't want him to come in the house so I told him he could sleep out there." Things would settle down with Rob, some of his buddies went off to college or were working and as he matured his drug issues slowly went away but it sure was a crazy time.

Chapter 15:

My Pal Sal

Late one evening Daisy was out for a walk with our dog, she just went down the block and then back home. When she got back to the house she noticed the front door to the house was open. Knowing she had closed the door when she left she didn't want to walk back in by herself. She walked around the corner to see if any neighbors were out and saw her brother-in-law (Vinnie's brother) Phil talking with one of our neighbors Sal. She told them her situation and Sal told her he would come check it out. He walked through the house but didn't find anything unusual, they talked for a while and then Sal went home.

A couple of weeks later Daisy felt like going for a car ride, she always enjoyed just cruising down the road taking in the fresh air. While she was pulling out of the driveway Sal happened to be walking up, he poked his head into the car and inquired where she was heading. She told him she was out for a cruise and invited him along. They went out to Englewood Cliffs, a real scenic place that overlooked New York City, which is when they officially started dating. Some years later when I went back to New Jersey to visit my friend Peter, we went up to Englewood Cliffs with some girls to hang out as well, not realizing until reading her notes some 20 years later that we had the same make out spot as my mother, a little weird to say the least.

Daisy and Sal were really hitting it off, he started coming over every night after work for dinner. Daisy would always make extra food so there was some for Sal's father. Sal lived in the same house he was born and raised in. His father, Augustino, was born in Italy and moved to the U.S. in the early 1900's, married and had four sons, Smokey, John, Tony and Sal a very proud Italian family.

I would bring Augustino his food every night after we were done eating. He would be sitting at his table with his glass of red wine, he didn't speak much English but would always say thank you and give me a pat on the cheek. He had mellowed in his old age; at that time he was in his late 80's. From what Sal said he was a tough father when he was growing up. Sal told stories when he and his brothers would constantly get whipped with the garden hose or anything else his father could get his hands on.

Sal's first wife had died about the same time as Vinnie and he was looking to move on in his life as well. He had pretty much raised his kids, he had four children; Bruce was the oldest, then Denise, Lenore and Pam. They were all pretty much on their own except Pam, she was supposed to marry John but he died in the car accident I mentioned earlier. Bruce was older and wasn't really part of the local group but Denise and Lenore were. Lenore and Rob actually dated for a while long before Daisy and Sal became an item.

Sal was about 5'5" tall and weighed about 165 pounds. Pound for pound he may have been the strongest person I ever knew. For years he was a bulldozer operator down at the local junk yard. After doing that for a while he went back into the scrap metal business, which was his father's business before he retired. Sal would go around in a pickup truck searching for scrap metal that he could strip down and sell. I saw him on numerous occasions squat down and lift an entire car engine into the back of his truck, right then I knew this was not someone I wanted to make mad. Even though he was not very tall many years earlier he played semi-pro football as an offensive lineman.

Just before Rob had really straightened up he and my mom were in a pretty heated argument when he raised his fist toward her and said, "I should just punch you in the…." Before he could finish the sentence Sal had stepped in front of Daisy and punched Rob right in the face. He was standing at the top of the stairs to our basement, after the shot Sal gave him he violently tumbled down all 15 stairs until hitting the wall at the bottom. Sal stood and the top of the stairs and yelled down to him, "If you ever raise your hand to your mother again I'll F—ING kill you!" Right then, Rob had new found respect for Sal, Daisy had a man she wanted and I knew this was a guy I wanted to call Dad.

Chapter 16:

What About The Other Kids

Steve was still working his butt off, either at the McDonald's down the road or waiting on tables at other restaurants. He even was a roadie for a local rock band. He didn't care he just wanted to make money, he needed the cash for his new passion, which at the time was taking flying lessons at the small local airport down in Teterboro, NJ. He wanted to become a pilot and was going to do whatever it took to achieve it.

He didn't burn up all his time on work, school and flying lessons, he saved some time for girls. It was evident even early on; Steve would not have any problems getting a date. He was good looking, had an outgoing personality, always had the nice things and knew how to attract the girls. As you will see later on, this was a sign of things to come.

Michele and I were just street kids, we had our local friends that we did everything with and we all got along great. Her friends were my friends and visa verse. Her best friend Suzanne would turn out to be my first real crush. We were just kids but it sure was some strong emotions as the first girl can be. It was nothing serious just the normal making out that boys and girls did at that age.

It seem like it lasted a while but I ended up dating a different girl from school. Suzanne went to the same private school as Peter did and dated someone she knew there.

Our gang was pretty much juvenile delinquents; we got into a bunch of trouble, nothing real serious, at least we didn't think so. One of our rituals was during the fall we would gather up all the dried up leaves in the park and light them on fire. The park was probably the length of three football fields surrounded by trees so there was plenty of leaves for a HUGE fire. During one of these fires would be the first time I would ever get chased by the police, they showed up at the front of the park sirens blasting as the fire burned out of control. The group would just take off toward the back of the park which had about six different ways to escape. I remember it like it was yesterday, my heart was pounding as I ran like the wind not wanting to get caught. I always wished someone had a stopwatch and would have timed me, I guarantee you it would have been a world record. Deep down I was a chicken, I wanted nothing to do with breaking the law but that's what the gang did and I was right there with them.

Some of our other activities that caused the police to chase us were illegal fireworks, fights, minor vandalism, you name it we did it. I can honestly say I lost count of how many times we ran from the police. It's not something I'm proud of but it just shows idle time for young kids is never a good thing. As for the police, looking back at it if they really wanted to catch us they just needed to have a police car at each exit to the park and we would have been dead meat, maybe they were messing with us as much as we were messing with them.

One night we were walking back from Red's Pizza, our local pizza place and pinball playing hangout. Red liked us, we never did anything wrong there, as far as he was concerned we were good kids and some of his best customers. We ate a lot of pizza at 25 cents a slice and drank a bunch of ten cent sodas. As me, Danny, Rob, Ralph, Tim, Ray and my sister Michele walked through the schoolyard heading back to the park we saw a man about 25 years old or so walking toward us. I knew something wasn't right, it was a cool fall night and he was walking with no shirt or shoes. As we walked passed him he had a mean look on his face and before we knew it he pulled a baseball bat out from behind his back, grabbed Danny (the biggest one of the group) and put him in a choke hold. He said if we didn't tell him who threw the bottle at his wife's car he was going to smash Danny's head open.

We didn't know what the heck he was talking about and told him that. He told us his wife drove past the park a couple hours ago and a bottle hit her VW Beatle. What we finally realized was we were throwing water balloons at cars earlier and she was one of our victims. There was a big tree at the front of the park with a thick branch that hung over the street; it was perfect for one of us to sit up there and as the car approached the water balloons would fly hitting the cars as they passed. What happened was after we hit her car, she jammed on her brakes and of course we ran out the back of the park. When she got out of her car she saw broken glass in the street and assumed we had thrown a bottle at her car.

This guy didn't believe our story and took Danny by the neck back to his house to call the police. The police came and took us down to the police station, age 11 and I've got my first arrest record. To think at that age I was out during all hours of the night was absolutely crazy, my mom trusted me even though I abused that trust. Being the youngest of four kids, especially with the oldest being Rob, Daisy's discipline by now had pretty much phased out.

When we were down at the station the police started asking questions of each of us one at a time. The other guys were all 15 and 16, except for me and Michele. When it came to me the police chief asked what the heck we were doing with these older boys. I told him they were our friends and they looked out for us. He told us we needed to have friends our own age which is the same thing Daisy told us when she came down to the police station to pick us up. Surprisingly she didn't make a big deal about it once I explained what happened. Again, that was the good thing about having an older brother like Rob, the shock element was gone as long as I didn't get killed and didn't mess with drugs all was pretty much forgiven.

The next episode happened when me, Danny and Ralph went down to Valley Fair which was the local everything store, sort of like today's Wal-Mart. Ralph had this jean jacket and asked me to hold it for him, when you're the little guy in the group you had to do what the older guys asked. Instead of holding it I put it on, the sleeves hung past my hands by about six inches and made me look like a midget. As we are walking in the store a couple of other guys walked by and made a snide comment about how I looked which set Ralph off. Ralph was a bit of a hot head and was always looking for a fight; having Danny by his side was not a bad thing either, he was a pretty tough dude. Ralph told Danny what the guy said and they agreed to follow these guys outside. Once we got out there Ralph jumped right in the face of one of the guys while the other guy ran back into the store. Ralph started pushing this guy around but he just stood there not saying a word, he didn't want any part of Ralph. This went on for several minutes until the other guy came back with a man dressed in a shirt and tie. It turned out he was the store detective, Detective Mudry, I'll never forget his name.

This was not my first run in with detective Mudry, a few years earlier he caught me stealing lipstick for my sister and her friend Barbara. The girls told me they really wanted the lipstick, I could just stuff it in my pants and nobody would suspect me. So I did it and within minutes Detective Mudry was tapping me on the shoulder asking me to open my jeans. Needless to say I almost wet my pants. He called Daisy and let us off with a warning. Truly, that is the first and last time I ever shoplifted.

Back to the fight, Detective Mudry (luckily he didn't remember my little shoplifting episode) jumped in the middle of Ralph and the other guy trying to keep anything from progressing. Ralph did not like this and in true New Jersey form yelled out to the other guy "I'm going to kill you." At that point the detective grabbed Ralph and told him "You're not going to kill anybody," he kind of pushed Ralph against those old aluminum railings that are for storing the shopping carts and actually pushed Ralph over the railing causing him to land flat on his back. Danny and I knew this was not going well and we just needed to get the heck out of there but Ralph said he now wanted to press charges against Mudry and went inside to call the police. Within minutes the police showed up and there I am in the back of a police car again, off to the police station for the juvenile delinquent and his friends.

This time it was the Little Ferry, New Jersey Police Station. For those old enough to remember, Little Ferry was home to Rosie's Diner, famous for the Bounty paper towel commercials where actress Nancy Walker proclaimed the brand, "The quicker picker upper."

Once we got to the police station the three of us waited in front of this huge wall until the police chief starting asking us questions. The first thing they wanted to know was our age, so Danny started "16," Ralph, "16" and then went it got to me and in my little squeaky voice yelled out "12" which the chief screamed out "Who the hell is that?" The problem was I was so small he couldn't even see me over the large wall. I got the same question as last time about why am I hanging with boys this age. The speech went on for a while until our parents were called and my mom came in to get me.

She seemed pretty calm as she assured the police chief this would never happen again and then we left to get in the car. This was strange because she was even more mellow then the first incident, that was until we got in the car. As I'm sitting in the passenger seat Daisy quickly grabbed me by the back of the head and proceeded to pound my head on the dashboard, "Why?!" screaming at the top of her lungs. I now knew I needed to change some things in my life before it got worse, I didn't like upsetting my mom like that, I loved her SO MUCH. All she's ever done as a single parent was work three jobs, morning, noon and night to make sure we had everything we ever needed.

For the next few months I didn't leave the house much other than going to school. I had heard from some of my other friends that Ralph was going ahead with pressing charges and I was going to be one of the key witnesses. I told Daisy this and said she would not let me go to court unless a subpoena was sent. I had heard that Danny and Ralph were looking for me which made me want to stay home even more. I figured if I ever ran into them a big ass kicking was going to happen because they heard I would not be going to court with them. One afternoon when I finally decided to go out, I was hanging out at Ray's house and we were playing basketball when Danny and Ralph came walking up. I started to sweat thinking I'm in deep trouble now but they were really cool, they just said they really needed me to be at court to tell the truth of what happened. I told them my mom was pissed off and wouldn't let me go. They said they understood and told me I should come back around.

This meant a lot to me, especially with Danny, he was our local sports hero. He was great at every sport, basketball, football and was a big time baseball player. I remember going to watch him play a high school baseball game where he pitched a no-hitter and hit a home run for the only run of the game and won 1-0. We were a group of school athletes that managed to balance school, home, friends and trouble making. Back in the early 1970s we were considered mischievous; today we would be sent to military school or worse.

It wasn't too much longer after running into them that I was sitting in class at school when a police officer came into my class and believe or not I was served a subpoena right in front of all my classmates. Not bragging but when a cop comes to your 7th grade glass and points you out in a crowd it does buy you some respect from your peers. With that being said, if that happened to one of my kids today I would beat the crap out of them. Again we are talking the tough streets of New Jersey in the early 1970s, I repeat A DIFFERENT TIME.

The court case came up and not surprisingly the two guys from the incident testified along with Detective Mudry that Ralph tried to go after one of the guys and while trying to break it up Mudry stepped in the middle of it. Trying to hold Ralph back while he was slipping over the railing, Mudry grabbed Ralph but he couldn't hold him and he fell. So who was the judge going to believe, some punk kids or the store detective with two witnesses that happen to also work at the store? Cased dismissed.

Chapter 17:

The First Move

Daisy and Sal started to get real serious in their relationship. They were dating for a couple years now, unfortunately Sal's father had passed away but this gave Sal and Daisy more freedom to do something that would become their passion, travel. They took a trip to Florida for a vacation and left Michele and me to be watched by Steve. This was funny because we never saw Steve when they were home; we sure weren't going to see him while they were gone. Rob was off doing his thing and wasn't responsible enough to be in charge so Steve was the only choice. Michele and I were 13 and 12 at this point, Steve was 17. Today, most parents wouldn't ever consider leaving their teenage kids behind but back then it didn't seem like a big deal.

We were all pretty independent because Daisy was always working. We starting doing our own laundry and made our own meals by the ages of eight and nine, not dinner, Daisy always wanted to have a family dinner. While they were gone for a couple of weeks we just went about our normal life, went to school, did our homework and hung out with our friends. While they were still in Florida, Peter, Michele, me and her friend Angel were at our house when Steve walked in. We hadn't seen him in days and he was not happy when he saw the house was a little messy. He knew if Daisy came home and saw the house like this he would be in trouble because he was left in charge. He quickly ordered me to vacuum the house, not wanting to be pushed around in front of Peter and more importantly Angel, I told him in a very cocky voice "You do it." That didn't set to well with him and he proceeded to beat on me, knocked me to the floor, while on the floor he grabbed my legs, while holding me upside down, forcefully pounded my head on the floor and then gave me a kick in the side for good measure. After rubbing my wounds for a minute I decided vacuuming the house was a great idea.

Being the only girl Michele never had to worry about being hit by Steve, Sal, Daisy or anyone else. Me on the other hand, I took a few spankings, not a lot but the ones I got were memorable. The only time l got what I would call a real beating by Sal was one I would never forget. He worked me over pretty good because I had upset my mom, he didn't believe in kids disrespecting their parents, a policy I uphold today also. Today, people would be up in arms for treatment like that. In my opinion a little more discipline is needed with today's kids, everyone needs a little tough love. I'm not talking about the kind of beating I got but a good kick in the pants might straighten some kids up. I know I sure got it as a kid when Sal finally came into our lives and it made a difference in me.

I would get some other beatings as well, not from my parents but from Steve's friends. Steve would pop in the house with his buddies Tony and Larry. He would run upstairs to get a change of clothes while Tony and Larry would come looking for me. One would grab me and hold my arms open while the other guy would just beat on my chest. This got me motivated in the lifting weights at a young age, they would comment that I was actually starting to get a chest as they continued to beat on it. Steve would eventually come down and yell for Tony and Larry; they would throw me to the floor and tell me they'll see me next time. This went on for a couple of years but I got smart, any time I heard the front door open I would run to my room and lock my door to avoid the beatings.

Those guys seemed to be big and strong to me at that age. Some 15 or so years later I met Steve for a drink at a restaurant in Hackensack when we both happened to be back in town. I was on my annual visits to see Peter and his family and I think Steve was there on business. Steve said he was meeting some old friends to catch up. When I walked in I saw Steve talking to a real short guy, when they turned around to greet me I realized the short guy was Larry. I had grown to 5'10" and about 180 pounds and Larry was all of about 5'4" and 120 pounds max.

Steve, always being the one to stir the pot, said, "Hey, Larry do you remember when you and Tony used to beat on Ronnie?" (my family always called me Ronnie). Larry quickly responded by saying "No, not really." Steve asked me if I remembered, for which I replied "Yeah, it was no big deal." My gut reaction was to squash Larry like a bug but I guess the fact of knowing I could was better than the act of actually doing it.

Just before Daisy and Sal returned from their Florida trip Daisy called to let us in on a big surprise, "WE'RE MOVING TO FLORIDA!!!!!" That hit me and Michele like a ton of bricks; we had no desire to move anywhere, on the other hand Rob didn't care, he actually wanted to go. Steve was a senior in high school so they agreed to let him stay at the house until he graduated. My mom had rented the basement apartment of our house to a co-worker of hers and felt OK with Steve staying upstairs with her there to make sure everything was taken care of.

Daisy told us Florida would be great, we would buy some land and have horses; it would be a new way of life. She tried to paint the best picture she could be we still were not buying it. Within a few months we packed up some clothes and south we went. Daisy and Sal had bought a few different types of campers, motor homes and pull trailers those first few years they were together and we had traveled quite a bit with them, going to Canada, down to Florida a few times. The trips were a lot of fun, we all really enjoyed traveling and spending time at the different campgrounds around the country. You want to meet some nice people check into a campground. I'm not sure if it was just because everyone was on vacation but the people we met at the campgrounds were super friendly.

The current camper of choice was a Chevy van with a bubble top on it and we had one of those pop up trailers we pulled behind it. This was going to be our home for the next few months. On our journey down I-95 through the south we had stopped for gas somewhere in South Carolina and I had to go to the bathroom real bad. It was one of those old style gas stations with the bathrooms around the side of the building. As soon as we stopped I ran out to go the bathroom and saw the first door that said "Women," the next said "Men," and then I realized there was a third door and my curiosity made me look to see who that door was for. I wished I never looked because what I saw opened my eyes to something I didn't realize existed, hatred. What was on the door was the "N" word. The hatred I had only read about was still very real. It's not like I never heard the word before, growing up a street kid in New Jersey I had pretty much heard it all. As kids we were picked on and picked on others for being fat, skinny, Jewish, black, white, ugly, good looking, having a girlfriend, not having a girlfriend and anything else we could think of. It wasn't prejudice it was kids picking on kids. But to see a work like that, displayed in public, I was shocked. I just froze. I got so scared the fact that I had to use the bathroom so badly was no longer an issue I didn't even have to go anymore. I ran as fast as I could to the van and jumped in. Sal was still pumping the gas as I sat there praying he would finish quickly. About 30 minutes later I asked if we could pull over on the side of the road as the urge to go to the bathroom had returned but this time I just went in the woods. My parents asked "I thought you just went?" I didn't tell them what I saw I just made up some story about having to go again.

Growing up in the north in the 60's and early 70's race wasn't that big of a deal, not to kids my age. We went to school together, played sports together, it just wasn't an issue. I surely never saw anything like that in a public place in New Jersey. It was my first run in with real racism and it scared the crap out of me.

We eventually made it down to Perrine, Florida, truly the middle of nowhere. This was south of Miami, just north of Homestead and not too far from the beginning of the Florida Keys. We moved into a KOA campground which would be our home for the next six months. Yes, we lived in our little van and pop up pull trailer. To my surprise there were quite a few families living in the campground. Daisy enrolled me and Michele in school and we caught the school bus at the entrance to the campground with about 15 other kids that lived there. This was new to us because back in New Jersey we didn't have school buses; we actually took the public bus to school. It was bus route 165 that came out of New York City that commuters would take to work. So we would get on the same bus as business people, this made for some interesting rides including some gross old men exposing themselves to the school girls. Most of the girls weren't even fazed; a lot of them were tougher than me including Michele.

Nobody would ever mess with her or me for that matter fearing they would have to deal with her. She wasn't big but she was just tough as nails. She used to kick my butt on a regular basis until we got older when puberty and a growth spurt finally kicked in for me.

As for living in the campground, it turned out to be a ton of fun living there, albeit a little like living in the Stone Age.

We didn't have a phone, if you wanted to call someone you would have to go to the little convenience store up by the campground office. There was a clubhouse with a game room and a nice big pool so there was plenty for us to do and of course the weather was great, it was getting close to winter but still warm down there.

Even though we had to go to school it felt like we were on vacation. The atmosphere was very laid back, a lot of people moved there and it seemed like time just stopped. Short term, that was a great lifestyle, long term, it could suck the ambition right out of you. I have to say Daisy and Sal were very happy; this may have been the happiest my mom had ever been. All the troubles of Sam were behind her, the stress of her mother and second husband dying was over as well. She was working at a restaurant in Miami and Sal had bought an old pickup truck to start a little junk business just like he was doing in New Jersey. My mom worked the night shift so she could be there in the mornings to feed us breakfast and see us off the school. She would then go to sleep and wake up when we got home from school, make dinner and then head off to work.

She liked the night shift and the evenings always brought out some interesting people. She would take the van to work while Sal, me and Michele would sleep in the pop up trailer. When Daisy got off work she would get in the van and change clothes, she had about a 40 minute ride back to the campground and she wanted to be comfortable so she would put on her nightgown.

One night while driving home she was going through the toll booth to get on the highway and while trying to put the coins in the shoot she missed. She got out of the van to pick up the coins, put them in the shoot and went on her way. Within a mile a man in a car was flashing his lights behind her, he quickly drove up next to her on the highway and was making hand gestures for her to join him somewhere. Daisy just ignored it and he eventually drove away. It took a few minutes but she finally figured out why the man was so eager to meet her, when she got out to put the coins in the shoot at the toll booth she gave the man a show because she didn't have anything on under her nightgown. So when she bent over to get the coins he got a full viewing, Daisy was not easily embarrassed, she laughed the rest of the way home and couldn't wait to tell us the story.

We enjoyed our stay in the campground for those few months but Daisy and Sal decided they needed something more permanent. They looked at a nice new mobile home park a few miles from the campground. These mobile home parks were popping up all over the place in south Florida, they were reasonably priced and very family oriented. . They were ready to buy in the mobile home park but we needed to go back to New Jersey, sell the house there and make the final move. Michele and I went back to our old school in Hackensack and our friends were surprised to see us thinking we had moved away to Florida. We stayed a few months, and then packed up and this time we made the permanent move to Florida.

Rob decided he would come with us, this would make about the 10th time he had moved back in with us. We all loved Rob he was just a pain in the butt to live with. He was real messy; you could tell when he was in the kitchen because of the mess he left behind, that would drive my mom crazy. His favorite meal was fried bologna sandwiches; the interesting part was how he made them. He would take the bologna and put it on top of the toaster to heat it while he toasted the bread, this almost caused a fire every time he did but that never stopped him.

Steve went off to college in Colorado, and this started a period of several years where we would not see much of him. He loved snow skiing and was very good at it. During that year in Colorado he went on a trip to Europe and somehow ended up doing some trick skiing on local TV there.

Chapter 18:

Welcome To Quail Roost Mobile Home Park

At the beginning it was a bit of culture shock for all of us, we needed to make new friends and the adults needed to find new jobs. Daisy knew she could work anywhere; she was a real pro when it came to being a waitress and Sal would continue his junk business. With over 300 homes in the park there was a bunch of kids so making friends happened pretty quickly. For me it was David, James, Gary, Tom and Doug. For Michele it was Cindy and Cheryl.

The first thing that surprised me was what these kids were into. Things were pretty crazy back in New Jersey but these guys were talking like they were already having sex, doing drugs and well on their way to some trouble. As always with teenagers, some of it was just talk but there was some truth too. David and I quickly became very good friends; his father was the park manager and seemed to be a nice guy but was not very well liked by the other kids. I guess he had to enforce the rules around the clubhouse and pool which didn't set well with rebellious teens. James was a good buddy too but after a little episode with his father I was real nervous being anywhere close to his house.

We were sitting in his front yard one day and the paper boy came by for the morning delivery. The paper boy and his family had just moved into the park and was the only black family that lived there. He set the paper down by the door and just as he was getting ready to drive off on his bike James' dad came out and yelled, "Hey. boy, don't ever set foot on my property again, I don't want no "the N word" around my house." I don't know who felt worse, me or the paper boy; I wanted to crawl under the house. I found out later that James' father was in the KKK. To me, that was a group that you just read about while living in the north but to be that close to it, having someone right in your neighborhood was very unsettling to me. Luckily that was the last episode like that I witnessed.

One thing we did to occupy our time was riding dirt bikes. We loved being out in the middle of nowhere there was a bunch of trails to ride on without ever having to go on the road. My mom bought me a little motorcycle to try to ease the pain of the move and it worked for a while. Michele started to get into some trouble in school, some girls began picking on her being the new girl but she was not one to sit back and take it and got into some fights. Daisy got called into school a few times before things finally settled down. The first move to the campground was fun but now we knew this was final, the house in New Jersey was sold and there was no going back. That didn't set well with Michele and me. She missed her friends; I missed mine and also missed Suzanne (the first crush). I don't care what anyone says it takes a while to get over your first crush.

Rob pretty much went with the flow; he could live anywhere. He liked Florida, it was a free spirit lifestyle, and there were tons of biker bars, which is where he loved to hang out. He swore he was a biker dude; the truth was he was more a lover than ever a fighter, even though one of the tattoos on his arm was "Saturday Night is Alright for Fighting." He loved woman and had a real weakness for them, if a woman came up to him and said she liked his T-shirt or his tattoo he was ready to marry her. Nobody knew this tremendous weakness for woman would eventually be his demise.

One day Rob came home and was acting a little different, this could mean a lot of things with him. Is he drunk? Is he stoned? What was it? When he took off his hat, his famous Humphrey Bogart hat, I knew something was up, his head was shaved completely bald and he told us he was going in the next day for some tests. When Daisy questioned him he told her some drug company was going to pay him $300. He had signed up to be a human guinea pig for some experimental drugs and shaving his head was one of the requirements. Luckily Daisy talked him out of it but he had to live with short hair for a while.

A few months later Rob came home and out of the blue he started preaching gospel and Bible verses to us, he had met somebody that introduced him to Jesus. This was all we needed, all the other crap we had to put up with from him and now he's a "Jesus Freak." He would pick his spots when to preach to us but just like most things he spoke about, we just ignored him. He seemed very passionate about this topic, more so than anything else before, but we just said, "Hey that's fine if it's your thing." We figured it was just another faze he would go through.

Daisy had always raised us to believe in God although we would not be considered religious by any means. We were Jewish but we celebrated all the Christian holidays as well. We as kids never fasted or anything like that during the Jewish holidays but based on what mom had survived as a child we knew we were Jews. The fact that Rob was talking more about Christianity than being Jewish kind of made Daisy mad, her feeling at the time was "I was born a Jew and I will die a Jew." Rob talked about being a "Completed Jew" which was a Jew who believed in Jesus, Daisy wasn't buying it. He periodically would continue his preaching but we just tuned him out.

Life in the trailer park was going OK, no real earth shattering moments. The big change was for Daisy and Sal; they ran into a business opportunity they thought would be a good one for them. There was another mobile home park on the other side of town and the owner of the park wanted someone to open a convenience store in the park. Daisy and Sal figured this was a great thing for them and started the process. They converted a single wide trailer the owner had into the store. They put in shelves, freezers, refrigerators and made it a nice little store. Everything seem to be fine but there was one small detail that nobody cared to tell them, this park had a bunch of ex-military people living there. Normally that would not be a problem but with the Homestead Air Force Base being just a few miles away most of the residents went there to shop because of the cheap prices they received for being ex-military.

It didn't take long to figure out this would be the downfall of the business. My parents were furious, they felt the owner of the park, Max Berger, knew this would be a failure, he just wanted the rent from the old trailer that he had sitting there. Sal never liked him or trusted him; he called him "The Jew Bastard." Daisy would just laugh, racial slurs didn't upset her, and she knew Sal was just spouting off.

You had to know Sal, he was not a racist. To me, he was the closest thing to Archie Bunker from *All in the Family* fame, he didn't hate the Jews, Pollocks, Blacks or Indians, he hated everyone.

Even though he was not even my stepfather, he and Daisy never married, most people thought he was my real father. They would say I looked just like him, we both had a small gap in our front teeth, I since had braces to have that fixed, rather large noses, no surgery yet to repair that, and we both were short and stocky. It wouldn't be until many years later that I realized what a huge influence he would have on my life although I would end up being very different than him.

He always considered me his own son, he liked Rob and got along with him but he was older and the relationship was different. Steve and Sal never really hit it off; they had a run in when Daisy and Sal first started dating. It was something where Steve, like the rest of us had a wise guy mouth and said something disrespectful, they pretty much kept their distance after that, it would be years later before they became close. Steve never lived with us once we left New Jersey so they didn't see much of each other. Michele and Sal were close but he wasn't allowed to discipline her so that made it tough on Sal because he was all about discipline. What discipline the other three didn't get I made up for, he was tough on me and my mom wanted it that way. Don't get me wrong, I was not an abused kid, Daisy loved all of us a ton. I had a bunch of freedom to do what I wanted; I could pretty much come and go as I please. That is the benefit of being the youngest of four kids and for Sal he had raised his four already too.

By now Michele had met a guy named John; he lived in the same park as we did. To look at him you would think this guy was a thug, he was older, long hair and drove an older type sports car. I wasn't crazy about my sister seeing this guy but there wasn't anything I could do, if I said anything to him he would knock me out. Daisy just kind of went with the flow, she wasn't crazy about the idea either as they started to get closer but she let Michele do what she wanted. This was a perfect example of don't judge a book by its cover. John turned out to be one of the nicest guys you would ever want to meet.

During this time our father Sam would try to keep in contact with us. Periodically he would revert back to some of his crazy behavior during a phone conversation, that was the way to figure out if he was on his medication or not. When he wasn't he would say something about the government listening in on the call so he had to be careful about what he said. Or we would go about two weeks where we could get several dozen letters from him, none of them made any sense of all. They would have all this chicken scratch writing, some words would be underlined, some would have lines connecting the words to other words, either way it was senseless babble that was hard to make out.

You could always count on the letters having some reference to whomever the current president was, Nixon, Ford, Carter, Reagan, Bush, Clinton, he didn't discriminate. He thought they were all in on the conspiracy to kill the family or to make sure we would never see him again. He would also mail dozens of letters to the White House accusing the president of these things as well. I have no way to verify this but I would bet if you asked the Secret Service if they knew who Sam was I guarantee you they did.

Sam would also send birthday cards and Christmas cards. An interesting note about the Christmas and birthday cards, when we were still young kids Michele would open hers and there would always be a $5 or $10 dollar bill in there. When I opened mine it was always empty. It used to hurt pretty bad back then, I just didn't understand it. Today it's something Michele and I share a laugh about.

Chapter 19:

It's Vegas or Bust

With their business going under and Florida kind of wearing out its welcome, it was time for Daisy and Sal to decide where they wanted to go to next. Sal's late wife had a brother who lived in Las Vegas so they decided to take a trip out there to visit them and see what it's like. Michele didn't go on the Las Vegas trip so it was just me joining Daisy and Sal on the cross country journey out west. It seemed like it took a month to get there but I guess we made it out there in about three days. We stayed at my parent's favorite place Motel 6, originally named because it was only $6 dollars a night. I would stay in the motel and watch TV while they went out to the casinos and gambled. They weren't big time gamblers but they did love the slot machines.

While visiting with Sal's brother-in-law Ed and his wife Dottie the conversation came up about moving there. Dottie had worked at the MGM Hotel for years, she was a seamstress for the showgirls. She told Daisy they should move here, she could get her a job as a waitress in the MGM where she could make big money. That was all Daisy needed to hear, we were still going to check out California where my uncle lived but I think the decision was done. We stayed a few more days in Las Vegas and then packed up and went to see Uncle Herb in California. We hadn't been out there since Vinnie died and it was good to see everybody. We stayed with them for a few days as we checked out the city to decide if this would be our next home even though Las Vegas was all but a done deal. After the brief visit it was back in the van for the long journey back to Florida. I think by the time we hit Texas they knew we would go home, get our things in order and pack up to make the move to the Las Vegas. Oh, if it were only that easy.

By the time we got back from the long journey out west it was July of 1976. Before we moved I went to New Jersey to spend the rest of the summer with Peter and his family. Pete's mom, Doris, was the best, she was one of the nicest and most generous people I had ever met. My visits were not just a week; I always ended up staying about six weeks. She would feed me, clean my clothes and make me feel like I was one of her own. Pete's brothers, Bernie, Paul, Donnie, and his sister Rita would do the same. Pete's father had died a year or two earlier and was very much missed by the family.

To me, they were my second family. During my visits I would do everything with them. If they had a scheduled beach trip, they took me along. I even went to some of their relative's weddings. It was a lot of fun because it also allowed me to reconnect with my old New Jersey friends.

The house they lived in was in Doris' family for years. The front of the house was actually a butcher shop and candy store that was run by Doris' brother Johnny. The back of the house and upstairs was where the family lived. Back when we still lived in town my mom had an account set up at the store so any time Michele or I needed anything we could go there and charge it. With Daisy working all the time this was handy for us; Johnny made fresh sandwiches and had all kinds of good stuff to eat. Daisy would go in at the end of the week and settle up the account. Unfortunately I don't think these types of family stores exist anymore. I remember that being a great summer, there was a beach trip where Peter and I had a sole mission of meeting girls. There was one problem, well maybe two. I had a double ear infection and it was so bad the doctor said to be sure not to get any water in my ears. This meant I couldn't shower. So there Peter and I are strutting the beach and boardwalks of the Jersey Shore, Peter was tall, tan, curly blonde hair and a good looking kid. Then there was me, greasy hair and cotton balls stuffed in both ears. The good news was when we would go up to talk to girls I didn't know if they were saying "hi or drop dead" because I couldn't hear a thing. This frustrated Peter to know end and we ultimately gave up on our mission and decided to find some beer instead.

Pete and I are still best friends today, more like brothers. We vacation together every summer, our wives have become great friends and their children and our children are pretty much like long distance cousins. We rekindle some of the crazy stories from our youth and all the kids get a real kick out of them realizing "hey our parents weren't such dorks after all." Well I finally returned to Florida after an extended fun vacation and was there long enough to say good bye to friends before the next big move.

Now the question was who was going with us? Michele and I were for sure going, we had no choice. Rob decided Vegas sounded like fun so he was in; John really loved Michele so he asked if he could come out with us, which we were all fine with because we all really liked John and we knew they were going to get married. Then there was Pam and Denise, Sal's daughters. They had moved down to Florida about a year earlier, they decided they would stay there. Pam and Denise had gotten real close with our family and they were just like sisters to me. Even though Denise was like 13 years older than me we had a great relationship, partly because neither of us acted our age, she much younger and for me much older.

The next question was how do we do it? The easy way was to rent a big U-Haul truck and pack our things in there but that would be too expensive. So they decided they would buy an old step van, like the UPS trucks. They could fix it up and once we got out to Las Vegas they could sell it to get their money back. Now it was time to decide the driving partners. We had Daisy and Sal in their little AMC Hornet, Michele and Rob were in his 1951 Buick (another one of Rob's crazy cars), that left me and John in the step van. What we hoped would be a three day trip turned into over a week on the road. The problem was a different vehicle would break down each day. Some were minor problems and some were big. The worst repair was on the van, one of the wheels almost came off when one of the lug nuts broke and we ended up being stranded for several hours. While Sal and John took one of the other vehicles to get the wheel repaired Rob decided to educate us on the sun; he made a little sun dial out of some sticks in the dirt to show us he actually learned something during his short time as a boy scout.

During one of our other vehicle repairs we were stranded in Winslow, Arizona. That's when Rob starting singing "standing on the corner in Winslow Arizona." It was amazing that Rob never seemed to get stressed, I truly believe his blood pressure was 2 over 1. The trip at the time seemed painful but in retrospect I think it brought our family closer, I know I got to know John much better after spending that much time together.

When we did finally made it to Las Vegas, went to a cheap motel and rested for a day. The weekend was coming and the motel manager told us the weekend rate was much higher so Sal called his brother in-law Ed and asked if we could stay there, which he said was fine. When we got there we found Ed's wife Dottie was temporarily stuck in a wheelchair from a car accident. Daisy and Michele waited on her hand and foot while we were there, which they didn't mind, but after a few days we knew we needed to go get our own place. Before that Daisy wanted to go ahead and get that job at the MGM Dottie had talked about. When she asked her who she needed to talk with, Dottie told her, "I can't help you with that you have to go through the union." Daisy was ready to explode, she had based the entire move on that job, now we moved to a new city, with limited amount of money and no jobs.

The next day Daisy rented a three bedroom apartment for us. Rob and I were now roommates for the first time, although he wouldn't stay for long. Daisy went to the union to find out the details of getting a job in the hotels and found out it wasn't that easy; she would have to wait her turn. Not being one for sitting around she got the newspaper, got a job at a little deli making sandwiches and working the cash register. Sal, John and Rob all went to work at a big local gas station chain called "Terrible Herbst." They had the biggest gas stations I had ever seen, there must have been at least 100 pumps, all self service, so you had to constantly be looking around to make sure nobody drove off without paying. They would have at least three guys for each shift and still people would be able to get off without paying. This would come right out of the pocket of whoever was working at the time. I think Rob lasted a few days and decided to quit, Sal and John stuck with it.

Rob hung around for a little while longer before hopping in his old Buick and driving back to New Jersey. I enrolled in the local high school and I got a job at K-Mart as well. That was my first real job, I had cut lawns before and shoveled snow but that was always on my own. This was the first time I actually worked for a company. They told me I would need to wear nice pants and a nice shirt, neither of which I owned; it was all jeans and T-shirts for me. Daisy bought me a couple of the finest polyester pants and shirts you could find. Her thinking was to never buy anything you couldn't throw in the washing machine. I was fine with that; I just wanted to make some money working after school.

The first few days as a stock boy started off pretty routine, stocking shelves, basic clean up and odd jobs. I think it was day four when the manager came up to me and told me the ladies room toilet was clogged to which I replied "Yeah." He replied sharply "Well go fix it." Without grossing you out as much as I was, this was disgusting work. I had unclogged a toilet before when it was my own doing (no pun intended) but doing it for someone else was awful. I was gagging as I plunged away trying to get this mess to go down the drain, all while cursing like a sailor thinking about my manager and what I really wanted to do with this plunger. That was the first time in my life that I realized having a big nose with a strong sense of smell was not a good thing.

Day three of week two would prove be the end of my K-Mart career. As soon as I got in my favorite manager told me to grab a lawnmower out of the lawn and garden department, put some gas and oil in it and cut the grass in the back of the store. I'm thinking to myself, "Since when does a stock boy, who had to wear nice clothes, have to cut grass?" Not that I cared, I've cut a million lawns what would one more be. Little did I know, this lawn looked like it hadn't been cut since the early 1960s, the grass had to be two feet high and thick as a jungle. I cranked this piece of junk K-Mart mower up and tried to make my way through the high grass with very little success. The mower stalled every two feet, the grass was just too thick. This was the beginning of summer in Las Vegas so the temperature was in the high to mid 90s and I'm sweating to death. They say you don't sweat in the dry heat, I proved that theory wrong. I decided I didn't care what my manager thought so I pulled my shirt off and rolled up my pant legs and tried to cut my way through the thick grass. After about an hour of trying to get this job finished I realized I was about 10 percent done. I thought about what to do for a minute and my first thought was to go back to my New Jersey roots, go inside and kick the crap out of my manager before I quit. Instead I continued cutting even as snakes were coming out of the grass left and right, finally, after several hours, I finished the task. I promptly put my shirt back on, rolled down my pant legs, brought the mower back in the store, put it on the shelf, clocked out and never went back. I did call them and asked them to mail me my last check.

The high school I went to was divided into two groups, kids from families that had money and those of us that didn't. The school itself was pretty good, it was an open campus so you could come and go as you please which most kids did. Our apartment was right down the street so I could walk to and from school. Within a few months I would be finishing up 10th grade. I was a pretty quiet kid to begin with and being new on top of that I didn't say much at all. The class where I kind of stood out was gym because I was always a good athlete. One day after gym a kid came up to me and introduced himself as Pete. We struck up a conversation and hit it off pretty quick. I would always look forward to gym and now even more because I had a friend. The friendship took off surprising fast and before long we were hanging out all the time. We finally figured out why we hit it off so well and had so much in common; we were born on the same day of the same year.

Meanwhile back at the apartment things got a little strange. Michele had made friends with a guy that my parents knew back at the convenience store they had in Florida. He kept in contact with Michele by writing letters to see how things were in Las Vegas. I guess Michele told him it was great and invited him to Las Vegas and stay with us never thinking he would ever show up. Next thing you know he shows up at our door step and now I'm sharing my room with this total stranger, stranger to me at least, Michele and my parents knew but I didn't. The first few nights I tossed and turned wondering if he was going to wake up in the middle of the night and butcher me with a knife. I guess I watched too much television and horror movies back then. I asked Michele what the heck she was thinking inviting him out here, her comment was "I was just being nice, I didn't think he would just show up."

After a week or so John and Sal got him a job at the gas station which seemed to be going fine. He was working there a few weeks and living with us just like one of the family, but it still felt pretty weird to me. Then one day I'm walking home from school and see a police car in front of our apartment and realized they are at our door. So I walk in to find out what was going on. While at work the night before this guy, his name was Joe, told John and Sal to turn their heads while they were by the cash register. Not knowing what he was talking about until he said, "If you don't see it happen you aren't part of it" sure enough he cleaned out the register, opened the safe and cleaned that out too. He threw the money in a bag, drove off in his car and we never saw him again. The police riffled through the few things he left behind in my room and then went on their way. Being that he was my roommate, the good news was he was a thief not a murderer.

We were all settling into our new life in Las Vegas and Daisy finally got the call from the union for a job at the old Fremont Hotel. After working a few months there she was very happy and decided it was time to buy a house. They looked around for a while until choosing this nice house a few miles outside of town. Rob had returned from his brief trip to New Jersey which didn't set well with me because I didn't want a roommate anymore. He and I started to argue a lot and before moving out of the apartment we had a knock down drag out brawl. I was 15 and he was 23 but I could hold my own, again he was never a fighter and that's all I was forced to do growing up. Sal was there but he just let us duke it out, I don't remember the specifics but I was wrong in the matter and Sal was hoping Rob would kick my ass. This fight went on for quite a while with each of us getting in some good shots as we wrestled throughout the apartment. Just about when we were worn out we heard a banging on the door which Sal opened to see a couple of police officers with their guns drawn. One of the neighbors had heard the commotion and told the police somebody was being killed in our apartment, as I said it was quite the fight. Sal explained it was two brothers in a little disagreement and they left without saying much.

In the meantime Steve had transferred from a college in Colorado to an aeronautics college, he was dead set on being a pilot and continued that pursuit. He never got a dollar from Daisy, at that point she didn't have it to give, so he worked nights while going to school during the day and also took out some school loans. He did it all on his own which really made Daisy proud.

We moved into our new house which we all really liked; it was nice to get out of the apartment. This was the summer of 1977; I was a couple months away from my 16th birthday and most importantly my driver's license. I needed this now because we lived several miles from school. . We looked around at several cars in the price range my mom was willing to spend which was about $500. We ended up getting a 1972 Chevy Vega, also known as the worst car ever made. The 4 cylinder engine they put in the car had aluminum heads and ran extremely hot which also caused them to burn oil. So every time I gassed up the car I had to add oil. Don't get me wrong, I loved that car, it was all mine and would give me the freedom to do what I wanted. It was not a chick magnet to say the least but it was transportation.

Summer was now ending and as 11th grade started, Pete and I were now hanging out all the time, at least when we weren't working. He worked at one of the hotels on the Las Vegas strip which was run by his father and I was now working delivering pizzas. Delivering pizzas in Las Vegas was an interesting job, you never knew who or what you would find when someone answered the door. One of my favorite stops was to Wayne Newton's ranch. At the time he lived in a large circular house, I never had a chance to meet him, the pizzas were always ordered by his ranch workers.

There was another delivery stop that was a little more exciting. I knocked on the door of this apartment and a woman answered the door in a sexy nightgown. As she opened the door the smoke from inside the apartment flowed out the door and she wasn't just smoking cigarettes. The first time I went there I was in shock as I walked back to the car thinking if I should have just invited myself in. The conservative part of me said if she wanted me to come in she would have invited me. I made that delivery several times and each time it was the same thing, the nightgown, the smoke filled room and the door closing in my face. I think she was a show girl from one of the hotels and enjoyed teasing young teenage boys.

Daisy liked her job at the Fremont and the crazy people she worked with there. Sal had quit the gas station and went back to the junk business; John also quit there and was now delivering furniture. He and Michele were getting along great and decided to get married. I think John was a little homesick for Florida and his brothers and sisters but knew Michele didn't want to leave her mother. Rob and I were roommates again at the new house and were finally getting along pretty good. Daisy got him on at the Freemont as a bus boy and kitchen helper so he was making pretty good money. He stayed with us for a while until finally moving out on his own, and I finally had my own room again. Daisy eventually got me on at the Fremont Hotel as well; I worked as busboy after school. We all worked together and enjoyed every minute of it.

Chapter 20:

Married To The Mob

As for Pete, Las Vegas Pete that is, he turned out to have quite the interesting family. He had kind of told me some stories about his dad, past and present, his uncles and their Italian Chicago roots. After hearing all those stories and the fact that his father ran one of the bigger hotels in Las Vegas I pretty much figured out the rest, he's in the mob. I had not met his father yet, he was always working. I met his mom a few times and she was very nice, a little crazy but nice. One day we decided we were going to cut out of school a little early and go back to Pete's place to hang out. Within a few minutes of getting there we heard the front door open and close which caused a look of panic on Pete's face. I quickly wanted to know what the problem was and to my dismay he said, "Oh, shit, I think my father is home." This very quickly put me into hyperventilation, I had not met his father (we'll leave his name out for obvious reasons) and at this point I did not want to. Remember, I watched way too much TV and I figured if he caught us skipping school Pete would be beaten and I would be killed and never found again. Even though this sounds farfetched if you saw the look on Pete's face you would of thought the same thing. We waited a minute or two and heard the master bedroom door open and close which gave Pete the idea it was time to bolt out the door.

I was never so happy in my life to go back to school; I just knew I was safe from the mob.

Pete and I continued our friendship and like any of the family friends, he became part of my family. Sal and Daisy loved him from day one; he was always polite and loved to hear Sal's old time stories. Daisy always cooked enough food just in case someone dropped in, if not, we lived on leftovers. I think this was something that went back to her childhood where there wasn't enough food to eat: she wanted to make sure that would never be the case at our house.

I eventually met Pete's dad and he was a great guy, intimidating, but great. After he got to know me he was always very nice although we didn't hang around a bunch when he was home. One day while at his house, we were sitting talking to Pete's mom and the subject of school came up. She asked me what classes I was taking which I told her. When she heard I was taking a drama class she told me she was a drama student as well. Little did I know what she was going to say next, she said "Why don't we plan some time together so I can teach you some acting techniques?" I was speechless; Daisy had always raised us to respect other adults which left me with only one reply "That would be great." We went back into Pete's room and he was laughing hysterically which made me feel even worse. I told him he needed to get me out of this which just increased his laughing. Pete's mom was a lovely woman although she had some psychological issues and had been on medication for years, telling her no was not an option.

Several days later while visiting again she came up to me and told me she had bad news, "I'm sorry Ron but I won't be able to help you with your acting." I wanted to jump up and kiss her until I heard the rest of the sentence. "When I told my husband what you asked me to do he got very upset, yelled and screamed so I can't do it." She walked away as I just stood there in shock. I figured that was it, he's going to kill me for sure now. Pete was out of the room while this happened; when he walked back in and saw the look on my face he thought I had seen a ghost. I told him what happened and he assured me it was nothing to worry about, his father had dealt with her crazy ideas and he would know it had nothing to do with me. I didn't feel good about it until seeing his father again a few weeks later and he never mentioned it.

Years later after we had moved away Pete had called up to let me know his father was in trouble. The hotel where he worked was taken down by the FBI. His father and several other managers from the hotel were arrested. His father spent very little time in jail but could have gone to prison for a long time. They were accused of skimming money off the top for which I don't believe anyone was ever convicted or spent any real jail time. The real problem was, due to being arrested he could no longer be bonded which pretty much ended his casino career.

Financially I think they were in pretty good shape but he still wanted to work. The family would have been set for life with the brothers and Pete working their way up to management in the hotel but all those plans went down the drain. Pete's older brothers were both making big money working as casino dealers but after the arrest they were pretty much blackballed from all the major casinos. They had to go way out of town to work at some of the smaller casinos and went from making over six figures to making about $25K a year.

A few years later there would be a film version of what happened at the hotel. The movie starred Robert DeNiro and Sharon Stone, *Casino.* Ironically, the actor who had played the role in the movie loosely based on Pete's father was none other than by my favorite guy, Don Rickels.

Las Vegas Pete and I continue our lifelong friendship, it's one of those relationships where we don't talk as often as we would like but when we do we pick up right where we left off and it always involves a lot of laughing. Pete, like me, married well, a wonderful, caring, giving person. Janine is great and she and Pete still live in Las Vegas raising their two daughters.

As for the rest of the crew, Daisy was having a blast at the Freemont Hotel and made a new best friend, David. She had talked about him quite a bit which kind of confused me, she was with Sal, and I think it made Sal a little jealous. That was until he came over for dinner, he was very open about the fact he was gay, quite honestly it would be impossible for him to hide it. When he was a few years younger he worked on the Vegas strip as a female impersonator. He was an extremely nice guy and my mom loved him which was good enough for me. Sal didn't feel the same way, remember he hated everyone and that included homosexuals. There was not much he could do about it, when Daisy made a friend it usually was for life. This friend would come in handy for Sal.

He was out working searching for scrap metal and came across a construction site. He noticed some big nail spikes that he needed for a project he was working on at our house. He saw a security guard there and went up to ask him if the spikes were being thrown out because they were in a big junk pile. The guard told him he could take all he wanted which is what Sal did. Before he finished a police officer came up and asked him what he was doing. Sal explained the guard told him could take them but the officer didn't want to hear any of it. He stated that the guard didn't run the job site; he quickly handcuffed Sal and took him down to the police station to book him on larceny. This was late on a Friday, it was about 6:00 PM by the time he was able to call Daisy to tell her what happened and ask her to come down to bail him out. There was a small problem, the bail was $1000 and Daisy didn't have that kind of cash, the banks had just closed and it was Friday. There were no money machines in the mid 1970s so this meant Sal would have to spend the rest of the weekend in jail unless Daisy could somehow come up with the money.

She didn't tell Sal that there was a problem; he thought she was on her way down to handle the bail. In a complete panic, she tried to figure out what to do. She made a call to David to see how much money he had. He didn't have the cash either but he did own his home outright and had the title. He assured Daisy they could use that as collateral for the bail and made their way down to the jail. They did accept it and Sal was now free on bail, when he found out it was David who saved him he was now his best friend too. That didn't mean Sal wouldn't pick on him like he did everyone else but it was all in good fun. By the way, the charges for theft were dropped and David got his title back.

Chapter 21:

Goodnight Johnboy

Michele and John had since married and were really doing well considering they were so young. We all loved John; he was everything you would want in guy for your sister or daughter to marry. We had a little above ground pool in our backyard and Michele had her bathing suit on getting ready to go for a quick dip. We were both in the kitchen getting something to eat at the time and I noticed her belly was sticking out some. Michele was always skinny as a rail so it was obvious she had gained some weight. We were always very close and could say anything to each other so I told her she was getting fat which made her look down to her stomach. Nothing more was said until a few weeks later as her stomach got bigger and she eventually went to the doctor which confirmed she was indeed pregnant. We were all thrilled, even though they were young. Daisy was beside herself, she was going to be a grandmother, even better than that, she was going to be a "Nanny" the same name we called her mother.

In the mean time Rob had fallen in and out of love with every woman that he saw but nothing ever lasted. He really wanted to settle down, he wanted someone to take care of but more importantly he wanted someone to take care of him. As for Steve, he had now finished college, made it through a year early by taking summer classes and graduated very high in his class. He moved to

Washington, D.C. and took a job as a lobbyist on Capitol Hill for the FAA (Federal Aviation Administration).

He really liked the job but it didn't pay much and just like when he was younger he still wanted the finer things. He made friends with a guy named Mike and they became roommates. Mike came from a wealthy family and his father opened a big disco in downtown DC called "The Appletree." This was now the late 1970s, disco was big and this club was a hotspot for the up and comers in DC. For extra cash Steve's roommate got him a job working the door at the disco.

He met a ton of people while working there, but it was a chance meeting with a guy that would change his life forever. His name was Ed; they called him "Airplane Ed." He was in the jet business; he actually sold jets for a living. This fascinated Steve in a big way mainly because Airplane Ed waived one hundred dollar bills around like they were pennies. He would also show Steve his commission checks after a sale and the numbers blew him away. He kept telling Steve he needed to give up on Capitol Hill and jump in with him. Steve was tempted, he had since given up on the idea of being a pilot, he didn't want to fly the plane anymore, he wanted to sit in the back of a private jet and have someone else do the flying. The big problem was that jet sales was a straight commission job, no sales, no money.

He thought about it for a while and after watching Airplane Ed continue to live the good life he decided it was time to give it a try. Ed got him a job with the same company he worked for and Steve's concerns were right on. He knew this would not be an overnight success; it was going to take time. He would share the sales calls that came into the office along with the other sales people and most of them turned into nothing. He no longer had the paycheck from his day job on Capitol Hill and money was tight. He was now working nights as a waiter to pay the bills. This went on for months and still no deals in sight, he would get close on one here and there but no luck.

Steve had pretty much decided he would have to give up on this career, he liked it but he figured he just wasn't good at it. Ultimately he gave himself one year and if he didn't sell anything in that time frame he would give it up. It came down to just about the last day of that year commitment and sure enough he finally got his sale. His first commission check was almost $15,000; this was more he than his yearly salary was working on Capitol Hill. Needless to say he was hooked. Once he got that first deal business really started to pick up for him, the sales became more consistent and he was on his way in his new career.

Back in Las Vegas Michele was getting ready to have her baby; she got as big as a house. Knowing that I was a little squeamish, she would show me her stomach while we were eating dinner and that would do it for me, my appetite was gone. That wasn't easy to do, especially how much I loved to eat. Then it happened, it was time to have a baby. We all went to the hospital, Daisy, Sal, Rob, John, Pete and I were sitting in the waiting room. They didn't let a bunch of people in the delivery room back then like they do now. I truly believe I was the most nervous one of the crew, I was pacing up and down the hall until we finally got the word, it's a beautiful and healthy baby boy. They named him after his father, John; his middle name is George, named after our grandfather, early on he got the nickname Johnboy and it stuck. Johnboy was the new apple of Daisy's eye; she doted over that boy like he was gold. Even though it was a little noisy in the house it was fun to have a baby around.

Things got a lot crazier when Sal's grandchildren came for a visit. Michelle and Dana were Denise's daughters who were being raised by their father, Keith. Denise and Keith divorced several a few years earlier; Denise originally had custody of the girls before

Keith wanted to take them. Denise had tried to make it on her own with the girls but financially just couldn't do it so her ex-husband had custody. Keith called Sal and asked if we would watch the girls for a couple of weeks while he and his new wife went to Mexico on their honeymoon. Sal looked forward to seeing his granddaughters but had a hunch something was up. The girls came for their visit, they were about eight and nine years old and were good kids. They really liked staying with us, they swam in the pool and enjoyed being with our family.

Two weeks had come and gone with no communication from Keith. Sal told us he knew he was not coming back and we would need to prepare to have the girls stay with us. Daisy thought there was no way Keith would not come back for his girls even though she was completely OK with the girls living with us. Another week passed and Sal decided to call Denise who was back in New Jersey and told her what was going on. Denise jumped in her car and pretty much drove non-stop all the way out to Las Vegas to reclaim her girls. They stayed with us for a while before Denise rented a house on the other side of town. She went to work in one of the casinos as a change girl. It would be a few weeks later before Keith called to let us know he was not coming back, his new wife didn't get along with the girls and he wanted to make a life with her. Sal cursed him out on the phone like I had never heard before and then just slammed the phone down. Even though it didn't happen the way anyone would have liked Denise was thrilled to be back with her daughters and the girls felt the same way.

Chapter 22:

We're Moving Where?

John had gotten a call from his father who was in the construction business back in Florida. He told him there was a ton of work and he could make a bunch of money as a carpenter building houses. John was tired of delivering furniture and wanted to make more money now that they had another mouth to feed. He and Michele talked about making the move back to Florida; even though she did not want to leave she knew it was the best thing for them financially.

Shortly thereafter Michele, John and Johnboy packed up and took off back to Florida. Daisy cried like the world was coming to an end and for her it was. It never took much to make Daisy cry, I would always tease her and say she even cried when the bad guys died in the movies. But this time, these were real heartbroken tears, she had never lived away from Michele and now with her new grandson leaving as well, she was devastated.

John went to work with his father and was doing well building houses in a small town called Port St. Lucie, a town about 45 miles north of West Palm Beach on the east coast of Florida. Michele would call Daisy every day to give her the updates on Johnboy and any other news of the day. She started giving Daisy the sales pitch of what a great place it was, very reasonably priced and the weather was great. Michele was doing the same thing Daisy did to us when she tried to convince us of a move. It didn't take a rocket scientist to figure out what was going to happen next.

This was now the summer of 1978 and I went for my annual six week stay in New Jersey with Peter and his family. The joke during this visit was "How many people live in Las Vegas and come to New Jersey for vacation?" I had a great time with Peter and his family as usual but now it was time to go home. When I got back to Las Vegas Daisy hit me with the news, "We're moving to Port St. Lucie, Florida." I was PISSED OFF to say the least. I did not want to leave, I had made a great friend in Las Vegas Pete, kind of had a girlfriend named Kathy (she didn't know it yet), either way I just didn't want to leave the life we made in Las Vegas. I was getting ready to start my senior year of high school, I didn't want another new school, especially not my senior year.

None of that mattered; Daisy had made her mind up. She wanted to be with her daughter and grandson and that was that. Sal was ready to leave for a different reason, he was going broke. Daisy would send him out for a gallon of milk and he would come back cursing like crazy. We would ask him what was wrong and he would say "That milk cost me $28." That meant after he purchased the milk he used his spare change in the slot machines. Every store, 7-11s, grocery stores, it didn't matter, they all had slot machines and Sal never missed a chance to throw in a few coins, the problem was he couldn't stop. Daisy had the same problem, she would leave work with all her tip money and in the slots it would go. Neither of them smoked or drank alcohol but gambling was their addiction, those slots drove them crazy.

By the time I got back from New Jersey it was the beginning of August. I had about two weeks to say my goodbyes and we moved back to Florida. Back on the road, this drive was a little better because I was actually old enough to drive one of the cars.

This time it was just me, Daisy, Sal and of course Rob was making the trip as well. It was a much smoother trip, this time we rented a U-Haul truck and didn't have any breakdowns.

Michele had arranged for us to rent a house two doors down from her so we had a place already set up. All these houses were pretty much the same, three bedrooms and two bathrooms, around 1500 square feet. These were the houses that John and the company he was working for were building. These things were popping up like mushrooms; they sold for around $35,000 and were selling like hotcakes, it was a little boomtown. I'm not sure what the appeal was, there wasn't much going on in Port St. Lucie. It was pretty much a retirement town.

School was getting ready to start so I enrolled in the local high school, Fort Pierce Central High. Fort Pierce was the next town over; Port St. Lucie was too small at the time to have its own high school. My first day there I realized something was different; this was the first time I was the minority. The school was predominantly African American, they said it was a 50/50 mix but it was more like 70/30. I wasn't prejudiced; it was just the first time I was part of the minority. After a few days I overheard some conversation about race riots and predictions of when this year's version would happen. I got to know a couple of students so I inquired what that was all about. They told me every year the school would have a big fight, "The whites against the blacks." My first thought was with the whites being outnumbered at least 2 to 1 this would be ugly. Then take in consideration half of the white kids would just run from a fight it would be more like 4 to 1. I didn't mind fighting, I had to do it all my life, I just wanted a fair shot at winning and being outnumbered 4 to 1 wasn't a fair shot.

This is not how I envisioned my senior year, for the first time in my life I could honestly say I was not real happy with my mother. I was perfectly happy in Las Vegas and now I was stuck here.

I was desperate so I came up with a great idea; I could move back to Las Vegas and live with Denise. Denise had her own place with her daughters and would gladly take me in. Daisy and Sal were having no part of that suggestion. When Steve got wind of this he called from DC and told me if I quit school he would be on the next flight to come down and kick my ass. Then Michele came up with her own idea, "How about private school?" She knew some neighbors who sent their kids to this little private school just up the road and they really liked it.

At this point I would have tried anything, I was just miserable and maybe a different school would make me happy. Daisy took me down to enroll in the new school, Faith Baptist School. Everybody was all smiles as we got the sales pitch from the principal and that had Daisy writing her check to get me in the school. The principal sold us on how great the school was and how I would fit in perfectly. I was kind of excited until he told me my hair was way too long and I would need to have it cut off before starting school on Monday. This was 1978 and long hair was in, by that afternoon my long hair was gone, cut above my ears.

I had no idea what I was in for when school started that following Monday. The good part was the girls, they looked at me like I was fresh meat, and they actually came up to me and asked me out. That had never happened in my life, I liked it. Also I was guaranteed a starting spot on the basketball team after the coach saw me play in gym class. The school had a total of 300 kids and that was kindergarten all the way through 12th grade. So the choices for boyfriends and athletes were slim but I figured I would use that to my advantage. I'm thinking this was the best decision I ever made.

When I came home that day from school Daisy and Michele were eager to find out how it went and were thrilled to find out it went well. Day two was a complete different story. Tuesday was church day; we had to go in the church for a little gospel preaching.

I figured I was open minded, I had been to church a few times with Pete back in New Jersey, even been to a few Catholic weddings. How different could the Baptist be? Well, VERY different. After asking all of us to bow our heads the preacher started screaming at us telling us we were sinners; we needed to pray for forgiveness. Then he asked us something that I had no idea what in the world he was talking about. He asked for us to raise our hand if we were not "Born again" or "Saved." I'm sitting there with my head down saying to myself "Born again?" I didn't die yet so he can't be talking to me." Then he starting yelling real loud "I know some of you are not saved and you need to confess your faith to Jesus Christ." Now I started to break out in a cold sweat, "Saved, from what?" I didn't know what he meant but at this point I was now sure he was talking to me. I just kept my head down and I prayed alright, I prayed to get me the heck out of this church and get me out of this school.

When I got home that day Daisy and Michele again wanted to know how it went. I figured once I told them the whole religious thing, especially with us being Jewish, this would be my out. When I told them the church story they started to laugh. I explained how I was scared and it wasn't funny, they just told me, "Hang in there it will get better." Daisy said, "You need to stay there because I paid the money for the whole year and if you leave they don't give any refunds."

Day Three would not be any better, and the school work started to pile up. I had a few book reports due and several other projects as well. I started thinking this wasn't such a good idea anymore. OK, the girls thing was cool but that was not enough to offset the rest of the junk. I also realized that this was not a school for religious people; it was for "Rednecks" who couldn't deal with normal society and wanted to be isolated with their own kind. A couple of the other guys in my class talked about how they hated blacks, their parents did as well and would never have them go to school with them. One of them even talked about how his father was in the KKK.

By the time I ended that week I was begging my mom to send me back to public school. I was not crazy about all the extra school work; it was much easier to cruise through public school. The racism and KKK stuff made me think they weren't so fond of Jewish people either. Most people didn't know I was Jewish, most thought I was Italian and I kind of went with it, and it made life much simpler. I'm ashamed to admit that I was ashamed of being Jewish, I guess I just wanted to blend in; I didn't want to be a minority. Since that time I've grown to appreciate and fully embrace my heritage.

Daisy was not happy about losing the money but ultimately she didn't like seeing me this upset and let me transfer back to Fort Pierce Central. My first day back in Fort Pierce Central went well, the few people I knew wanted to know where I went and why all my hair was cut off. I lied, I told them I got into some trouble and went to jail for a week, it was a lot better story then the truth. After everything was said and done the school wasn't so bad. Was it perfect, no, but it wasn't as bad as I made it out to be. I made some good friends, both white and black and really ended up enjoying my senior year. As for the big race riot, it never happened.

Chapter 23:

Rob's got A Girlfriend

In the meantime Rob was going through a career change; he decided he wanted to be a truck driver. Somehow he talked his way into a job as a dump truck driver with zero experience. He liked it as much as he thought he would but his real desire was to drive the big tractor trailers and go cross country. The big news was he met a woman and decided to move in with her. It would be a while before we met her but when we did we were a little surprised. He brought Faye over for dinner and it caught us off guard to see how much older she was than Rob. He was 25 at the time and I think she was in her early 40s, but because she had a very tough life she looked even older than that.

Faye had six children and her oldest was actually older than Rob. She was from the mountains of Georgia and starting having children at age 13. Her ex-husband went to prison and she had to raise the kids on her own. Rob and Faye seemed to get along great; we really liked her even though we thought the age difference would be a challenge. My thoughts were she was the mother image he was looking for.

It was that time again, Daisy and Sal needed to come up with new business venture. They figured with all this new construction going on they could start a little lunch truck and go around to the job sites to feed the workers. They bought a van and had it converted with a steam table, propane tanks and everything it needed to do business. Their little venture started off pretty good as they made their rounds. The tough part was Daisy wanted to make everything fresh so the pre-work was brutal. She would wake up about 4:00 a.m. and start cooking the meatballs, steak and cutting deli meat for all the sandwiches, if Daisy was serving food only the best would do. Sal did all the grunt work, loading the truck, cleaning it and did all the driving. They seemed to enjoy what they were doing. They fought all the time but that was nothing new, this gave them something else to argue about.

Business was good enough for them to start looking to buy a house. They found one off the main road in town which I was against, like with most things my vote didn't count and they bought it anyway. Life seemed to be going along pretty good for all of us. My folks had their business, Rob had his woman, Steve was doing well in DC, Michele and John were doing good and I was a week away from graduating high school after a bumpy start.

Chapter 24:

Time to Grow Up

It was the Sunday morning before my final week of high school, graduation would be Thursday and I was thrilled. I was just hanging out watching TV when John came over and said, "Let's go waterskiing." We had this little old boat which we used to go waterskiing in the St. Lucie River. The problem was it was a cloudy, misty, rainy day and I didn't want to go. John was bored and he was going whether I went or not.

With out any real friends at school John was not just my brother in-law he was my best friend. We also worked together, after school I would help with some of the grunt work with John and his construction crew.

I gave in and decided I would go skiing with him. We stopped by to pick up a couple of his buddies, David and his roommate Smitty. We got to the river and the four of us jumped in the boat on this ugly rainy day. The question was who wanted to go first, nobody was that eager to do it. We knew the river was loaded with alligators but when there are a bunch of boats speeding through the waters you felt a lot safer. With the weather being what it was the river was very quiet, we were the only boat out there. After nobody volunteered to go first John decided he would do it. He put on his life jacket and jumped in the water. I was driving the boat and when he gave the signal we took off. We were cruising down the river and John was doing well, that was not a surprise, he was a great skier.

After skiing for a few minutes David said "Turn around John fell down." This kind of shocked me because this was the first time he ever fell. We would go for miles and he would just let go of the rope when he was tired but he never fell. I slowed the boat down and started to turn it around when the engine just stopped. I tried to start it but it was not doing anything. We periodically had problems with the old boat, it picked the most inopportune times to act up and this was one of them. John was about 70 or 80 yards back and when we looked for him we saw his head was in the water face down. We started to freak out, the boat wouldn't start and John's face down in the water.

I didn't know what to do; I kept trying to start the boat but no luck. David took off his shirt, jumped in the water and starting swimming toward John. I have to give David credit, we knew that water was infested with alligators but he still jumped in. With no boats around and with our boat not running it was a ballsy move to jump in. What seemed like forever but was only about a minute or two I did get the boat started and we drove toward John. David got there about the same time as us, I got out of the boat and we tried to pull John out of the water. This is when we realized he was not breathing and totally blue. My brother-in-law was dead! We pretty much dragged him in the boat and I started to give him mouth to mouth resuscitation. Miraculously a few months earlier we had a Florida State Trooper come into our school and teach a class on how to do it. If you never had to give mouth to mouth before consider yourself lucky, it was the worst experience of my life. I was freaking out but I just continued to do it.

We tried to start the boat but it was not working and now we're stuck in the middle of the river with John fighting for his life.

After a few minutes we were elated and surprised to see another boat speeding around the corner and we waved them down. They pulled up and we told them what was going on. The three guys in their boat helped us transfer John into their boat so we could get him to shore. I stopped the mouth to mouth for a moment until we got him secured in the other boat and then started again.

One of the guys said John was still not breathing so I just kept doing mouth to mouth. One of the guys realized I was emotionally breaking down and relieved me for a moment. We needed to make it back to the marina and get John to the hospital to see if we could save his life. These guys had a radio in their boat and called for an ambulance. We were back to land within a few minutes and the paramedics were there waiting for us as well as the Marine Patrol. The Marine Patrol are the kings of the Florida waterways, they had a well earned reputation for being very tough.

The paramedics got John out of the boat and on to a stretcher, they did get him breathing, hooked him up to an oxygen mask and started poking and prodding him all over. They also secured his neck with a brace while strapping him to the stretcher. I was asking them if he was going to be ok but they wouldn't say much, they did confirm he was breathing but nothing else. They took a sharp object and poked him in the bottom of his feet, I wasn't sure what they expected he was unconscious.

The two Marine Patrol officers came over and asked to speak with me. I told them I would talk with them later I was going in the ambulance with my brother-in-law to the hospital. They told me they just needed to speak with me for a minute and would make sure I went in the ambulance. The paramedics continued to work on John while I told the officers what happened. I went over everything that happened, he was skiing, he fell, when we got to him he was face down in the water, got him in the boat, I performed mouth to mouth until the other boat got there. Before I could continue on the ambulance was starting to pull away, I told them I needed to go. As I tried to walk away, one of the officers grabbed me by the arm and said "Kid, you ain't going nowhere, if you don't start telling us the truth we going to arrest you for attempted murder."

I know I should have been afraid but I was more pissed off than anything, my best friend was in trouble and these guys were keeping me from being with him. That's when I blurted out "Listen you cold hearted son of a bitch, I'm going to the hospital and check on my brother-in-law, after that you can do to me whatever the hell you want with me." At that point they told me they would take me to the hospital and continue their investigation there. We raced to the hospital which was just up the road a few miles. When I got there I made the tough call to my mom who called Michele and they quickly drove up to meet me. Just as Daisy, Sal and Michele walked in a doctor was coming out of the emergency room and belted out to the nurse at the front desk "That kid who was in the boating accident, he's a vegetable, he'll never walk again." I actually saw my mom's knees buckle; Sal grabbed her before she fell and eased her into a chair. Michele started crying as we just all stood there in disbelief. I'm not sure what would make a doctor do something as cruel as that but if I ever saw him again there is no telling what I would do to him.

A nurse came out and had to sedate Daisy while another doctor came out to give us the bad news. John had a broken neck and indeed was paralyzed from the neck down. We didn't know what to say or do. After getting this news the Marine Patrol officers no longer needed to talk to me and left. At the time I didn't know why all of a sudden the whole attempted murder thing was forgotten but later found out. They thought I was lying because of telling them we found him face down in the water. He had a Coast Guard approved life vest on and they are made so if you are left unconscious in the water it keeps your head out of the water. What they didn't know was that his neck was broken and I guess that was why the vest didn't do what it was supposed to do.

When we finally were allowed to go in and see John they had already drilled holes in his head and put a steel crown on him to stabilize his neck. He didn't regain consciousness for several days, when he finally came to he had no idea of what had happened and no memory of the accident at all. When I went home that first day I had to go see my one year old nephew Johnboy. I walked in and hugged him so tight he almost started to cry which is exactly what I did. I was so sad knowing my nephew's life would never be the same based on what had happened to his father. I knew what it was like to grow up without a father, I didn't know how this would turn out for Johnboy but I didn't want that for him. From that day on he became the little brother I never had.

Michele stayed at the hospital around the clock while family members helped take care of Johnboy. We all went back and forth from the hospital to check in on John as well as Michele. During one of my visits I took a break and went in to a little waiting area. There was an older woman sitting there and she asked why I was there. I told her the story of what happed and she told me why she was there. Her husband was dying, it was a prolonged disease and now it was his time to go. I was amazed by the way she was so calm and almost at peace with what was happening. When I asked her how she was handling things so well, she said, "Sometimes you have to realize what happens is not really in your control." I said to her, "It wasn't fair what happened to my brother-in-law, I don't understand why this would happen to such a nice guy." What she said next is something I would take away with me forever: "You can never question God, don't ever ask why just pray for strength to get you through it." I left the room feeling a touch better; I wasn't sure why but I did.

It took a few days for the reality to hit us all, this was going to be a long tough road ahead. Michele was only 19 years old, had a one year old baby and now a husband who would require 24 hour care. Almost a week had gone by and it was now time for me to graduate high school. What was supposed to be a time of celebration was a time of "Let's just get this over with." I tried to have fun and did manage a few smiles but it was just too tough, I ended up at a party but called it a night early.

After staying in the hospital for a while John had to go to Orlando for therapy to see how much use of his arms and hands he could regain. Michele had to go with him so she could learn how to care for someone in his condition.

Shortly after graduation Steve came back to visit the family which was a rare occasion. We hadn't seen him in over a year prior to him coming in to see John. He rented a little four passenger plane which he flew himself down from DC. He convinced me I needed to get away; John's accident was really weighing on my mind. "Was it my fault? Did I do something wrong?" They never found a scratch on John and could not figure out what really happened. Maybe he skied over a log or an alligator which caused him to fall and the impact of hitting the water is what broke his neck? Did he black out while skiing? We really never knew. The question I had is how much more did I hurt him when we were getting him out of the water, did we make things worse? Those are questions that will go unanswered for the rest of my life.

I jumped in the plane with Steve and we flew to Washington DC. We stopped in Jacksonville to get gas and then took off again for the nation's capital. I stayed for a week and every night was a new party. Steve's life had a fast pace that I was not used to. He took me to his favorite hang outs and we had a great time. It was the first time I had spent any real quality time with Steve and I really liked it. From what I could see he was living the good life and doing very well for himself. After a week of partying it was time to fly back home. I booked a commercial flight and it was back to the reality of Port St. Lucie.

After being in Orlando for a few months Michele and John came back and tried to get into some type of normal routine life. Michele got a lot of help, not only from our family but John's family as well. His mother, Millie, was a big help to John and Michele but it was still a very tough time for them.

As for Rob and Faye, they seemed to be doing well but I knew something was up when we would get together. He had changed companies and finally got the trucking job he wanted working for Flowers Bakery. He worked the night shift delivering bread to restaurants and grocery stores in the middle of the night. He would come over and visit on his way to the gym; he finally decided he was going to get into shape. He had never lifted weights in his life but before long he got as big as a house. Faye was not happy about this because she was always nervous that he would leave her for a younger woman.

Over the years Rob and I had become real close, and we would have long deep conversations about a lot of different topics, but not about God which had surprisingly stopped for a while. He would tell me he really loved Faye but he did have a hard time with her age. My advice was always the same, "if you're not happy you need to make a decision". He didn't like my advice because he was afraid to leave Faye. He knew Faye was perfect for him, she did everything, cooked, cleaned, ironed his clothes, and took care of things at the house while he worked. He worked the night shift; he went to work at about 8:00 PM and wouldn't get home until 6:00 a.m. the next morning. He did this for several years but could never get used to the crazy hours. He had to put dark shades on all his bedroom windows because he had to sleep during the day.

Daisy and Sal's business was doing OK, they were not getting rich but they were paying the bills. Sal ended up getting a hernia from all the grunt work. He was now in his mid 60's and even though he was still a strong guy his body was telling him it was time to slow down. Sal now realized he could no longer do all the lifting so Daisy asked me to go to work with her so I quit my construction job and became the driver and grunt worker for their business.

It was fun working with my mom, she loved being around the people and her face would glow when they bragged about her food. She was a great cook and was happy to share it while making a living at the same time. Most of the day was a leisure pace until the lunch hour, that's when we went out to the Hutchison Island Nuclear Power Plant. This was a huge construction project where a few thousand people worked, they had 30 minutes for lunch and it was a feeding frenzy. There was another lunch truck out there; Matty was the guy who ran it. When Daisy and Sal first started going out there Matty told them it was his spot and they needed to back off. If he knew Sal at all he wouldn't have said that. Sal jumped off the truck and told him where he could go and what he could do with his truck. I've seen Sal mad; it's not a pretty sight. This was a guy who came up the hard way in a working class Italian family. He then went to serve in World War II and was a prisoner of war for several months where he was beaten and tortured before eventually escaping. He also had a chance to join the mafia; they wanted to run a numbers phone ring out of his basement and were willing to pay him a good bit of money. His father wanted no part of it and told Sal "that would not happen in his house." Even though Sal was paying all the bills and it was really his house he respected his father's wishes. He told me years later he really wanted to do that, it would have set him up financially for life. All that being said, Matty did not make him nervous when he made his demand. Over time they actually became friends and realized there was enough business for both of them.

This 30 minute rush of business was insane, Daisy would handle the food, and I would handle the drinks and the money. Most of the time it was so hot outside, like in the 90s and we were in the truck with those steam ovens and no air conditioning. By the time the 30 minutes was over Daisy would almost pass out, she would just start yelling out "I need a drink, quick, I need a drink". I would quickly get her a cup of ice tea or soda before she would fall over. After a while I got used to it but the first time it happened I started to laugh before realizing she was serious. The few months we worked together was quite the experience, it was fun and we got really close, not that we weren't close already but when you're that age (18), you don't usually spend several hours a day with your mother.

I eventually got a job at that same nuclear power plant after hearing how much money those guys were making. It was all union work so the pay was really good. I joined the laborer's union and my starting pay was $11 an hour. This was 1980, that was a lot of money for a young kid, plus we worked a ton of overtime at the plant which was always behind on deadlines. I worked the nightshift which was 3:30 p.m. to 11:30 p.m. It was difficult to work those hours at that age because you basically had to give up your entire social life. By the time I got home, took a shower and got something to eat it would be close to 1:00 a.m. There was nobody to party with at that hour; most people had to get up early the next morning for work. We worked just about every Saturday and sometimes Sunday as well, the money was great but socially it was tough, it was all work and very little time to play.

A couple years had passed since John's accident and Michele was doing her best to keep her family together but it was becoming very clear they weren't going to make it. John's mom, Millie, was at their house all the time and she really wanted to take care of John herself. Michele was busy trying to raise Johnboy which was a fulltime job by itself. Unfortunately they eventually decided to separate; John and Michele knew it would be the best thing for both of them. John moved in with his mother and step father, Bunny. Millie and John's father had divorced many years earlier. I'm not sure how Bunny got his nickname but to see him it didn't fit. He was about 6'2" and weighed about 350 pounds. He was a big beer drinker and had one of those 100 pound bellies. He was just a huge man but a very nice man and did everything he could to help Millie take care of John.

A bunch of people John and his father had worked with got together with a few companies around town and had a custom house built for John to move into. I think he just had to pay for a small portion of the cost, whatever it was it was well worth it. Michele and John remained on good terms and Johnboy would spend a lot of time with his father. Daisy would often cook extra food and bring it over for John, which he loved.

I've thought of that day many times over the years. What if I just didn't go with John? Would he have canceled? If he did still go would he still have had the accident? Would he have died because I wasn't there to give him mouth to mouth? Lots of questions unfortunately very few answers. The good news is John is now in his early 50s and living a full life. He's remarried, works full time and is a productive part of society. He has managed to live quiet well with his handicap including learning to drive a specially equipped van. His son, now is his 30s, keeps in contact with him and they have a great relationship. I lost touch with him over the years which I regret but do get constant updates from my nephew.

As for the power plant years, they were very interesting. I worked there for over three years and the guys that worked there was a hard core group. A lot of them would move from state to state going where the jobs were. They would stay for three or four years, however long it lasted and then move on to the next one. I was just a laborer and made good money, but there were electricians, plumbers, carpenters who made the real big money. It was not uncommon for them to get close to or even over one hundred thousand dollars a year. For blue collar work in the early 1980s that was a great living.

With the great living came the hard core lifestyle. Being on the night shift a lot of guys would go out to the parking lot during their dinner break and grab a few beers, or something even stronger than that, smoking pot or snorting cocaine was pretty common as well. It didn't seem like a big deal until you realized a lot of these same guys would come back from their partying and start welding on pipes that would eventually run the nuclear reactor. I always thought one day I would read about a problem at the plant but thank God nothing major ever happened.

Chapter 25:

Daisy and Sal's Last Business

Daisy and Sal had since shut down the lunch truck and turned to a new business venture, they ran the restaurant portion of a truck stop. Daisy could not get away from the food business, it was all she knew. Sal was pretty much retired but would help out around the place. He mainly would talk with all the regular truckers that came in. They would sit there for hours, drink coffee and smoke cigarettes. When you walked in, the smoke would almost knock you over. Daisy really liked having her own place; she had several good people that worked for her. The problem with the business was the expenses were more than the business could justify. The rent was real high but the prices had to be low because the truckers were not big spenders.

Daisy and Sal didn't make a lot of money but they did make a lot of friends. This is a crazy story about one couple who were local truckers. Daisy knew these people pretty well, so she thought. One day while watching the local news they were talking about the police having a shootout in town. It turned out this couple, they were in their late forties with a twenty something year old son, were big drug dealers and the cops came to their place to make a bust. The husband did not want to go down without a fight, he ended up getting shot and killed by the police, the son went to prison for several years but they could never connect the wife to anything so she was set free. This made for some good coffee talk for several months.

I started working a few night shifts as a waiter to help out and also make some money while I was going to the local college. The power plant went into operation so about 99 percent of us were laid off; they kept just a handful for maintenance work. Being that it was a truck stop it was open 24 hours a day, which was a challenge, anytime someone would call in sick Daisy had to work their shift. This would eventually take a toll on her. I had to work the graveyard shift for a while from 11:00 p.m to 6:00 a.m., mostly on Friday nights because they couldn't get anybody to work that shift. The truck stop was just across the street from the local strip club, "The Jokers Wild." What a dump that was, just an old beat up building but it was a cash cow for the owners.

When the place would close for the night a lot of people would make their way across the street for a bite to eat before calling it a night, this included some of the strippers and their boyfriends. Most of the girls were biker chicks and their boyfriends were some tough looking individuals. They made them work there and at the end of the night the girls would give all the money to their guys, some life. Some of the girls who were just working girls, no biker boyfriends, would come over as well. The crowd would start staggering in between 2:00 a.m. to 3:00 a.m. While waiting for their food they would pull out cocaine and snort it right off the table. It was just me and one cook in the back running the place and I sure wasn't saying anything, these guys would have killed me. Daisy and Sal would have had a fit if they knew this was going on. You knew when some of the girls had a slow night; they would want to trade drugs or other favors, so to speak, for food. Thanks, but no thanks, as I said, it was a rough crowd.

Saturday morning after work I would go straight to my college radio station. That was part of my communications class during one semester. It was a long day after working all night at the restaurant. The college station was publicly funded and played all classical music, for me it was the perfect sleeping pill. I would open the station shortly after 6:00 a.m.; I had to check the satellite to make sure it was pumping in that riveting classic music. Once I had it tuned in I would pull up a chair, prop my feet on the desk and go to sleep for a few hours.

That seemed to be working fine until one Saturday I got a phone call from a listener. They asked me if the format of the station had changed, I told them not to my knowledge. They complained that some type of contemporary jazz was playing, I said "Listen, I just put the station on I don't choose the music." The guy was very upset and state he would stop sending donations and hung up the phone. I tried to go back to sleep but that call was bothering me. I decided to check the satellite to see if something was wrong. Sure enough I had it tuned incorrectly and the music was jazz. I quickly fixed it and never said a word to anyone about it.

I had made great money during my power plant days and bought a 1969 Corvette. It needed some work but was a fun car to own for $3000. I wanted to establish my credit so I went to our local bank for a loan but without any credit they wanted one of my parents to co-sign. Sal agreed to do if for me but told me if I was ever late on a payment he would kill me. Daisy had taught us all about the importance of having good credit, she never had a lot of money but she was never late on a bill in her life. Any time she wanted something she knew she could get a loan for it. This was some of the best advice I ever got.

After owning the Corvette for a while I decided I wanted to sell it. I didn't want to put the money into it the car it would take to make it a cream puff so selling it was the best idea. The car wasn't running as good as it should so I took it to our local mechanic. The young guy that worked there was the one who worked on my car previously, I told him it just wasn't running right. He suggested we take it for a test ride. It was a typical Florida afternoon, hot, humid and it had just stormed a bit so the roads were a little wet. We went cruising down the road and my mechanic told me to hit it so he could hear the engine. I gunned it and we were going about 60 MPH down this side street where the speed limit was 35. As we were flying down the road one of my tires hit the grass median and the car started going sideways. I tried to regain control of the car but I was going too fast. The car slid one way then the other before we went off the road and slammed right into an electric wire pole.

My door is what hit the pole; we flipped over and cut the pole in half. What occurred next is the stuff you read about but you don't think ever really happens. We are upside down in the Corvette, my head is kind of halfway out of the broken door window and I can see the electric wires from the pole sparking just above the car. My mechanic is pulling his way out of his broken window as I try to do the same until I realized I am pinned by the steering wheel and can't get out. I took another look at those wires hanging over me and knew I had to do something and fast. This is when the adrenaline kicked in; I somehow got the strength to bend the steering column with one hand to free myself and crawled out of the car. It was like one of those old Superman TV shows where he bent a steel bar, that's how the steering wheel was; I just bent it out of the way and got out.

We both crawled out of the mud and onto the street where several cars had already stopped to see what happened. My mechanic had a pretty bad gash on his arm that was bleeding like crazy, I was bleeding from my hand and arm but the pain in my ribs was the worst. The police and ambulance showed up within minutes and that's when I collapsed. The next thing I knew I was in the ambulance heading to the hospital. It could have been a lot worse, I just need a few stitches in my hand and arm but the bruised ribs were what hurt the most.

Daisy and Sal showed up shortly after I got there and Daisy came running in crying like crazy which of course made me cry (I inherited the sensitive gene from her). They kept me for a few hours and then I was free to go. Before leaving the police wanted to know what happened, after explaining the wet conditions were the issue, I left out the speeding part, they didn't even give me a ticket. The officer's comment was "He wrecked his Corvette, that's punishment enough."

He was more right than he knew, because I had taken out a signature loan not a car loan, full coverage insurance was not required. So you can figure out the rest of the story, I had two years of payments left that I had to pay without even having use of the car. Not paying was not an option; Sal told me what would happen if I didn't pay. Also my credit would have been ruined, an expensive lesson to say the least. I was able to sell the car for parts but lost a couple thousand dollars.

Just a few months later Rob called and said he had to talk to me and Michele about something. With Rob there was no telling what this was going to be about. He told us he finally decided he was not happy with Faye and he needed our help moving out. He had this whole plan figured out; it would all happen without Faye knowing. We gave him grief for not telling Faye what was going on, he explained he was afraid of what Faye might do to him. Even though Faye was a small woman she was tough as nails.

We met Rob at his apartment at the designated time, when Faye would be out for a while. Rob had a rented truck which he would drive, Michele had to drive his Ford LTD and I would drive his little project car he was working on, an old Chevy El Camino. He had already moved his prized possession, the 1948 Harley Davidson motorcycle that he had re-built himself. We loaded up the truck with just his stuff, Rob was running around like the place was on fire, you could tell he was nervous and knew what would happen if Faye would have shown up.

After we got everything out we started down the road back to our house, Rob would be moving back home again. As I'm driving about 45 miles per hour the El Camino didn't feel right when all of a sudden the car started weaving back and forth and forced me off the road. I started to panic because this was the same feeling of losing control when I crashed my Corvette just a few months earlier. Luckily I got control of the car and slid to a stop in dirt on the side of the road. Rob and Michele eventually circled back when they saw I was no longer behind him. When I got out of the car I saw that one of the rear wheels had fallen off. What happened was Faye was smarter than Rob thought, she knew he was planning to leave and she had loosened the lug nuts on one of the wheels which caused it to coming flying off.

Rob ended up staying with us for a few months before realizing he wanted to go back to Faye. They rekindled their relationship and rented a nice little house in Fort Pierce. Deep down he still wasn't happy, but he loved how Faye took care of him.

Chapter 26:

Time to Leave the Nest

Fast forward to Christmas of 1983 and Steve came to visit for the holidays. Steve saw that I was going nowhere living in what he called a nowhere town. Steve was a big city person and the thought of living in Port St. Lucie made his skin crawl. During a visit if he sat down for more than 10 minutes he would fall asleep, the town bored him to death. With that, he looked at me and said, "You need to get the hell out of here; you need to move to DC." Deep down I knew he was right and told him if he could get me a job I would do it. Before he left to go back to DC he told me to be ready to make the move when he called.

Sure enough, shortly after the first of the New Year Steve called and said he got me a job with his old college roommate. I would be a stock boy for a small computer company. Within two weeks I had packed all my stuff in the back of my Datsun (now called Nissan) 280ZX and was ready for my new life. It was very emotional to say goodbye to my mom and Sal, they were my whole life and were great to me. I had already stayed much longer than I should have but they made life too easy on me. Even though I had paid rent for a few years, it started at $50 week and ended at $75 a week, living with them was a bargain. When I was working all those hours at the power plant I was actually making more money than they were with the lunch truck. We hugged and said our emotional good bye that early January morning and off I went.

The journey to DC started around 6:00 a.m. The first several hours was easy, just straight highway driving. By the time I got about two hours from northern Virginia, where Steve lived, it started to snow a little bit. By now I had been driving for a good 12 hours and each mile I drove north the snow seemed to be coming down a little harder. Within the next 30 minutes it was a full blown blizzard. Even though I had grown up in the north I left long before I was old enough to drive. So this was the first time I had to deal with these driving conditions and it was not fun. The first problem I had was the windshield freezing up, I had the defrosters on but I didn't like the heat on because it made me feel like I was suffocating so I had the temperature on cold. I didn't know you had to have the heat on to clear the windshield; this made visibility a bit of a problem.

After driving for so many hours my eyes were burning from being tired, couple that with these conditions and I thought I was going to lose my mind. I guess I had about 10 miles to go, driving 30 miles per hour it still took forever. I was putting my head out the window so I could see because the window was just about frozen over. I finally got to the exit and basically slid down toward the light, luckily there were no other idiots on the road but me. Steve had told me when I got off the exit to stop at a gas station and to call him. Even though the station was closed I saw there was a payphone outside. I called Steve and he was excited to hear my voice. Based on the conditions, he told me to stay where I was he would be there in a few minutes to lead me back to his place. Steve showed up in his beautiful black two door convertible Mercedes Benz, I then followed him up the hill to his building. We first had to pass through the security gate where you use your card to get in. We parked the cars in the underground parking garage and made our way up to the top floor in the elevator.

It may not sound like a big deal but from where I came from this was like paradise. When we entered his penthouse apartment I knew this was a place I could get used to real fast. Remember Steve liked the finer things and the apartment was no different. It was professionally decorated with no detail left out. I was sitting on the couch resting after the long drive from Florida; we had called Daisy to let her know I made it there safely. That was a rule since we were kids, she didn't care where we were, what time it was as long as we called to let her know we were fine. She could not go to sleep without knowing where we were. There were many times we all had called from strange places and situations, she never questioned it, she just said, "Thanks for calling."

Just as I was catching my breath and about to fall asleep sitting on the couch Steve gets a phone call and tells me, "Come on we're going out for a drink." I told him "you're crazy, I just got here, I need some sleep, need a shower, and need a lot of things but going out in a snow storm for a drink is not one of them." Steve has always been very convincing he said, "Get your ass up, you're not in Podunk Florida anymore, you're in DC," so we went out for a drink.

We went to a local restaurant that was only a mile away; the people he was meeting had been there a while and already had a few drinks in them. They wanted to discuss renting a jet for the weekend to fly to Tampa to watch the Washington Redskins play in the Super Bowl. The guy was a big local auto dealer and had plenty of money; he had some nice looking young ladies with him and a couple of buddies. After discussing some of the details and a couple of drinks, Steve told the gentlemen he would handle the jet for him and we went back home. I should have known that this first night would be an omen of what living in the big city with Steve would be like.

Chapter 27:

The Fast and the Furious

The next two years living in Northern Virginia (we called it Washington DC because it was a 20 minute ride to downtown DC and the White House) was a lot of fun, a lot of parties, spent a lot of money I didn't have, learned a lot about life and met a lot of crazy people. The best part of living there was finally getting to know my brother. He was never home when we were kids living back in New Jersey and he went out on his own when we first moved to Florida.

The first thing I found out was he was very generous, he always picked up the tab for me when we went out, dinner, drinks, it didn't matter he was paying the check. Granted he was making a lot more than me, he was in the jet business and doing very well. I was working for a small computer company making about $30,000 a year, which was good money in Florida but not much in DC. I went out and bought a used BMW and had the big car payment that went with it. I also had to go out and buy a bunch of new clothes. I came to DC with mostly jeans and T-shirts, although I did have one polyester suit that Steve sent me many years earlier, I thought it was still a good looking suit, little did I know. Within a few weeks of moving from "The sticks" of Florida I was going to a black tie party with Steve and his friends. His friend George was making big money in the computer business, and he was driving us to the party in his company car, a Rolls Royce. Yeah, I liked this lifestyle even though I was riding the coat tails of many others.

While Steve and I were living the high life in DC the rest of the family was getting on with their lives back in Florida. Rob and Faye were doing OK, Rob was still driving a truck for the bakery and Faye took care of the house. I didn't talk with Rob much while I was gone but the few times we spoke I could tell he was just going through the motions of life.

Michele was doing good while working and taking care of Johnboy. He was the one I missed the most, I spent a lot of time with him as Daisy, Sal and I all helped raise him. He was a great kid and I really did miss him. I think he missed me too although I gave him the same abuse I got from my older brothers, my theory was it would make him tougher. Daisy and Sal were still working away at the truck stop restaurant, business was not doing great but they hung in there.

After being in DC a few months Steve wanted to make sure I was meeting enough girls so he always made his place available for a social gathering. Late one night about 2:00 a.m., the phone rang, I just turned over and ignored it because it was a work night and I had to be up in a few hours. A few minutes later my door flies open, the light flips on and Steve yells out, "So you want to meet some girls, here you go." I open my eyes and see four good looking girls standing in my room. They told me I need to come out to the living room and have a drink. Before I had a chance to say anything they threatened to pull my covers off if I didn't agree to come out. I quickly replied by saying, "I sleep in the nude so go ahead and pull off the covers if you want to." With that they all moved to the living room and waited for me to come out.

Even though all the girls were very pretty one stood out to me, Carol. She was a tall, olive skinned dark haired beauty; I knew I had to get to know her better. They had come over with Steve's friends George and Kay. One of Carol's friends was George and Kay's live-in nanny. The crazy part was they would get a baby sitter so they could take the nanny and her friends out to party. We would have frequent late night visitors at the apartment, we were close to one of the local clubs and once they would close the only place left to get a drink was Steve's place. Steve would never say no to anyone and everyone knew it. It was a lot of fun and I got to meet a lot of people but I sure didn't get much sleep.

I called Carol a few days after meeting her to see if we could do something together. We started out as friends, having lunch, playing racquetball and stuff like that. I really liked her because she was very easy to get along with. I had a feeling this could grow into something so I was taking it very slow. We were both casually dating other people so we didn't see each other often. I had been in town for several months now and my 23rd birthday was quickly arriving. Steve decided to give me my birthday present early and what a present it was two tickets to a Bruce Springsteen concert, not just regular seats but sitting in the luxury suite and on top of that he rented a limo for the night. This was by far the best present I had ever received; Steve loved to give great gifts. There was only one caveat; I could not take a buddy, I had to take a girl.

So now the pressure was on, I didn't want to waste the tickets on just anyone. I needed to make the most of the tickets and I figured now was the time to see if I could take the relationship with Carol to the next level. I called her and asked her to go, she told me she was already going. I then told her I had luxury suite tickets; she hesitated but then said she couldn't. I fired the last bullet letting her know we would have champagne and a limo for the night and that closed the deal, she finally said "yes."

This would be a great official first date, we had our champagne and limo ride to the show, great seats in the luxury box and more champagne. Springsteen was his normal awesome self (this was the "Born in The USA' tour). After the show we had a relaxing ride home in the limo, traffic never felt so good, we were now officially dating. Part two of that story is a couple years later Carol and I went to another Springsteen concert. We go to our seats very early to beat the crowd and as we are sitting there a couple people with a microphone and camera approach us. They said they were from MTV and wanted to ask us a few questions. We told them about how the previous Springsteen concert was our first date and a few other boring tidbits. A few weeks later we start getting phone calls from friends in New Jersey, Florida and locally telling us how they saw our interview on MTV. They said it was pretty funny but unfortunately neither Carol nor I ever did see it.

A few months later Steve got transferred to his company's home office in Detroit but he still flew back on weekends. The weekdays didn't matter to him because he traveled all the time anyway. He definitely wanted to be home on the weekends because that's when the fun started. I was really enjoying the big city life and more importantly I had finally got to know Steve as we became real close. Steve knew most of the bartenders at some of our favorite places which made for lots of fun and reasonable bar tabs. He would just tip them a ton when it was time to settle up and the next time it would be the same deal. Carol and her friends would meet us some times as we all started to hang out together, we all had a big time.

With Steve being gone a lot I moved into his room and rented out my room to my friend Mike. I met him through some other people after he moved down from a small town in Pennsylvania. He was blown away by the big city just like I was several months earlier. When Steve came home on the weekends we just took turns sleeping on the couch. I had to offset my expensive lifestyle somehow and taking in a roommate just made sense.

Chapter 28:

The Real Bachelor

What would happen next started a crazy series of events that truly are hard to believe. If there weren't other people there to witness it nobody would have ever believed me. Steve was written up in his college newspaper, they were doing follow up stories on some of their graduates, sort or a "Where are they now." It really wasn't any big story; it highlighted his success in the jet sales business and few extra words about how he did it, no big deal right?

One of the magazines for pilots and people in the aviation business, *Flying Magazine* saw the article from the college and decided they would do a story on Steve. This article was a little more in depth and really talked Steve up big time. Someone from that magazine knew someone at *Cosmopolitan Magazine* and suggested they consider Steve for their "Bachelor of the Month" feature. Someone from the magazine called Steve and asked if he was interested. Like most guys, he didn't know much about the magazine but figured it could only help his business. They asked him a few questions about his likes, dislikes, what he thought was attractive in a woman and what would be his perfect weekend with the girl of his dreams. He was contacted by a photographer to take his picture for the magazine and after that he pretty much forgot about it.

I guess it was a couple months later when he was featured in the magazine. Little did he know what would happen next. We got a copy of the magazine and quickly looked for his picture. When we saw the picture we all laughed, it may have been the worst picture of him I've ever seen. My brother is a good looking guy; he even did some professional modeling when he was younger to help make ends meet, trust me this guy made women's head turn when we walked into a place. But this picture, yikes!

The write up was one paragraph that read something like "Steve is a very successful jet salesman, he likes to cook, loves good food and his ideal weekend would be skiing up in the mountains with a nice little snow bunny." It ended with his name and a PO Box address. That's not word for word, but pretty close.

It seemed like within hours of the magazine hitting the newsstands our phone starting ringing. Steve was there to get the first call; it was a woman asking for him. He said, "Yes this is Steve." That phone call and the hundreds of others that followed were all the same, "Hi, my name is Jane Doe and I saw you in this month's *Cosmopolitan Magazine* and I think you're wonderful, handsome, and gorgeous," you name it, they used it. We were all blown away by this; we had no idea the impact this little article could have. Within a week Steve went to empty his mailbox at the post office and he came home with well over 1000 letters. They were the same as the phone calls; some even sent nude photos, panties, lipstick and all kinds of other crazy stuff. Steve just decided to have fun with it. He knew nothing serious would come out of it so he just kind of played along with most of them. Nothing to hurt anyone just a little harmless flirting; the funny thing was Steve was the last person who needed help getting dates.

My roommate and I decided to have some fun as well. When Steve was out of town we would take turns answering the phone. I would get the same thing most of the time when I told them I was his younger brother. "You must be just as good looking as Steve right?" "Sure I'm taller and richer too." Truly nothing came out of any of this, Carol and I were starting to get serious and very happy, but it was fun to play along on the phone.

Steve got some local media attention and was asked to go on a local TV talk show. The host was Maury Povich, this was way before his show went national. Steve used his 15 minutes of fame to do some good. He had heard about a young boy who was in failing health with heart problems. He teamed up with some people and organized a huge benefit party for the American Heart Association. The party was a big success for raising money and on top of that we all had a great time at the party.

Local media covered the party and Gary Collins, who at the time had a national talk show, had a camera crew there and put the highlights of the party on his show. They interviewed me during the party, and they asked me what I thought of my brother. I bragged about him saying what a great brother he was, very generous which of course led to the party. Unfortunately they got to me pretty late in the evening and I may have slurred a few words which left me on the cutting room floor. Either way it was for a great cause and a great time for all who attended.

Earlier I said nothing came out of all the phone calls; there was one caller who decided to continue calling long after all the hoopla had passed. She talked with me, Steve and my roommate Mike. She was an interesting character to say the least. She swore she was a sheltered girl from the Midwest and was the heir to a very wealthy family. We all played along for a while, heck it was her dime she was calling on. She said she wanted to come visit, we didn't have any problem with that, both Mike and I spelled out that we were both in steady relationships but she was welcome to come sleep on the couch. Steve was back to his busy traveling, not that he minded anyway.

We really didn't know what to make of her; we surely didn't think she would actually visit. Within a few weeks, she showed up at our front door. She was an attractive black woman in her early twenties and just as pleasant in person as she was on the phone. Carol, Mike and I took turns entertaining her for a few days, taking her to the mall, to dinner and the like until the weekend came, that's when things got really interesting.

This was the fall of 1985, in the middle of football season in the home of the fan crazed Washington Redskins. The young lady, let's just call her Mary, asked if we could go downtown and pick up a friend of hers. Again, we were easy to get along with, we were all in our early twenties, up for a good time and looking back, very naive. We still had no idea who this girl really was; she didn't have the appearance of a wealthy person. No expensive jewelry, no fancy clothes, no limo to get her around and no identification which we really found weird. She said she had to travel very low key due to the threat of being kidnapped. Okay, sure. Well we wanted to believe she was wealthy.

When we inquired who her friend was we all were shocked when she said "Tony Dorsett". He was the star running back of the Dallas Cowboys and he was in town to play the Redskins that Sunday. This was the Saturday night before the game; this is when the visiting teams always arrive at the city where they are going to play and check into a local hotel. Mary told us she spoke with him earlier and we needed to go to the team's hotel to pick him up, he would be ready about 8:00 p.m. It was just Mary, Carol and me at this time. Carol and I didn't know what to think but we jumped in the car and headed downtown. We pulled up to the hotel and there was a ton of people there. They were all Dallas Cowboy fans hoping to get a peak at their favorite players. I looked at Mary and said "What now?" She said "I can't go in there due to security concerns, you go in and tell him you're with me and bring him out to the car; he is expecting you."

Before I go on with the rest of the story you need to know I might be one of the biggest NFL football fans in the world. I can probably count on one hand how many Sundays over the past 40 years that I didn't sit down and watch at least a little of a NFL game. For me to walk in the hotel and potentially meet Tony Dorsett, the best running back in the game at that time and a future "Hall of Famer" I was going to fulfill a lifelong dream.

I jumped out of the car and walked up to the entrance of the hotel, I walked right past all the fans that were chanting and waving their Cowboy signs. A security guard quickly stopped me and asked me if he can help me which left me with only one reply "I'm here to pick up Tony Dorsett." This is when I figured the whole thing would blow up, we would finally figure out Mary is a fraud and I would be thrown out on my butt. The security guards asked me my name and then said, "Follow me, they are just finishing their team dinner and he should be out shortly." We took the elevator up a couple of floors and walked toward one of the big conference rooms. He then handed me over to another security guard and told him who I was and what I was doing. He told me to stand right in a certain spot and he would be right back. I stood there for a couple of minutes which felt like an hour until he returned. As he approached me I started thinking how was I going to get out of this one, they'll think I'm some kind of stalker and take me right to the police. He finally got back to me and said words I'll never forget: "Mr. Craig, Mr. Dorsett said they are almost done, he'll be out in a few minutes." I don't know what my facial expression externally looked like, but internally I felt like someone was standing on my chest and then finally jumped off.

Now the fun part: within a couple of minutes the team finished their dinner and the players started walking out. Quarterback Danny White, Defensive lineman Ed "Too Tall" Jones, Randy White , the legendary coach Tom Landry, I was beside myself, but I knew I had to keep my cool. Then as most of the team had filed out walks Tony Dorsett. The security guard pointed toward me and they started walking my way. He extended his hand and said, "Are you Ron?" I give him a firm handshake and nervously said, "Yes." He asks where I was parked and then suggested I pull in to the underground parking lot due to the crowd out front.

I raced back out to the car where Carol and Mary eagerly awaited my return. When I got in the car they both quickly asked "Where is he?" I told them the plan of picking him up in the underground parking deck and quickly drove around. When we got there he was waiting with a security guard, he hurriedly got in the car and I started to drive. I did a quick introduction to Carol and then he strangely enough introduced himself to Mary. This threw me for a loop because I assumed they knew each other but not so. We had some small talk during the 20 minute ride back to my apartment and then made our way up to our place.

The four of us sat there, had a couple of drinks, a few snacks and acted like we knew each other forever. He was one of the nicest guys you could ever meet and he was a perfect gentleman to both Carol and Mary. There was no romance between him and Mary, it turns out he met her the same way we did, via the phone. After about 30 minutes of chatting he said he needed to get back to the hotel due to curfew. As we are getting ready to leave my roommate Mike walks in. This is one of those moments you see on TV. He looks over and says "Hey Ron, Carol, Mary, Tony Dorsett, TONY DORSETT!" He runs over to where we were to shake his hand and exchange a few words and then we took off back to the hotel. We dropped him off at the same spot where we picked him up, shook his hand and that was it. I have to say those few hours were some of the most fun I've ever had.

I'd love to tell you we solved the mystery of Mary but we never did. She flew out a couple days later, continued to call for a few more weeks and then the phone went silent. Dying from curiosity, we tried calling her back and the number was no longer in service. Who was she? Was she really a rich heir?

My guess is she was a bit of a crazy person which fit right in with the rest of us at the time. Although she did have some type of connection, I found out months later when I received a phone call from one of Tony Dorsett's financial advisors. She asked if I knew how to reach Mary, when I told her how we met she offered a similar story where she received a random call and next thing she knew Tony and Mary were speaking on the phone. I guess that is one mystery I will never solve but it sure has made for some great conversations throughout the years.

Chapter 29:

This City Will Eat You Alive

All the wild parties and crazy events had finally quieted down, real life was settling in. During all this I also had a job to do, I had moved up to sales from the stock room with the computer company and was doing pretty good. Even with my brother's generosity I was still living way above my means. I had bought an expensive car, a bunch of new expensive suits, fancy shirts, ties and shoes to go along with it. After about two years of this lifestyle I had burned through all the money I had saved up prior to moving to DC.

My main function at the computer company was to handle this large house account my boss had given me. They did a lot of software design and consulting for this account and I handled all their small computer purchases. After doing this for close to two years their contract for services had run out and all of my business, which accounted for about 95% what I did, had come to a screeching halt.

The next day I went to work figuring they would put me on another account and all would be fine. Within an hour of being in the office my boss called me in and gave me the news. "Sorry Ron, we don't have enough business to justify you staying on, we have to let you go." WOW! Boy was I naïve, I thought for sure they would take care of me. I went from this humble kid that moved from small town Florida to a bit of a cocky son of a gun who came to take on the big city.

After that shocker I went on a job hunt. Finding a job was not that tough, the problem was I did not want to stay in the computer industry (smart move, I know).

I interviewed with quite a few different companies but I couldn't find what I wanted. I wanted the same cushy job I had before, give me some accounts and I'll take care of them. That is not what was out there, most of the sales jobs I ran into were cold calling (knocking on doors), straight commission with no salary. Welcome to the real world.

I tried a couple different things but found myself bouncing around from job to job. I sold debt collection systems, truck training classes (trying to convince people to buy $5000 worth of truck driving lessons so they could become a professional truck driver), office supplies, I tried everything but nothing was working.

I was broke and in my mind had only one choice left, move back down to small town Florida and regroup. Steve, who was the ultimate big city person, did not think this was the right thing to do. He tried to talk me out of it and said he would cover me financially until I go back on my feet. I knew that was not the right thing to do, so my decision was made.

One big item that still had to be addressed, what happens with me and Carol? We had become very close, we were in love. This was the person I wanted to spend the rest of my life with, she was by my side for the good times and now she was there during the not so good times. We had talked about the options and we agreed I would go down to Florida, find a job, get settled in and she would follow in about a month. She had 30 days to figure how to break the news to her parents.

It was the spring of 1986, I packed up all my stuff and headed back Florida. I had mixed emotions, I finally got close with Steve and really enjoyed having him as a roommate, and we had become best friends. I had to come to terms with the fact that the big city kicked my butt. It was a big money town and I was out of money. That was the bad news; the good news was I really did learn a valuable life lesson. Just when you think you're invincible and you get a little too big for your britches, life will punch you right in the gut. I was glad to learn that lesson at an early age. Over the past 25 years I saw this happen to so many people, they walked around sticking their chest out, and eventually they all get knocked on their butts. The lesson is quite simple, stay humble.

I moved back in with Daisy and Sal and boy was that different. After being gone for over two years I realized how much I had changed, I saw things completely different. The little things they did which never used to annoy me were now driving me crazy. They had moved out of their house, they were tired of the maintenance and yard upkeep, and were now living in a very small and very old mobile home in a small and somewhat rundown older mobile home park in Fort Pierce.

All I was thinking about was "When was Carol going to get here?" Daisy and Sal were asking the same thing. They loved her, they had met Carol on a couple of occasions, we flew down for Thanksgiving one year and they also saw her on their visits to see Steve and me. I knew all would be fine once she got there. In the mean time I starting looking for a job and landed one right away. It was for in home sales selling water purification systems. This was big business in Florida because the drinking water throughout the state was horrible. The first week into it I did great, I had made several sales and earned $1500, I was ecstatic. I called Carol to give her the good news and also asked how the talk with her parents went. She told me she was going to tell them she was just coming down for a long vacation and then break the news to them later.

I didn't think it would be a big deal but her parents were very different than mine. Her father, Oscar, was originally from Lima, Peru, definitely old school Latin American thinking. Her mother, Martha, was from Buenos Aries, Argentina (her family was originally from Italy and migrated to Argentina during the World War 1) and much more open minded. Carol also had a sister, Brenda, she was three years younger. She and Carol were always very close, I got to know her well too because she and her friends would go with Carol and me to parties and clubs even though they were under age, amazing what fake IDs would do back then.

A month had gone by and I was starting to settle in to my new low key lifestyle in Florida. I had rekindled some of my previous friendships and also got back on my league softball team. If you have ever seen any of these competitive softball leagues you know how crazy it can get. More importantly I was able to see my sister, Johnboy and my brother Rob more often. Michele was doing well and my nephew was turning into a great little kid. Johnboy's father, John, was doing well also. I felt bad that I had not kept in touch with him. He and Michele had a great relationship as he saw his son all the time and Daisy and Sal stayed in close contact with John as well. For Rob, he had finally decided it was time to leave his wife, he loved her but ultimately he just wasn't happy. This time it wasn't a sneaky thing, he told Faye exactly what was going on.

I think what made him finally decide to move out was one night he wanted to go out for a ride on his Harley Davidson. Faye, being very jealous and insecure about him going any place because he may run into some younger woman, told him she didn't want him going out. He told her it wasn't a big deal and he wouldn't be out late, he just needed to get out for a while. This erupted into a fight with a lot of yelling and screaming. Rob told her to let him be and he jumped on his bike. Faye quickly ran inside as Rob fastened his helmet and just as he was getting ready to start the bike Faye came back out with a gun. She put it against the gas tank and said "I dare you to start this bike, I'll blow the both of us up right now, go ahead, I dare you!" Rob, being a non-confrontational guy, sat there for a moment and then got off the bike. She may have won that little battle but Rob knew it was over for him, I think within a few weeks he moved out. He rented a small house in town and left with his stereo equipment, a bed, his clothes, a pickup truck and of course his classic 1948 Harley Davidson.

During my breaks from sales appointments I would stop by Rob's apartment to see how he was doing. It was very weird but any time I would be there I would have this very secure feeling, like I was safe from the world. I wasn't really sure why but it was a feeling that I would experience numerous times over the years. It didn't take long for Rob to realize he needed a woman again; he never liked being alone. He tried going to the singles clubs but that wasn't his environment, so he stayed alone for quite some time. By now he had gone back to learning more about Christianity, was growing pretty strong in his faith and no longer believed in pre-marital sex.

Rob and I had become really close at this point, closer than we had ever been. I was 25, he was 33 and we finally understood each other. I would get burnt out on the sales calls, to just to get away for a while and get that safe feeling I would stop by his house just about on a daily basis. We would get into some deep conversations, he would get a little strong on preaching to me but I learned to shut that part of him out. It would always come back to him finding a woman. I used to tease him about being so desperate for a woman he would take just about anyone. The big joke between me and him was when I would say "If I had boobs you would marry me."

Carol was now ready to leave Northern Virginia and make her way to Florida. I was real excited to say the least, my mom and Sal were as well. She called and told me the day she was leaving and to look for her some time that evening. I went to work that day and that night I had a softball game. Carol had made the long journey and went to my mom's little mobile home. She sat with Daisy and Sal for a while to get caught up and then came to the ball field to catch the last part of the game.

This would be a real eye opener for Carol, again these were pretty competitive guys playing and their wives where very vocal fans. Carol was sitting in the stands watching the game as the other woman would yell and scream for their guys. If there were any close calls by the umpires the gals would let them have it, the four letter words would be flying. Carol knew right away, "I'm not in DC anymore." This will be a whole new world and it was going to be a bit of an adjustment.

The game was over and I was thrilled to see Carol. We went back to my mom's place, had a nice dinner and the four of us talked for hours. It was a great evening and I thought our new life was off to a good start. I had my old friends back, back with my family, Carol and I were together, and the job thing I figured that would somehow work out.

We all went to sleep that night with smiles and all was good. After falling asleep I woke up about an hour later and heard Carol sniffling. I asked her if she was OK only to find out she was crying. She said she was already homesick and wasn't sure this was the right place for her. We talked about it for a bit until she settled down and we eventually fell asleep.

The next morning I woke up and when I rolled over I realized the bed was soaking wet. My first thought was, "Oh, no, Carol wet the bed." The weird thing was the wetness was ice cold. Carol then woke up with the same look on her face as I had "Oh no, Ron wet the bed." After a brief moment we both realized that the window air conditioner unit had frozen over and leaked on to the bed. We laughed so hard and were relieved to know that neither one of us were a bed wetter.

The wet bed thing would happen just about every night as well as Carol crying herself to sleep; she was desperately homesick. We loved living with my folks but I knew if we were going to make it we needed to get our own place. Carol had found a job pretty quick and was working for a law office down in West Palm Beach, which was a 45 minute ride each way. It was a good job but the ride was a killer, I don't think that helped things so she looked for something closer to home and eventually got with a local real estate company as an assistant.

The early success I had selling in home water conditioners did not last and I was now job hopping from one place to the next trying to make some money. Every job was straight commission and I would have good weeks and then some bad weeks.

We didn't have any money but wanted to try to get a place of our own so I called my brother Steve for a loan. He said, "No problem, how much do you need?" I think he sent us like $900 for the first month's rent and security deposit.

We had picked out this nice little two bedroom apartment about 10 miles down the road from my mom's place. Carol and I were really excited as we reached move in day. My mom had let us take some of her furniture, a TV as well as the bed from our room, this was enough for us. I thought this was now the true beginning of our life together.

Chapter 30:

Would You Buy a Used Car From This Guy?

We did enjoy having our own place even though we were struggling financially. I continued to hop from sales job to sales job, until I saw an ad in the paper "Make Big Money Selling Cars." I figured I liked cars and I'm a pretty good in sales, it's got to be a good fit. I went to the interview and it seemed to be going pretty good when all of a sudden the manager asked me "When do you want to start?" Without thinking about it I said "Right away" which is exactly what he wanted to hear. So I was now in the car business, not a big deal at the time but a decision that would eventually have a big impact on my life.

There were 11 of us "new hires" that went through a few days of sales training which included a great lesson in car sales or sales in general for that matter. The 11 of us were sitting at a conference room table when the sales manager who was doing the training asked us, "What constitutes a good deal for the customer?" He went around the table asking each one of us our opinion. The answers varied from "Cheapest price on the car," "Lowest monthly payment," Lowest interest rate," "Best trade-in allowance" and so on. He looked at the 11 of us and said, "There is not one of you that will make it in the car business." My jaw dropped along with everyone else, we thought at least one of us had the right answer. He then told us his version of what constitutes a good deal for the customer, "When they sign the buyers order and agree to buy the car."

I wasn't really sure I knew what he meant. He went on to say "Have you ever agreed to buy something when you knew you were being ripped off? If they agree to it then it must be a good deal, right?" After I thought about it for a few minutes, he was right, if you don't stick a gun to someone's head and they agree to the terms they must think it's a good deal. It was one of the best sales lessons I ever learned, it works in all sales situations and in life as well.

Carol and I were settling in to living together and we were getting along great. Money was still tight as the car sales world was not an instant success. I knew we had hit rock bottom when one night we decided we would rent a video for the evening but we didn't have the two dollars (the price at the time) we needed to do it. We looked at each other, just turned on the TV and we were OK with that.

I started getting the hang of selling cars and the sales started to pick up although you never knew if it would be enough to stay employed. They told us from the beginning that we all were on a 90 day probationary period and we would get no benefits, vacation time or anything else until that time frame. I was also learning it was a ruthless business and whoever negotiates best wins. A rule this dealership had was to never take an offer from a customer without some type of commitment (also known as a down payment of some sort). Luckily this practice has changed through the years along with a lot of other archaic traditions of how to sell cars.

My manager wanted something from the customer and I was not allowed to present an offer without it. Most times this was not a big problem as they would have cash or a check but one time this guy did not want to give me a check, no matter what I said. I told him I wanted to sell him the car but I couldn't present his offer without something proving he was serious. I happened to notice he had a very nice watch and I asked him if I could borrow it to show my manager he was serious. After looking at me like I was crazy he took off the watch and gave it to me. My manager was very impressed with that and we did actually make a deal with the guy. We were all working six days a week and if you wanted to take Sunday off (you worked every other Sunday) they looked at you like you were crazy. My manager said to me "If you want to make it in the car business you have to be willing to work seven days a week." I stated wondering if this was the right business for me, I didn't mind working hard but I liked my time off as well.

The big day was now approaching; I was 89 days into my car sales career. I was sure I had sold enough as well as proved that I had potential. How wrong was I? 10 out of the 11 of us were fired one day before our insurance kicked in. I was unemployed again, I had to go home and tell Carol and I knew she would be crushed. Me and one of the other guys stopped by the bar first and knocked down a couple of drinks before heading home to break the bad news.

Carol actually took it well, but we both knew it was time for more of a drastic change then just another job would offer. We talked about it and said it was time to leave Florida. I didn't want to go back to DC; it was too tough for young people to get started up there, everything was so expensive and I had already tried to make it there. Similar to Daisy, I was always ready to try a new city. I didn't want to go to DC and Carol didn't want to stay in Florida so we needed some type of compromise. I remembered reading an article about Atlanta being a great place for young people, a thriving city that had a reasonable cost of living. I mentioned that to Carol and she was all for it, now we needed a game plan.

I mentioned this to Daisy, at first she was heartbroken because she loved having us close by. One of the ways we survived was going to her truck stop restaurant for free dinners just about every night. Deep down she knew this was not the place for us and told us she would help in any way. The first thing that came to mind was her best friend, crazy Toby, her oldest son Stewart lived in Atlanta and happened to be in the car business as well. She suggested I give him a call, which I did the next day and he built up Atlanta as a great place. He also told me he could get me a job selling cars at the same Chevy dealership where he worked. This sounded like a no brainer, cool place to live, and a big enough city but not too big with a job almost guaranteed.

Before we packed up and made the move I took a drive up there to interview at the Chevy dealership and also look for some apartments. The interview went good so I went ahead and secured an apartment for us to move into in a couple of weeks. Carol was excited and so was I, another fresh start. Moving to me was no big deal; I had done it so much with Daisy and Sal that I actually looked forward to a new adventure. Carol gave notice at her job, I made arrangements for the U-Haul truck and we were ready to go. It was time to say good bye to Daisy and Sal again, this time I knew there would be no coming back. The saying "You can never go home again" is so true. You think and want it to be the same as when you left it but not only has the place you left changed but you have changed as well. Another lesson learned.

Chapter 31:

Atlanta, Save Me!

We started our journey, Carol driving her car (I had sold my car to get rid of the payment) and I was driving the U-Haul truck. We had since added a little dog to our family, Bogy, our little chewing and peeing machine. He conveniently chewed a big hole in the wall in our apartment before we left and had the habit of peeing on your shoes when you petted him. It was a long journey to Atlanta but we finally made it. We quickly unpacked our stuff in our new apartment, a nice two bedroom place about 20 minutes north of downtown Atlanta.

We loved our new place and liked our first impressions of Atlanta. Carol started doing some interviews and I went ahead and started selling cars at the Chevy store. I got off to a great start, even though they had a veteran sales force with guys that had been there for 15 and 20 years, I ended up number four out of 30 in total sales for my first month. The managers, Buddy, Bill and Pat all took a liking to me, it didn't hurt that Stewart told them to take care of me. They all thought the world of him because he was one of their best sales people even though he left to work at a bigger store in town; he eventually came back.

Carol landed a job with a technology company working in customer service; it was a small company with just a handful of people to start. She took an instant liking to her boss, Frank, he was a great guy, a fun loving northeast Italian gem of a guy. Over time and through some social events at her work we all became friends. We also got very close to Frank, his wife Kathy and their family. Because we were there without any family they began invited us over for Thanksgiving and Christmas dinners. They were about 10 years older than us and looked after Carol and me like we were family; it is a friendship that we still cherish today. Carol was working hard but liked what she was doing. Things were going pretty good at the Chevy dealership; I was making decent money and even got a new car to drive for free. We stuck with this life for a while but I got the bug, I wanted more.

Before we made any changes we decided it was time to get married. We called our families to break the news and set the date. We didn't want anything big plus we were on a small budget. We decided the reception would be at Carol's parent's house, they had a nice sized basement that would hold a bunch of people for the party. The good news was my future father-in-law Oscar, was finally talking to us again. He was very upset about Carol and me living together without being married but now that the date was set he was fine. He and Martha put on a great party for us, there were about 60 or so family and friends, including Daisy and Sal, my brothers Rob and Steve, my best friend Peter from New Jersey made it down with his wife Maureen as well. We danced well into the evening and a good time was had by all. The actual marriage part we handled the day before in front of a judge at the court house. Just the immediate family as well as Peter (the best man) and Maureen were there. Talk about informal, my brother Rob always laughed because right after we said our vows the judge said "That will be twenty five dollars, please" we even have it on tape, Daisy loved recording everything.

Carol and I jumped on a plane the next morning after the reception and spent a week traveling the entire coast line of California. Staring out in beautiful San Francisco and ending in Los Angeles. We even managed a quick visit with my Uncle Herb and Aunt Eleanor. Other than landing in a hooker hotel on Sunset Boulevard in L.A. we had a great time. My first clue was when we checked in the clerk asked how many hours I needed the room, I went for the 12 hour rate based on us just needing a place just for a night.

Once we got back in town from our honeymoon I knew I needed to take my career to the next level, the car business was good but I hated the nights and weekends. I would go to work on Saturday and Carol would have to do things on her own, she was OK with that sometimes but not every Saturday, we wanted our weekends together. The problem was Saturdays were the busiest days at the dealership and if you wanted to make any money that was a key day. Sometimes I would sell two or even three cars in one day. Then there were those days I worked 10 or 12 hours and didn't sell any. I would come home and Carol was ready to go out to dinner or see a movie, all I wanted to do was have a drink and shut out the world. Yes, I needed to make a change.

I decided to call my brother Steve and see if he could get me something with all his contacts. Carol and I decided to give DC one more shot and figured Steve was a good place to start. He called me back a few days later and said he was working on something and would let me know. That was the worst thing he could have told me, I was and still am the worst at juggling more than one thing in my head at a time. All I could think of was this deal he was working on and I could no longer sell cars, my sales dropped to basically nothing. Luckily he called, gave me a guy's name and number and said to call him when I got to town, it was all set up. The guy was a big shot in commercial real estate and my guess was he would take me under his wing and teach me the ropes of the business. Carol made arrangements through her company to go to work with one of their customers who was in the DC area. We were now all set to go, again. We packed up the U-Haul and made the trek back to DC.

Chapter 32:

I Said There Was No Going Home Again

How right that statement is. We ventured back to Northern Virginia to try to make another go of it. Steve had set me up for a promising job interview and Carol was good with her new company. We moved in with Carol's parents, which was not a big hit with my father-in-law. The problem was Carol started her job right away; I had to wait to get my meeting. I called the guy several times and his assistant kept telling me he wasn't in, and then he went out of town for a week. This went on for several weeks, I decided I needed to get a job somewhere so I got on with a local Honda dealership and went back to selling cars. For anyone that has ever been in sales or is considering a career in sales one of the first keys to success is the mental aspect. If you are not in a positive frame of mind you can't sell anything to anyone. I wanted that appointment with Steve's buddy so bad I couldn't think of anything else. I hated that I was still stuck selling cars, so my results or lack thereof proved it, I couldn't sell a thing.

Things were getting very uncomfortable at my in-laws house, and at the time I didn't understand it or appreciate it. Looking back now, I completely understand, I was waiting on something that to them looked more like a dream than a guarantee of a new career. This turned into a screaming match with my father-in-law which caused Carol and me to decide to take the few dollars we had left and get our own apartment.

I decided to leave the dealership and took a job as a courier; I delivered packages from one business to another all over the DC area. It didn't pay much but it was enough to cover the bills while I waited for my big meeting. After several weeks of waiting and the guy traveling I finally got the interview scheduled. I called in sick for my courier job, put on a suit and tie and headed downtown for the interview. I walked into this beautiful office, nice furniture, fancy desks and all, it even smelled good. I walked up to the receptionist and introduced myself, I was told to have a seat and I would be brought in shortly.

After waiting for a while I finally was signaled that he was ready for me. I nervously followed the young lady back to the man's office and walked in. He was on the phone so I sat a waited for a couple of minutes until he finished. I didn't care at this point I was finally in his office and ready for my new career. From the time we left Atlanta first knowing about this meeting to now were a couple of months so what was a few more minutes? He hung up the phone as we introduced ourselves, I handed him my resume and he looked it over in about 10 seconds then put it down. I figured he didn't care much about that as I was going to be trained anyway. Well, with all this build up you can probably predict exactly how this went. He looked at me and said, "You have a sales background, we don't have a need for you in our company, not only that we are moving our office to South Florida in two months, but thanks for coming in."

As I tried to get my jaw off the floor he walked me to the door and I was in the parking lot before I knew what hit me. I've had disappointments during the first 26 years of my life and have had many during the 20 plus years since that day, but I have to say that was rock bottom. I now had to figure out a way to tell Carol what we bet our future on has crashed and burned. I also had to swallow my pride and tell my father-in-law that he was right.

I knew Carol was downtown at a meeting not far from where I was. So I crawled that way with my head down wondering not only how I was going to tell her but what the heck are we going to do now. We had started to look for a house; we talked about starting a family, all that was out the window based on that meeting. Just as I was walking in the building where she was I saw her walking out, I slowly headed toward her and without saying a word she saw the look on my face and asked in a sad voice "What happened?" I told her the whole 30 seconds of the story and then she asked "What should we do?" I just blurted out with very little thought behind it "We need to go back to Atlanta." Carol thought about it for a second and said, "I agree let's do it." I let her go back to her meeting and I headed back to the apartment to get a game plan together. When she got home we sat down and talked it out. We decided we would stay at our jobs for a few more weeks, save some extra money for the move and make the transition back to Atlanta a little easier. OK, so we would break the rule of "No going home again." We figured we really didn't give Atlanta a chance so it really didn't count.

If you're wondering what went so wrong in that meeting when Steve had it all set up for me. What Steve thought was a friend at the time turned out to be a big jerk. Steve didn't find this out until about a year later when this same guy had the chance to help Steve with a big deal he was working on, he ended up screwing him over instead. The real issue, Steve was in his early 30's, very successful, good looking and was living the life most men just dream of. This other gentleman, I use that word loosely, was older, had taken years to get where he was, twice divorced and extremely jealous of Steve's lifestyle. Steve had no idea this guy felt that way toward him or he would have never set up that meeting for me. Live and learn.

Chapter 33:

You're Giving Me a Heart Attack

During this time of confusion, a bit of depression and just feeling down and out, I was in constant communication with my mother. Daisy always wanted to know what was going on with her kids, good or bad. As I said before, if we cut our hand she would bleed. I got such comfort from talking with her, she was always so positive; one of her favorite lines was, "Don't worry about it, things always work out."

What I didn't know was the emotional and physical toll it was taking on her. Not only was I struggling, Michele was having a tough time as well. Her older son was now nine years old and her new son, Ramon, was several months old and had colic so bad he never slept, just screamed. This was wearing my sister out, the lack of sleep and stress that went along with it was tough on her and tough for Daisy to watch.

Rob was still searching for his new wife which was driving us all crazy until one day he told us he finally met, as he would say "The woman of my dreams." They met at church so he figured it was divine intervention and it must be right. Her name was Sheila and she had a nine-year-old daughter. Rob brought Sheila to the restaurant to meet Daisy and Sal. One thing about Sal, he could read people better than anyone I knew and he didn't like what he saw in Sheila. Daisy was much more open as usual but still felt a little uneasy. One thing that concerned her was during their conversation the question of age came up and Sheila pleaded the fifth on that. Now we all know it's not polite to ask a woman her age but this was an older woman asking and potential mother-in-law as well.

Either way Rob was head over heels in love and nothing would change his mind. They were only dating a couple of weeks but he told Daisy they were getting married. That threw our mom for a loop but this was Rob and the shock element had long been over. Sure enough two weeks later, knowing Sheila just a month, they got married. No big ceremony or anything just in front of a judge to make it legal.

They decided Florida wasn't for them, they wanted to live in upstate New York, that's where she was from, and Rob had been there before and liked it. Rob had received a settlement check for a back injury he suffered while working on the job and the plan was to use that money to put a down payment on a house when they got to New York.

They packed up a truck with their stuff and took off to New York, or so they thought. They ended up stopping a couple days for a break from the road in Roanoke, Virginia; they liked it so much they decided to stay. They stayed in a hotel for a while as they looked for a house and jobs. Rob went back to trucking and Sheila went to work at the local hospital as a nurse.

Within a very short time Rob found just what he always wanted, an old farm house on a couple of acres. They put a contract on the house and shortly thereafter they moved in. Rob and I talked a few times and he seemed very happy and I was happy for him even though I hadn't had the chance to meet his new wife yet.

Steve was doing great; he no longer sold jets for a living. One of his jet clients, a CEO of a large corporation, liked him so much he hired him to be his right hand man. He handled everything from his personal real estate, company jets, security and many other aspects of the daily business. The company was based out of New York but then moved down to Palm Beach, Florida. Steve made the move with the company and bought a house in Palm Beach. There he was, my brother, living in the same neighborhood as the Kellogg family, the Mars family, the Kennedy's, you name it, the heavy hitters all had a place there and my brother was their neighbor. Yes I was proud and told anyone who cared to listen. One of the smart things Steve did was keep his business to himself. Sure he would share some of his highlights with Daisy but there were some tough days for him too, and he never burdened her with that. I wish the rest of us would have done the same.

Carol and I were within a week or so of heading back to Atlanta and I got a call from Steve. He shared some news I was not ready for, mom had a heart attack. I was floored, all my problems were nothing, my mom was sick and I was scared for her. I also was scared for the rest of us, what would we do without our mother? She was our rock! I asked Steve how bad it was and he made it sound like she would be OK. Luckily he and Michele were both down in Florida and with her at the hospital; I didn't know if I should fly down or not but Steve told me to sit tight, she should be fine.

After I hung up the phone Carol looked at me and wanted to know the details. After filling her in I made a commitment to her, "I will never, ever let my mom know when we are struggling." I truly believed then and still do today; our struggles were a big contributor to her heart attack. Yes, she didn't have the best diet, no exercise and was a big woman, and maybe this was inevitable, but not now, not yet.

I called Steve and Michele; I told them both my commitment and asked if they would do the same. It would be tough for Michele because they lived in the same town and mom was part of her day to day life, but for me, I was done singing the blues to her, as far as she was concerned everything was just great.

Daisy's health was not good; the heart attack triggered other issues, the main one being the onset of diabetes. We would find out that disease is not one to mess around with. The best thing that came out of all this was Steve told Daisy he didn't want her working any more, we were all concerned for her health and it would be a good idea for her to retire. He was in a position financially where he could support both her and Sal, as I said before; Steve was always generous especially when it came to taking care of mom.

They both had a little retirement money coming in; Steve sent them a check every month to offset their other expenses. They didn't need much, they had their little house, both cars were paid for, so the main expense became Daisy's medications. The doctors put her on all kinds of stuff from blood thinners and blood pressure medicine and of course insulin for her diabetes. She didn't think she could do it but she learned to give herself a shot every day, actually it started off with three shots a day. The first time I saw her do it I thought I would pass out, she jammed that needle right into her thigh. Daisy's health seemed to stabilize for a bit while she and Sal got used to their quite relaxed retired life style.

Chapter 34:

The Biggest Bluff of All Time

Carol and I made our move back to Atlanta. Carol's old company loved her and welcomed her back with open arms. For me it was back on the interview hunt. I was sending out resumes all over the place, calling head hunters and going to job fairs, but nothing was happening. A friend of mine was working at a Volkswagen dealership as a sales manager and told me to come to work with him. I had to do something so I did it. For some reason I was surprised, I still HATED SELLING CARS!!! I didn't last too long, my buddy knew I didn't want to stay any longer, he understood. I went back on the hunt and then one day it happened. Carol and I got home and there was a message on the machine, answering one of the many resumes I sent out. Quite honestly I didn't even remember sending it to this particular company, World Omni Finance.

I called them back and set up an interview for a couple days later. I was so excited; it seemed like a good opportunity. They wanted someone who had retail car sales experience but not the typical car salesman, so I figured that was me. Carol said, "I know this is it, this is the job for you, this is the break we have been waiting for."

I went for the interview; it was in this beautiful high rise building not far from our apartment. Up the elevator I went, and after seeing all these clean cut, good looking people I knew I wanted to work in this building. I went in for the interview and met with several of the managers before meeting the assistant branch manager, Roy. For some reason Roy and I hit it off great, he really liked me, although I wasn't really sure why. We met for the better part of two hours, he would take phone calls in between our conversations and then we would talk some more. He told me he wanted me to go for a physical and drug test, if everything came back good from that I would meet with the branch manager and he felt like the job would all be mine. I left there on cloud nine; I couldn't wait to tell Carol the good news. As expected, she was thrilled; we had a big glass of wine to celebrate. Even though I didn't have the job yet, it was a move in a positive direction, something I haven't had in a long time.

Roy called back a few days later letting me know all was good and we set up the final interview. He made it sound like the job was mine, I just needed to meet the branch manager and the rest was just a formality. I showed up for the interview and while waiting in the lobby Roy finally came out and said he would have me in shortly. He also told me they had a new candidate who was referred to them today and he was interviewing right now. After he went back in I began to shake, what I thought was just a formality now might be slipping away. .

About 30 minutes later Roy came to get me, and we went to the conference room to meet the branch manager. His name was Ron as well and we seemed to hit it off pretty good. He told me that Roy had really spoken highly of me and after talking for about 20 minutes or so they said they needed until the following Monday to make a decision, this was on a Tuesday. My mind usually doesn't work this fast but I figured it out pretty quick, they needed until Monday because the new candidate had to take the physical/drug test and the results wouldn't come back until then.

This would be a HUGE risk but I had to do it. I had to bluff, I told them "Unfortunately that puts me in a bind, I have another job offer that needs an answer by Thursday, I really want this job, it's a great company and know I would be successful but I can't risk turning the other job down and then come Monday not have this one either. I need to know today." Ron looked at Roy and then looked at me and said, "I like your aggressiveness; we can give you an answer later today, is that fast enough?" I replied "Yes, that would be great" and that was the end of the interview. Before I walked out Roy looked at me and gave me a wink and a smile that had me feeling like my bluff may have worked.

I went home and waited on that phone to ring. Carol was still at work so I just sat there waiting and waiting until it finally rang, I almost fell over before answering it. Sure enough it was Roy; he said the words it seems like I had been waiting my entire life to hear, "Congratulations, you got the job." It took me a minute to catch my breath then I told Roy how much I appreciated the opportunity and how I wouldn't let him down. He told me my pay would be $25,000 base salary and commissions that should have me make about $35,000 my first year. I made that years earlier working construction but duplicating that amount in the white collar world was proving quite difficult, until now.

After I hung up the phone I let a few tears out and realized I finally did it, I got a great job and I would actually have a salary not just straight commission! I quickly called Carol at her job and gave her the great news; I think she yelled so loud that everyone in her office heard her. Now it was truly time to celebrate, our life together was finally on the right track.

Chapter 35:

Another Life Long Friend

The job was great, good people to work with, nice building to work in, I loved it. My job was the Lease Termination Supervisor, it even sounded good. We were an automotive finance company and I handled all the cars coming off lease. The main business for the company was distributing Toyotas in the southeast. They had several other divisions including the finance arm that I worked for. The owner of the company, Jim Moran, has a great story of his own. He was a big car dealer in Chicago back in the 1950's. He was the first dealer to ever advertise on television, way ahead of his time. He had his dealerships until the late 1960's when he was diagnosed with a rare disease. The doctors told him there was nothing they could do; the best thing for him was to go relax in the warm climate of south Florida.

So he moved to Florida pretty much waiting to die. I guess a year goes by and he's feeling fine, another year goes by, same thing. Somehow whatever he had was gone; he went to the doctor and got a clean bill of health. He was still young, in his early fifties; he wanted to go back to work. A Japanese company approached him about distributing cars in the south, he said, "Sure why not, I guess these little Toyotas will sell pretty well." As they say the rest is history, Southeast Toyota Distributors has gone on to be one of the most successful distributors in all Toyota and is still thriving today. Unfortunately Mr. Moran recently passed away after living to his early 90s.

As for me, I was clicking along when all of a sudden this new guy shows up, Hank. He wanted to change everything, he reviewed all the departments and after looking over my little one man empire he pulled me into his office. He looked at me and said, "You better straighten that department up or you'll be out on your butt." That knocked me for a loop; I thought I was doing OK.

When I started I was handed a desk, a phone and a list of customers who had leases terminating in the next 12 months. There was no department, and I had to make something out of this mess. Whatever I was doing was not good enough for the new Mister Big. The crazy thing was this guy was about my age, how did he get to be such a big shot? The good news was he had me working harder and smarter and my income actually jumped up drastically. He saw that I was doing good and called me back into his office to let me know. After a few of these meetings, surprisingly, we started to become friends, even to the point where he wanted these meetings to continue but I had a bunch of work to do. He figured he could fix that, I still made all the phone calls but he gave me an assistant to handle my paperwork. We worked together for another year and became best of friends. He was just a great guy who was very much like me, grouchy on the outside but big softie on the inside. What started as work buddies is now, some 20 years later, a friendship I truly treasure. I consider Hank my spiritual brother.

With work going as good as it was for both Carol and I we decided to buy our first house, a little ranch style home with a basement. The next big move would be a family. We both felt pretty secure in our jobs so we figured now would be as good a time as any. One thing someone told me several years earlier, "If you wait to have kids until you think are ready you will never have them." I was 29 and Carol was 26, the time was right to start our family. Shortly thereafter, we got the news from the doctor, we're pregnant!! At first it doesn't seem like a big deal but as the date got closer it got a lot scarier.

The entire family seemed to be doing well although I was getting concerned with Rob. We stayed in touch on a regular basis; he loved that fact that I had an 800 number at work so he could call for free. He started telling me stories about his wife that didn't make sense. He said she didn't want to work anymore even though she was making good money as a nurse; she made more than Rob but she just didn't want to do it anymore. Rob would ask my advice and I really didn't know what to say. She would tell him if he made her work she would just pick up and leave. Rob wouldn't allow that to happen, he loved her to much, plus his building faith had him doing anything to keep his marriage together. My only comment to him was "I wouldn't like ultimatums like that."

There would be many more problems; it started out to be just financial problems. Sheila spent money like it was going out of style and Rob couldn't make enough money to keep up and eventually had to file for bankruptcy. This was crushing to him, he knew what Daisy had taught us about our credit and how important it was to take care of it, unfortunately he had no choice. We all tried to talk to Rob but it didn't matter, Sheila just kept spending.

Surprisingly Rob still seemed happy just not as perky as when they first met. There is a reason you shouldn't get married to someone you've only known for 30 days and what follows is a terrifying example of what could happen when you don't know a person.

Chapter 36:

Skeletons in the Closet

As time went on Rob would call me at work and tell me more horror stories, he relied heavy on his faith and continued to preach to me. No matter how strong his faith was his marital issues were taking a toll on him. I would try to lighten things up with a joke and he would laugh for a second but that was it, the smile in his voice went away. One day he called and he was ecstatic, he told me he was a father again. Even though his wife's nine year old wasn't his he tried to treat her like she was. Another point of contention was she really didn't like Rob and was very disrespectful. When he told me the news I thought Sheila was pregnant, not the case. He said a young boy came up to his door asking for his mother. Rob told the boy he must be at the wrong house, and then he asked for Sheila by name. Sheila had told Rob she had twins from her first marriage some 18 years ago but said they died at birth. Well this boy was very much alive, he was there to tell his mother he was going off to the military and he said his twin brother was doing fine as well.

Just to show how forgiving Rob was after he told me this story he started laughing and began to hum the theme song from "My Three Sons." For those of you who are too young, that was a TV series in the 1960s. I couldn't believe it; this woman lied about her children being dead, wow, that one threw me, what could be next?

What would happen next no one could have predicted or was prepared for. A few months later Rob called me at work to tell me how sick Sheila was, she was in bed and not feeling well at all. He said this has been going on for about a week, it started as a cold but just got worse. I told Rob that if it was serious she would go to the hospital; after all she was a nurse.

The next day Rob called again saying she was feeling worse but still refused to go to the hospital. I thought he was over reacting, she should know what is best. The next day, another call, this time he said he didn't care he was calling 911 for an ambulance to come get her, she was almost non-responsive. Now I was beginning to worry, this didn't sound good at all. I didn't know her, I just knew my brother loved her and he was scared.

He called me back from the hospital in a panic; he thought she was going to die. I tried to comfort him but he was a wreck. He kept me updated with calls every hour or so. The next morning he called and said it didn't look good. When I asked what the doctors were saying he just didn't know, they just said she was deathly ill. More update calls throughout the day until the final call; it was Rob telling me his wife died a few minutes earlier. I was shocked; I didn't know what to say. He was crying, he was at a loss and didn't know what to do. On top of that he now had her little daughter to take care of.

Daisy and Sal went up to help Rob and make arrangements for the funeral. Her family came down from New York and wanted her buried up there, so they had the body taken to New York. Before that happened Daisy urged Rob to have an autopsy done to find out what Sheila died from. Daisy, Sal and Michele went to the funeral, but I didn't go. I was really the only one that knew what crap she put Rob through in the short two years they were together. I should have gone to support Rob but I didn't.

After the funeral Rob drove with Daisy and Sal back to Roanoke. The daughter stayed in New York with her grandmother, Sheila's mother said it was best for the girl which Rob agreed. After being home for a few days he finally got the results from the autopsy, AIDS, Sheila died of AIDS. Rob was floored, his loving wife had told the biggest lie of all by not telling Rob what she had. She knew all along what she suffered from and that's why she didn't want to go to the hospital where she used to work. She had a secret and she wanted to take it to her grave.

It all made sense, why she quit work, why she spent money they didn't have, charged up credit cards, she knew she was not long for this world and she dumped it all on my brother. The next thing that needed to be done was to get Rob tested, they were together for two years, the test would be just a formality, Rob was HIV positive. It had not reached full blow AIDS, which is a matter of blood count, but it was still terrifying. This was the early 1990s, HIV, AIDS, it didn't matter, it was a death sentence for everyone who got it.

Chapter 37:

Now What?

Rob immediately went into depression, understandably so. Interestingly enough, he did not blame Sheila; he loved her and truly believed she was in heaven because she was a Christian. Me, I HATED her, she was a murderer, she ruined my brother's life and then she gives him a death sentence and checks out. Rob, being the better person, a strong Christian, a true person of God, loved her, forgave her and understood why she did it. She needed someone to take care of her daughter until she died, then she knew her mother would take over.

I called Rob every day, Steve, Michele, Mom, we all did. He was hurting, not only physically but mentally. He quit his job, he just wanted to sit there and die. This lasted a few months; he let his hair get long, grew a long beard and just hung out. He wanted to know more about Sheila so he started making some phone calls. He called back down to Florida; he knew her ex-husband's name and looked him up. He called the number and a man answered the phone. When Rob asked to speak with Sheila's ex the man, who was his father, told Rob he died a few years ago, yes, of AIDS. He was a drug addict, that's how he got it and then passed it on to Sheila. She knew he had died but kept the secret to herself. Another lie, she never told Rob but it turned out Sheila had been married three times before Rob, not just once.

That hurt Rob, to verify that she knew but he still forgave her. After a while when he realized he wasn't going to die over night he decided he would pursue his faith even stronger. He enrolled into Liberty University, a Bible College about an hour from his house; he wanted to become an evangelist. He knew he couldn't lead a church because he had a previous divorcé but he still could be an evangelist.

Rob was put on some medication, the only thing at the time was AZT. This stuff was toxic, I guess it kept the disease from advancing but had some strong side effects. It made him pretty sick, weak and tired. He eventually got off the medicine and starting taking natural herbs, he said they seemed to help and didn't have the bad side effects.

Rob really started to rely on his faith to get him through each day; he also started abusing my 800 number by calling me and preaching to me on a daily basis. He would start off light and then hit me with "If you don't commit to Jesus Christ you're going to hell." I didn't really want to have those types of conversations at work but he didn't care— he was on a mission. He told me his goal was to get each of his family members to become born again before he died. He started with me because we were the closest and I would listen, the 800 number helped too. He would haunt me with these calls to the point where I would just hang up on him. My excuse to myself was, "I'm at work, I can't have these conversations." The truth was I was afraid he was right and I didn't want to go to hell!

As he began to learn how to live with his disease he started to become more open about it. He shared this information with his church, he thought he would find compassion, what he found was he was being treated like a leper, and he quickly became an outcast. They didn't want anything to do with him, they assumed he was gay, cheated on his wife, gave her the disease and killed her. In the early 1990s this was a homosexual disease, nobody thought someone heterosexual could get it, and obviously that wasn't the case.

He left that church and found new church, one that accepted him. Rob told me he felt at home at the new church and wanted to do everything he could to support them. The problem was he was on a limited income, with a small amount of disability that covered his basic expenses. He asked me for money and I sent some, Steve and Michele did as well, we tried to help but money wasn't going to solve all his problems. One thing we didn't understand was how somebody with no money to spare could keep giving money to the church. He tried to explain it to me but I wasn't buying it. This was a time when the church scandals from Jim and Tammy Faye Baker and Jimmy Swaggart were fresh in everyone's mind; giving money to a church we knew nothing about was hard to swallow.

Rob never wavered, he loved his new church. I had a chance to go visit Rob and we went to his church. I could tell Faith Life Baptist Church in Montvale Virginia, led by Pastor Johnny Basham welcomed him with open arms. Rob said he was a true Christian man of God, accepting people regardless of circumstance. I didn't know what it meant to be a Christian but if this was it, I needed to learn more about it. I enjoyed my time with Rob; we got back into our deep conversations. He told me what he wanted to do next, he wanted to go preach to kids in high school and educate them about HIV/AIDS and that if it happened to him it could happen to anyone. He also shared with me he was part of the biggest minority in the world. He was born a Jew, who converted to Christianity, who was a heterosexual male that was HIV positive. What are the odds?

He wanted to share his story with the world; he said he was going to contact some national talk shows to see if he could get on. This made us all nervous, we loved him and wanted to help but we didn't want everyone to know our brother had this disease. That's how shallow I was, my brother was dying and I was worried about what people would think of me. Boy did I have a lot to learn.

Chapter 38:

Oh Baby

We all tried to have life go on as much as we could even with the thought of Rob's health in the back of our mind. I had gotten a promotion at work, Carol was doing great with her job and we were getting ready to have our first baby. Michele was working hard as she was moving up in her career as well while taking care of her two boys and keeping a close eye on mom's health too, which began to slowly deteriorate as the diabetes began to advance. Sal's health was starting to be an issue also as he began to have heart problems.

Mom had been warned years earlier by a doctor when we were still living in Las Vegas, she had the beginning signs of diabetes but if she changed her diet she could avoid big problems later. Problems like loss of vision, loss of circulation which could lead to amputation of fingers, toes, feet, along with worst case scenario: the loss of a leg. From where Daisy came from she always felt invincible and just ignored the doctor. Unfortunately the doctor's predictions were beginning to come true, she began to lose feeling in her hands and her feet, it was a slow progression but it was definitely happening.

Steve was going with his company over to Europe for a two year project. Before he left Palm Beach Carol and I had a chance to fly down for a vacation, where we met my friend Peter and his wife Maureen there. His house was amazing, several thousand square feet, professionally decorated and furnished, big pool in the back yard, all in spectacular Palm Beach Florida. We were going to miss him, even though we didn't see him much, just the fact he would be out of the country was a little bit weird.

It was now early in 1991 and our baby was on the way. We found out it was a boy a few months earlier. During Carol's last visit to the doctor they detected an irregular heartbeat on our baby and decided to induce labor. We had just completed our last birthing class, the one where they take you on the hospital tour of the delivery rooms and the nursery. We saw these brand new babies' just hours old, and that's when I asked the big question, "How soon after they are born do we take them home?" I was hoping they would say a week or two but the answer was within hours, 24 if everything goes well. That shook me up, we had no formal training in being parents, what do we do? The best comment someone said to me that put me at ease was "You'll be just like animals in the wild, instinct takes over and you'll know exactly what to do." It sounds crazy but it was true, if animals could do it why can't we figure it out.

We went in to the hospital on February 7th and within a few hours our boy was making his way into the world. The irregular heartbeat was gone, the umbilical cord was loosely wrapped around his neck and once he was delivered he was fine. He was a gorgeous, healthy boy that we named Marcus.

A few hours later we took him home, my mother-in-law Martha was there to help, he stayed with us for a few weeks and was a hug help. My father-in-law came down to see his new grandson also, he was a proud grandfather. We had long mended fences, he knew I was working hard and taking good care of his daughter. I became very close with my in-laws and we visited often. Daisy and Sal came for a visit as well; they wanted to see the third grandson of our family and wanted to spoil him just like the others. Carol and I were nervous new parents initially but in just a matter of days we loved our new life as mother and father.

Just a little over a year later, on April 29 1992 we had our second son, Lucas. He popped out just as fast as Marcus, Carol's labor was about 90 minutes and he came racing out. He had this glow about him, I can't think of any other way to say it, he was a good looking baby. A little tidbit about Lucas, the doctor who delivered him said "that boy has the loudest scream I've ever heard, he should be a singer." Well yes, now as college student Lucas is an aspiring musician.

I had called my father Sam after both boys were born to let him know. He was still off the wall and went off on his conspiracies with me, I just focused on telling him about his grandsons and ended the conversation. Sam went to visit Rob during all the craziness, and that didn't help Rob at all, it only stressed him out. Years earlier Rob used to eat up all of Sam's stories about government but now he didn't have the patience or desire to listen to them. After a two week stay Sam flew back to New York. Rob told me that he would never have him visit again and he never did.

Everything seemed to be going well for a while, our boys were growing like crazy, jobs were great, and the family was doing well. Carol and I did everything with our boys. If we went biking we put them in the kid seats on the back of the bike. If we walked we put them in a stroller or backpack. Grocery store, restaurant, it didn't matter they were with us and we loved every minute of it.

Rob was hanging in there, he really found strength in preaching to kids. He went to high schools to emphasize being careful. He wasn't naïve, he knew kids were having sex but he just wanted them to know HIV was real and it could happen to anyone. He was real proud when he made some of the local papers and mailed us copies. He was happy when he realized he had the ability to help people and make a difference.

For the first time in my life I could say I was VERY PROUD of my brother Rob. I have a strong belief that there are two types of people in this world, leaders and followers. Rob had been the ultimate follower his entire life and now he had become a true leader in every sense of the word. He was out there in front of some very tough audiences, exposing his own story, preaching Gospel as well as safe sex or even abstinence. I remind you at that time HIV/AIDS was the modern day plague, he was considered a leper and was not necessarily welcomed with open arms.

Chapter 39:

Born Again

Carol and I wanted to have some type of structured religious base for our boys, we both grew up believing in God but we weren't religious. I didn't know where to start but I knew who to call. I dialed up Rob and he was thrilled that I was calling him regarding what to do about finding faith. I could hear his voice cracking a little on the phone. His millions of phone calls, constant preaching and prayer were finally going to pay off. He told me to look for a church that preaches the blood of Jesus, I had no idea what that meant. He also said it wasn't about religion as much as it was about spirituality. Based on us living in the south he said a Baptist church would be a good place to start, conveniently there was one right down the road from our house.

The following Sunday Carol, the boys and I were off to church. We both had been to church before but not in a long time and always as visitors or for weddings.

After we checked the boys into their little daycare class we went in and listened to the service. For our first time it went well, no real surprises, although there were quite of few people yelling Amen and other words as the pastor preached. We went back a few more times and after we filled out the visitor's card that got us a knock on our door one night. The assistant pastor came to welcome us to their church and we invited him in to our kitchen for coffee. He handed us some literature about the church and God then asked us some basic questions about our background. He seemed very intrigued when I told him I was raised Jewish then I remembered what Rob had told me, it was a big deal in the Christian society to convert a Jewish person.

We talked for a while, Carol and I felt very comfortable with him, he was a very nice man and had a calming nature about him. After talking for some time he finally hit us with the big question, "Do you want to commit your lives to Jesus Christ and have him be your lord and savior?" Carol and I had heard the pastor preach this during the services we attended and we had talked about it, but we weren't ready to walk up in front of the church and announce our faith in front of everyone. In our own home, that was much more comfortable. We looked at each other and knew this is what we wanted, not only for us but for our children. We said a prayer together, a prayer of committing our self to Jesus Christ and once we both said Amen we were now "Born Again Christians." No, we didn't fall on the floor kicking our legs in the air or anything crazy like you may have seen on TV. We did have a feeling of peace, a calming feeling that we knew we were doing the right thing. This is not where it all ended; this was just the beginning of our journey, our long walk of faith, a walk that lasts a lifetime.

The next Sunday we were going to be baptized during the service in front of the congregation. We were nervous, being pretty private people and really not knowing anyone at the church. But we went for it, we put on these water proof gowns and we were dipped in there baptismal pool, we confessed our faith in public and according to the church we were Christians and also members of the church.

This is where it can get confusing and controversial for a lot of people. Yes, I believe our sins have been forgiven, Jesus died at the cross for my sins and yours. But where is the line drawn? It's been many years since that day we confessed our faith and I can truly say I don't have all the answers, I don't know anyone does, except Jesus Christ.

Whose sins are forgiven and whose aren't? Who goes to heaven and who doesn't? Those are tough questions that I can't answer. Somebody with much more knowledge than me will have to answer those questions.

Do I believe my sins have been forgiven and I am going to heaven because I believe Jesus is the son of God and died on the cross for me? "YES"! Does that mean someone who doesn't have my same beliefs will not be forgiven on their judgment day and not go to heaven? I don't have that answer. If you believe God can do anything, which I do, then he can forgive anyone he wants regardless of their life here on earth. You or I are not the judge and jury when it comes to those decisions, God is.

The death row inmates that all of a sudden have found faith and claim to be Christians, are they going to heaven? Jim Baker, Jimmy Swaggart, what about those guys that used God as a front to commit their sins? If they prayed for forgiveness and truly meant it, not just because they didn't want to go to hell but really meant it for the right reasons, are they truly forgiven? That's God's call, not mine and not yours.

My good friend Hank, who I spoke about earlier in the book, also a Christian, always teased me about being a Jew who converted to Christianity. He would say, "With the Jews being the chosen people plus you're a Christian, you're going to heaven for sure." I would joke "I just wanted to hedge my bet and cover all the angles."

There are many religions and they all believe they are going to heaven to meet their God, and I respect them all. I just know what I believe and what the Bible says. Now for the people who claim to have a religion that believes in blowing up churches, hospitals or having planes crash into buildings and killing people, I have a pretty strong feeling about where they went when they died. I say this not to pick on Muslims; I believe they are a religion of peaceful people, but a very small percentage of radicals have nothing but hate for the people of the United States. As of this writing our BRAVE, COURAGEOUS and UNBELIEVABLE AMERICAN HEROES, THE NAVE SEALS have just taken out Osama Bin Laden and I think we can all guess where he went.

Chapter 40:

If You Don't Have Your Health…

Daisy had been up in New Jersey visiting Michele when she had a health mishap. Michele got a big promotion from the company she was working with and moved back to New Jersey. She was close to our old home town and had the chance to rekindle some old friendships. While Daisy was visiting her health became an issue, she had another mild heart attack and was rushed to the hospital. This started more severe problems with her diabetes, her vision started to become an issue and her circulation was getting worse. She had some infections on her foot that was causing some concern; if they didn't heal soon they would have to be amputated.

Diabetes causes less blood going toward the wounds which slows down the healing process. Luckily the doctors at Hackensack hospital were great, much better than the doctors in Florida; they were able to get the infections under control. After a few weeks she had recovered and her and Sal went back home to Florida. Now it was Sal's turn, he was having heart problems and ending up needing quadruple bypass surgery, not an easy surgery for a man in his early 70's. Luckily he was a strong son of a gun and in time recovered just fine.

Daisy starting getting these laser surgeries on her eyes, they were suppose to stop the blood vessels from leaking and keep her vision intact, again another side effect from diabetes. She would go what seemed like every few weeks for these quick little laser surgeries. They were done right in the doctor's office and she said the laser lasted about 10 seconds, some times less. They were billing her insurance company something like $1500 for each procedure, to me, it sounded like an insurance scam preying on the elderly who have good insurance. My mom was sure it was helping so she kept going. We found out years later that many surgeries indeed were not needed; unfortunately by then there were much bigger problems for Daisy to deal with.

A couple years would pass and now Daisy's new problem was congestive heart failure, her heart was getting weaker and was not able to pump the fluid out fast enough. Her diabetes had worsened to the point where the doctors would not perform open heart surgery. The fear was her heart was not strong enough to handle it and even if it was the circulation problem caused from her diabetes might keep the incision from healing. Daisy had to live her life dealing with this the best she could.

She didn't let it slow her down; she still did all her little activities, going to flea markets and auctions, although she never bought much she still loved to look around. The pain in her legs would get bad if she walked too much so she eventually got one of those scooters to get around, again, nothing was going to stop Daisy from living.

Chapter 41:

The First Cut Is the Deepest

The progression of this horrible disease known as diabetes would now take its first little victim. Daisy had an infection on her toe that just wouldn't heal; it was getting worse to the point where it turned black. The doctors had no choice but to amputate it, to which Daisy's response was, "What are you gonna do, I don't need the toe anyway." The surgery itself was not a big deal, she had it done as an outpatient and went home an hour after the procedure. The good news was, without much feeling in her foot there would be no pain; luckily, there was enough circulation to the foot so the incision would heal.

The doctors wanted to somehow help our mom with the pain in her legs and also increase her circulation; the option was to do a bypass in both legs. The surgery is similar to a heart bypass where they take veins from another part of her legs and use them to bypass the veins that have poor blood flow. This was major surgery and the recovery was not pleasant. Michele took some time off work and flew down to Florida to be with mom and help her through this. Michele actually had to clean the incisions and re-bandage them a few times a day. When I called to check in she gave me blow by blow of what she had to do, I was turning green on the other end of the phone but Michele needed someone to talk to and I was it.

It took a while but the circulation got better and Daisy's legs eventually healed. Unfortunately over time the problem would come back, diabetes is a relentless disease that just continues to take over your body. Before we knew it another toe was being cut off Daisy's other foot, being the good sport she just wouldn't let it get her down "What the heck, I don't feel nothing down there anyway" and life went on.

A funny story I need to tell regarding Sam, years earlier he made a visit to Florida to see Michele; this was before she had moved. For some crazy reason Daisy agreed to allow Sam to stay at her house, Michele wanted nothing to do with him and she sure didn't want him staying at her house. He would always stay with Rob but by then Rob had moved to Virginia.

So he flew down and stayed with Sal and Daisy. Sal didn't really care, he actually liked having Sam there because it was another person to talk to and Sal LOVED to talk. When lucid, Sam was very interesting to talk to; he was well versed in history especially when it came to Presidents and wars, the war conversations were right up Sal's alley being a veteran himself.

After a few days Sam decided he no longer would take his medicine, this would not be a good decision. His mental illness was such that without his daily medicine he was a mess. Daisy had a doctor's appointment and not wanting to leave him home along they took Sam with them. While they were in the doctor's office Sam decided to go for a walk, when Sal and Daisy came out they found him being handcuffed by a police officer. I guess he went into one of his crazy tirades out in the middle of the street and somebody called the police. Daisy quickly explained the situation and promised that it wouldn't happen again so with no laws being broken, the officer took off the handcuffs him and let Sam go.

While relaxing back at the house Sam asked Daisy if she had a pen and a piece of paper which she kindly handed over, this request happened another 75 to 100 times. Sam was back to writing his letters to the President again, about how the government cost him his family, why was he an experiment, when would he get his financial restitution. He wore out a path to the mail box mailing these letters over the next several days. There was just one problem; he never put any stamps on the letters. The mail man, who knew my parents, just kept bringing the letters to them; they would try to read them but it was mostly incomprehensible dribble and just threw them out.

Another day prior to him leaving he went for a walk and was strolling right in the middle of the street again when a police officer picked him up and brought him back to the house. Daisy again promised this would not happen again. Another problem, this visit had Sam wanting to rekindle his marriage to Daisy some 30 years after leaving. He saw Daisy in failing health and wanted to be the hero. The crazy part was he had enough trouble taking care of himself how would take care of anyone else? Ultimately he was too selfish to really consider it when he was of sound mind, but when he is off his medicine anything was possible.

He eventually flew back to his life in New York and began his fantasy about marrying Daisy again. He began calling me with his game plan. I would try to talk him out of it but it was no use, he knew what he wanted to do. He told me he wanted to move into that house in Florida, "After all, the money your mother got to buy the house came from the government, money that I suffered for." When I asked him "What about Sal?" he said "I guess he'll have to move out." After hanging up the phone I laughed my butt off, the thought of Sam going to Florida and telling Sal he had to get out the house he co-owned with Daisy, that would have been something, Sal would have beat the daylights out of him.

For the next several years I would have to listen to this nonsense about him moving to Florida, it would be off and on, off and on, which again was an indication of whether he was on his medicine or not. The problem was he would go to the VA (Veterans Administration) for his yearly check up; he received free medical treatment as a retirement benefit. During his checkup they would get him back on his psych drugs and for a few months he was fine. He just didn't like how it made him feel, they were just too strong. He would go to bed around 6:00 p.m. and wake up around 8:00 a.m., when he was off the medicine he would stay up all hours of the night writing letters, after a couple of hours sleep he's wake up at the crack of dawn ready to write some more.

I truly think he forced his mind to make up these government stories so he wouldn't have to take blame for abandoning his family. He was so lonely and miserable if he ever thought that was self inflected he couldn't live with himself.

Chapter 42:

The Last Supper?

Fast forward to Thanksgiving 1993, Carol and I were hosting the holiday dinner at our house that year. We were all there, Daisy, Sal, Rob, Steve, Michele and her kids; Uncle Herb and Aunt Eleanor came in from California as well. We had a great time; it was great to have everyone together again. We all updated each other on our life, who was doing what and so on. As for having all four of us kids together with Daisy and Sal, it had been quite a number of years since that had happened. The question I had at the time was "would it be our last?"

Rob and Steve were getting along better than they ever had and so were Daisy and Uncle Herb, which made the holiday that much better. Although Rob would try to preach to everyone, those conversations got very interesting and went in all different directions. Of course Uncle Herb and Daisy were Jewish, Aunt El and Sal were raised Catholic and Rob was preaching the Baptist religion, talk about dinner time discussions, that one was interesting. The good news was we all believed in God, just from different perspectives. After the weekend everyone went their separate ways and back to our day to day life. Steve was done with his overseas project and was now living in Miami.

A few months had gone by when I found out Rob's health was starting to deteriorate, his best defense had been his positive attitude and his faith. His faith was strong and it was his key to staying alive. The real problem was he was lonely again; he wanted to have a woman in his life, and having his disease made that difficult. He would never lie about it like Sheila did so if he met someone he would tell them the truth and that would pretty much end any chance of a relationship. He tried one of those personal ads, he put them in several papers and got a few replies but nothing came of them, except one. As Rob described her to me, a young, rather attractive woman came to his house to meet him. He said they hit it off right away, for Rob, I'm sure it didn't take much, as for the woman, I was a little concerned. Rob kept me posted saying the relationship was going well and I could tell his spirits were really uplifted. It was just a few weeks later and Rob said they were getting married. In his condition, I didn't want to deter him I was just very worried about this woman, what were her motives? The man has a disease, which at the time had a 100% death rate. Was it a pity thing? He had his house, could she want that? He didn't have any money, was she for real?

A couple of weeks later I called Rob and he confirmed he did get married. When I asked how it was going, he was a little hesitant in talking which told me something was up. He confessed and told me the truth; the woman had already left him. He came home one day and she was gone, so was her stuff and she conveniently took some of Rob's things as well. He was devastated. It turned out Rob had a small life insurance policy and she wanted to hang around long enough to get her hands on it. When she found out Rob was not as close to death as she thought she decided to take off. The marriage was annulled and that was the end of that.

What was now left was a man who had sunken into a deep depression, someone I was really worried about. I kept this and most of his health issues from Daisy, with her weakened condition I didn't want her upset too. He had overcome so much; he really became an inspiration for a lot of people including myself. Rob was in a bad spot and I wasn't sure he was going to come out of it.

I was surprised to find his spirits lifted when we talked just a couple of days later. He had called for my advice; he wanted to know if I thought cashing in his life insurance was a good idea. I told him "Why not, it would give you some extra cash and you do whatever you wanted with it, travel, buy something you always wanted, anything."

The deal was he would get a certain percent of the policy depending on the gravity of his illness. The only problem was he would need to have a blood test to determine what his blood count was. The reality was the lower the blood count the closer to the end you were. Rob had purposely refrained from taking this test since the first time he was diagnosed, which had been about five years. He didn't want to know if it was getting worse because there was nothing he could do about it anyway.

He wanted the money so he went through with the test. The results came back and he no longer was HIV Positive, he had FULL BLOWN AIDS. When you hear people say, "Your brain is very strong and capable of doing anything" this was very true with Rob. Once he found out the gravity of his condition his health began to fail almost overnight, he had convinced himself he was dying at a much faster rate than even the doctors said. The phone conversations had become very depressing, I would try to get his spirits up, talk about our faith, family but nothing worked, he was down and just about out. Each call would get progressively worse, he would be in and out of the hospital several times over the next few months with all kinds of ailments, none of which they could cure. They would just try to medicate him to put him at ease, which helped for a while but not for long.

Each trip to the hospital would incur a longer stay as the illness was getting more aggressive. My mind would keep going back to a conversation Rob and I had a few years earlier. I had just seen the movie *Philadelphia* with Tom Hanks. Regardless of what you thought about this illness and how people got this illness, this movie had to move you. I was horrified to think what my brother, a person that I love, was going to have to go through; I had a lot more compassion for Rob after I saw the movie. I remember calling Rob the next day and we talked about the movie for a few minutes as I told him how upsetting it was to watch.

But now I tried to put some type of positive spin on it but it wasn't working. He said "People have no idea how bad this disease is they think it's no big deal. They just see Magic Johnson walking around without any complications, that's not everyone's reality. He's a person who is in tremendous shape and has all the latest medical treatments that money can buy."

He was again back in the hospital and I was told by the doctors it was not good. My brother was dying and there was nothing I could do about it. I knew it was time to take another trip up to see him. Carol, me and our two boys jumped in the car and made the trip up to Roanoke. We were not ready for what we were about to see. I went in first and Carol stayed in the hall with the boys. Rob had been reduced to lying in bed, unable to talk, wearing a diaper and near death. It had only been a few days since I spoke with him; he had some type of episode or seizure that left him in this vegetative state. I don't even know if he could recognize me, his eyes would move but no speech or emotion, he just lied there. I wanted to leave the room because I felt the tears coming; I walked out to Carol and my boys. Carol saw the look on my face, the tears and knew it wasn't good.

To make matters worse as Carol and I were talking, Marcus, my older son, walked over to one of those carts that holds all the old used needles and stuck his hand in right where the old needles were. I let out a scream that could be heard for miles. I ran over to him to make sure there were no puncture marks on his fingers, PRAISE GOD, he never touched anything.

Carol wanted to go in and see Rob even though I suggested against it. She came out with the same look and tears as I did. She loved Rob, he was an easy guy to love, he never hurt anyone. When things like this happen it rocks you right at your core and makes you question a lot of things, including your faith.

I was still early in my walk with Jesus, even though that woman told me many years ago to never question God, I had some questions. I would learn even though we want answers sometimes they just never come. That doesn't mean you should waver from you faith, it's okay not to understand some things and you can question why things happen, just don't question or blame God, his plan is perfect even if it doesn't always seem that way.

Chapter 43:

No One Gets Out Alive

Rob had made this statement to me during one of our many discussions about faith. He said, "You think you can do it all on your own, when the reality is we don't control anything, God is in control. Remember we are just passing through this life, and then comes judgment day and we will all be judged by our God and no one gets out alive." Those words hit me like a kick in the head, he was right, no one is leaving this place still breathing. That may have been the strongest statement he had shared with me while he kept pounding away at my lack of belief. Wow, where do I go when I die? I always believed in heaven and hell but to know all I had to do now is confess my faith to God, believe that Jesus died for my sins and the pearly gates of heaven will open for me when my time is up here.

I know that's where the controversy starts for a lot of people. Some say "just be a good person and you'll get to heaven". Maybe donate a lot of money to good causes and heaven is there for you. Or go to church every Sunday and I'm guaranteed to get into heaven. Again, I'm not here to say that won't get you in to heaven, I'm not the judge and jury; I just know what the Bible tells me. The famous Bible verse John 3:16 states "For God loved the world so much that he gave his only Son so that anyone who believes in Him shall not perish but have eternal life."

Notice the words "God loved," not "will love if you." God loves us all; we are all His children, and are given His true unconditional love. He loves me whether I believe in Him or not, donate money to church or not, go to church Sunday or seven days a week or not. But to get into heaven He only asks that you believe in Him, a small price to pay for eternal life.

Someone once said "They'll be a load of compromising on the road to my horizon." To me it is talking about a faith walk, where you have to make some changes but the payoff is huge and well worth it.

The good news for Rob was he believed in God with all his heart. The bad news for us was Rob was near death and close to meeting his maker. I had made another trip back to Virginia to see Rob in the hospital knowing it was time for me to bring him to Atlanta to be closer to family. One problem, he had signed his medical proxy over to a woman (we'll leave her name out of this) he had met a few months earlier. They were just friends; something that Rob told me really bothered him. He wanted more out of the relationship, knowing Rob that was not a surprise. I truly believe she had Rob's best interest in mind but she just seemed to be a strange person to me. For some reason she couldn't face the reality of Rob dying and she thought he would get better. I knew that wasn't the case. I pleaded with her to sign over his medical proxy to me so I could take him back to Atlanta with me. She didn't want to do it, she wanted him to go back to his house and have 24 hour nurse care until he got better.

I wanted to bring him back to Atlanta and put him in a nursing home close to my house. I had checked it out, they would cater to his current needs and I could see him on a regular basis. The cost was much less than 24 hour nurse care at home and the reality of the situation was Rob had been reduced to lying in bed, unable to speak, communicate or move. If he knew anything I wanted him to know he was close to family at the end of his life.

I had considered moving him into my house and hire part time nursing help. But we had two young children, four and three years old and at the time the doctors were not completely sure how easy or hard it was to catch this fatal disease. I couldn't take that kind of chance with my wife and children, so the nursing home was the next best option.

After begging and pleading Rob's friend finally conceded to sign over medical proxy to me. In her mind she felt it had something to do with money. Again, Rob had no money, he had a house that was worth around $50,000 and he owed about $35,000.
The doctors had no idea how long Rob would live: it could be days, weeks or months. Rob had told her and other people that his family was all about money, we all wanted to be rich, except him. The reality was we were like most Americans working toward the American dream of financial security. Rob was not that way, he was a throwback to the 1960's, he had always been a free spirited guy that just wanted to live and let live. In 1960's speak, he was and would always be and hippie. That wasn't right or wrong it was just different than the way the rest of us lived. This was my brother Rob; we disagreed on a lot of things but we all loved him.

I went back to Atlanta to make the arrangements at the nursing home and a week later went to pick him up. When I got to the hospital the doctors had some concern, they thought he may have contracted tuberculosis. I didn't know what that meant specifically but I knew it wasn't good. They warned me it was highly contagious but didn't know for sure if he had it, and the test results would take some time maybe a few days. I was ready to go; they said as long as we both wear surgical masks in the car we should be fine. I got Rob in the car; we both had our masks and began our several hour journey to Atlanta. To say we got more than a few strange looks going down the highway wearing our masks was is an understatement.

I had packed a bunch of Rob's favorite CDs for the ride and played them along the way. It turned out to be a very nostalgic magical time. A lot of the songs had a special meaning or memory that I shared with Rob. I would say "Do you remember when we did ….." or "What about the time….." The problem was it was a one way conversation, Rob just sat there staring off in another world. My brother wasn't officially gone yet but he wasn't far off. I shed many tears during that long car ride knowing the end of our relationship was near. After many tough hours we finally made it to the nursing home; they were waiting for us and had Rob's room all ready. I got him checked in, chatted with the nurses for a while until they recommended I leave so they could get him used to his new environment.

I went to visit each day for the first several days. I would walk in and the nurses would be in with Rob rubbing his legs and arms trying to stimulate circulation. They doted over him, I don't know how nurses do what they do but it takes a special breed and in my opinion they are under paid. The doctors get most of the money and I understand that as well but I just think more should be shared with the nurses who do the day to day, hour to hour or even minute to minute care. They are the true caretakers.

I was out of town and didn't see Rob for a few days. I had called the nurses and they assured me he was doing fine. I was going to see him the next morning after I returned. I had finished showering when the phone rang, it was the nursing home they said, "We are unable to get a response from Rob." I didn't know what they meant; I asked, "Do you mean he won't talk? He can't talk!" They said, "No, he is unresponsive." I still didn't know what they meant and asked "Is my brother dead?" The next response said it all,

"I'm sorry Mr. Craig we can't share that type of information over the phone but you need to come in right away."

Now I knew exactly what she was trying to tell me, my brother was dead! I hung up the phone, tried to digest what had just happened and think about what I needed to do. The reality was I didn't think that far ahead, I had no idea what to do. I sat there for a moment and gathered my thoughts, shed some tears but I was anything but shocked, maybe even relieved. Relieved my brother's suffering was over. Another big problem was Daisy had no clue how sick Rob was we had all decided to keep that information from her due to her condition. To give her the depressing details was more pain than we all thought she could handle. Experiencing it first hand was brutal enough; to have her suffer with us was not necessary. I think she knew it as well, during our phone conversations she would cautiously ask about Rob. I would always say something like, "He's about the same, we just all have to be prepared for what may happen." To keep her from talking to him I told her he had trouble speaking so it was best for him not to get on the phone.

I now had to make that phone call and I was not looking forward to it. I first called my brother Steve and it shook him up pretty bad. He first was in disbelief, but eventually accepted it and began to make his arrangements to fly in for the funeral. The next call was to my sister Michele, pretty much the same reaction, denial then reality. We talked about telling Daisy and how we were going to do it. We decided it would be best if Michele called her, she was closest to her and knew her best. Believe it or not Daisy handled it better than we thought; she had mentally prepared herself a while back that this would be a reality some day.

I continued to make a few more calls, believe it not one of the tougher calls was to Peter in New Jersey. He and his brothers were the last real connection I had to Rob's past. I left him a choked up voicemail asking him to tell his brothers and say a prayer for our family. Rob had not talked with Peter's brothers in years but they would always ask me "How's Bogart?" (Rob's nickname, he was a big Humphrey Bogart fan). That group of the original Owls was a tight bunch and even though time and distance had separated them true friendship was not far away.

I drove over to the nursing home and mentally began to prepare myself for what I was going to see. When I got there the nurses comforted me and told me even though Rob had been there just a couple of weeks they could tell he was a special person with a big heart. I walked in to spend some time alone with him. I saw him lying there and in my mind I just kept repeating what he told me years earlier "When I die, don't cry for me, don't feel sorry for me, I will be in heaven with God happier than I have ever been." Quoting Rob he said he was now "Rocking in the Free World." I prayed at his bedside knowing that's exactly where he was, with God. All his pain was gone, no worries, he wanted so bad to walk the golden streets of Heaven with Jesus Christ and his wish was now reality. I could tell the spirit I felt while leaning on his bed praying was something that was not of this world. Not something you can imagine, just something I hope we all will experience in our lives, something I would get to experience a couple of more times over the next several years.

A pastor came in while I was still there and we prayed together for a moment then it was time for me to leave. I now had to make preparations for his funeral; even though the inevitable was coming I had not made any pre-arrangements for this. After making a few phone calls it looked like this would not be that difficult of a task, I was wrong.

When you go to funeral homes to begin the process it turns into one big guilt trip. They start showing all these different caskets which at the time ranged from several hundred dollars all the way to 15 and 20 thousand dollars.

Needless to say I was on a tight budget and not in a position to spend thousands and thousands of dollars. I still had to buy the plot and stone which wasn't cheap either. The only reason I bring this up, if you are a person who wants all the nice things for you or your loved one's funeral you better pre-plan. This way you know exactly what you're spending instead of trying to make financial decisions during a very emotional time.

When I started to focus more toward the less expensive caskets the funeral director starting saying things like "Well that one does not seal very tightly, bugs and other things can get into the box." After I thought about it for a moment I realized whoever is lying in those boxes are not going to know or care if bugs are coming in. My faith tells me the flesh and bones are there but my brother's spirit is in heaven. Yes, I have been a used car salesman during my career but there is no way I could ever try to up sell expensive caskets to people who are grieving the loss of a loved one. I did give in and spend more than I wanted to for a nicer casket but I have made it perfectly clear to my family, when my time comes I want to be cremated and throw my ashes in the back yard, ocean or anywhere else. Save the rest of the money for the real necessities of life.

I finally got everything organized and realized we were supposed to go out of town for a few days for a mini vacation we had planned months earlier. Pete from Las Vegas and his family were flying in to join us for the trip. I quickly called Pete and told him what happened and pleaded with him to still make the trip. We would have the funeral and then go on our little trip to the beach; it would be a great distraction for me and good to get away. He agreed and made the trip to Atlanta. This turned out to be great because one of the pre-funeral preparations was to meet with the pastor to tell him about Rob so he could share a few things about Rob with the family at the grave site. Pastor Gerald Harris was our Pastor at Eastside Baptist Church in Marietta, Georgia. I've been to a lot of churches over the years and I have to say I loved this man so much. He had this ability to relate to people of all ages, colors, gender, regardless of your background the message was always easy to follow, and he was a great communicator.

Pete arrived in time for that meeting along with me, my brother Steve and Carol. We sat there for just about 30 minutes and told some old crazy stories about Rob. It was interesting for Pastor Harris; he heard stories from all different perspectives. A younger brother who knew him very well, another brother who had deeper feelings for him than I thought, a sister-in-law who loved him in her own way and a friend of his younger brother who actually knew Rob better than I thought. Pastor Harris said, "He sure seemed like a special guy, a man of God with very strong faith, someone I would have liked to have known." I told him what time the funeral was and the time we expected to be at the grave site, and he assured us he would meet us there.

I had received many phone calls and requests to fly in but I told everybody it would be a small gathering of just family and a few friends. When the day came for the funeral Steve, Carol, Pete and I went to the funeral home to pay our respects. We told Michele to be with Daisy to support her; we didn't want our mom at the funeral since we wanted her to remember Rob differently, not the way he looked at the end. We had the casket open because it was just the few of us. Hank, my other good friend came as well. We had a short viewing time, I went up first to do a quick prayer and say a final good bye, and Carol was next, Hank, Pete and then Steve. When Steve was done and was walking from the casket I noticed a tear streaming down his face. I immediately went up to give him a hug. This was the first time I ever saw Steve cry. When you have two brothers and you lose one, the relationship with the remaining one takes on a whole new meaning. We were pretty close up to that point, but from that day forward our bond and friendship jumped to a new level.

The time came to close the casket and make our way to the cemetery. There was one little detail that I wanted to have for the funeral. The funeral director asked me if we would need a police escort to the cemetery for traffic purposes. My first response was "No, there wouldn't be that many people there." But then I had an idea and asked "Could it be a motorcycle escort?" He told me for $200 we could have four motorcycle police officers escort the hearse and the rest of us to the cemetery. I jumped all over that knowing how much Rob loved motorcycles. So as we made our way to our cars to follow the hearse there they were, four beautiful Harley Davidson motorcycles being driven by Marietta, Georgia's finest police officers. On a day where there were not going to be a lot of smiles, I managed to sneak a little one on the ride to the cemetery, four Harleys leading a hearse, two of Rob's favorite forms of transportation from his youth.

Pastor Harris met us at the cemetery and delivered a beautiful eulogy. In the short time we met with him to talk about Rob he managed to completely capture his spirit. He had talked about how not many things upset Rob, he would let things just roll off his back. The pastor also thoroughly understood Rob's deep faith and how much he depended on it in good times and bad. After Pastor Harris was done the service concluded, we watched the casket get lowered into the ground and made our way to the cars. Rob was gone, yet he was at peace with our Lord and Savior. We selfishly missed him but life must go on.

Chapter 44:

What's Next?

Life was normal for a while as we all continued on with our lives. Michele was promoted again with her company, had moved just outside of Boston and she met a great guy named Gene. He was a fellow executive at work, they hit it off and before you know it they decided to get married. Her oldest son was in college doing well and her younger son was around 10 years old. Soon there would be a couple more additions to her family, with two more boys born about 18 months apart.

Even though Michele was in Boston she still stayed very close with Daisy. They would talk every day and Michele was mom's nurse on call. With her health being up and down we stayed on pins and needles, any time the phone would ring we would answer it with caution. And if ever rang late at night or early in the morning I would almost jump out of bed.

We were surprised with Daisy and Sal getting up in the years when they hit the road for another trip. They stopped in Atlanta first to see me, Carol and the boys. It was always a treat when they visited; Daisy never came empty handed. It would be some type of cookies, cakes, breads or something she bought "For a deal." Mom was always about making a deal; she would buy stuff she didn't even need if the deal was good enough. Michele, Steve and

I all inherited that gene from Daisy; we liked to negotiate. For the first time I would finally see Sal starting to show his age. For years nobody could guess his age, he looked and acted so much younger. But his heart condition was taking a toll on him, he had the heart surgery years earlier but eventually the problems came back. I was nervous with them taking such long drives up and down the east coast but they weren't stopping, not yet. Flying was not an option, it was the only thing Sal was afraid of, he just hated flying. He had the greatest comeback when the conversation about flying would come up. They said "Sal if it's your time to go it doesn't matter if you're flying if your time is up." He replied as only Sal could "I agree, I'm not worried about it being my time but what if it's the son of a b—'s time who is sitting next to me?" How do you reply to that, you just shake your head and say "That's Sal."

From Atlanta they continued on to Boston to see Michele and her family. A strange fact about Daisy and Sal's relationship, they were always arguing about something, but when they when they were on the road they got along great, never an argument. As the trips would go on Daisy's legs would bother her from sitting to long from the lack of blood circulation. Sal's arthritis in his knees would act up on the long journeys as well. They didn't care, they would just take extra Tylenol and keep on driving, we were scared, not them they loved it.

Once they returned home from that trip Sal's health took a turn for the worse. He was not feeling good but didn't want to go to the doctor until Daisy finally convinced him to go to the hospital. The news was not good; he was in kidney failure, for Sal that was real bad news because he only had one kidney. As I mentioned before during World War II he was captured by the enemy and was held hostage for several months. While a prisoner he and his fellow Army brothers were beaten by the guards. I heard Sal tell the story a few times through the years about how they would take the end of their riffle and jam it into his side. After he and several others finally escaped and returned home Sal would have to have a kidney removed from those beatings. Funny thing he didn't really complain about that as much as he complained about being fed only turnips for several months. He would eat anything Daisy cooked but she knew not to bring turnips into the house. He swore if he made it out of there alive he would never eat another turnip and he held his word.

But now Sal being in kidney failure and only having one meant if he didn't bounce back he would have to go on dialysis. Unfortunately that's exactly what happened; he would have the treatment three times a week. A driving service would come pick him, he would have to go to the dialysis center and sit there for several hours as his blood was filtered, doing the job his kidney could no longer do. For most people this would not be a big deal, for someone who loved to jump in a car and take off for a couple of weeks it was a death sentence. He tried to remain upbeat about it and when we talked he made it sound like a road trip was still in his plans. After a year or so he knew that was not going to be a reality and his attitude turned very bitter.

Here's a man that came up the hard way, like many of his generation. He worked his butt off; I'm not talking about a tough day in the air conditioned office, hard physical labor. He was a son of an Italian immigrant who supported his family selling junk, literally selling junk. He never made a lot of money but it was enough to support his family. The problem was he had no retirement, just his very small Social Security check. I think that bothered him the most, he worked very hard and the end had very little to show for it. As I mentioned earlier, if not for Steve helping a bunch, Michele and I pitching in a bit as well, it would not have been such a good retirement for Daisy and Sal. We were glad to do it and felt blessed that we could. For what our mom did for us working three jobs when she had to, and doing whatever it took to make sure we had what we needed it was the least we could do.

With Daisy and Sal hanging in there and the rest of us doing our thing time started to fly by. My boys were getting older and getting into their activities. Carol and I were really enjoying being parents, yes there was stress especially with both of us working full time but we loved life raising our two boys. Steve continued on in his business and would periodically have some interesting stories. He would tell me about how he would run into all these celebrities. One time he was out in Colorado on a ski trip and through a business associate he was invited to dinner. He sat at the same table with Ed Bradley from 60 Minutes fame, Jimmy Buffett and Vanna White. I thought what an interesting dinner that must have been?

Not long ago Ed Bradley passed away and I saw on the news how one of his closest friends, Jimmy Buffett, was at the funeral, which seemed like a strange pair. As for Vanna White, her husband knew Steve's friend from previous business dealings.

Steve told me how he got to know all of them pretty good and if I ever wanted tickets to a Jimmy Buffett concert to just give him a call. Interestingly enough, it wasn't Jimmy Buffett tickets that would come up first. The TV show Wheel of Fortune came to Atlanta to film at the famous Fox Theatre for a week. It was time to call his bluff, I called Steve, told him the show was coming to Atlanta and it would be great if he could get us tickets, he said he would work on it. This was several weeks in advance so it gave him enough time to see if he could do it or was he just blowing smoke.

A few weeks would pass and it kind of fell to the back of my mind. I came home from work one day and just as I walked in the phone rang. I picked it up and said "Hi" when the voice on the phone said, "Is this Ronnie?" First of all only my family called me

Ronnie so that through me plus I didn't recognize the voice. I said "Yes it is" the person then said, "Hi this is Vanna White." My first reaction was going to be very typical for a kid from New Jersey and say something like "Yeah and I'm the president of freakin' United States of America." But for some reason I didn't and good thing because it really was Vanna White. She told me that Steve called her and she'd be happy to get us tickets for the taping of the show. She also mentioned how she heard so much about me and how her and her husband thought the world of Steve. Long story short she got us six tickets, Carol's sister Brenda and her husband Ed were going to be in town during that time. She told us to show up at the theater and who to ask for.

On the day of the show Carol, Marcus, Lucas, Brenda, Ed and I went downtown to see the show. We asked for the person who was to meet us and the lady came out to and she escorted us into the theater. We started walking back stage when she told us she was taking us to meet Vanna in her dressing room. We were smiling from ear to ear when at that point Pat Sajek walked by and gave us a quick hello. We then entered Vanna's dressing room and waited a few minutes for her to arrive. When she walked in she gave me a hug like she knew me for years, hugged Carol, the kids, Brenda and Ed. I know you hear this about celebrities but it's usually from other celebrities. I'm here to tell you Vanna White was one of the nicest people I have ever met. There was a big spread of food in her dressing room and she urged all of us to make ourselves at home and to take what we wanted, the adults nibbled on some snacks but Marcus and Lucas dug in like they hadn't eaten in days. We talked for a little while longer and then she needed to get ready for the show. She asked if we wanted to stay for the show, although she would have to sneak the kids in because there was an age limit. We actually had a bunch of fun just meeting her and that was enough for us. I called Steve and told him how we had a great time and what a nice person Vanna was.

During another phone conversation he told me how he met Pat Riley, the great NBA coach. He was working with him on leasing a jet to take him around on his motivational speaking tour. Steve was living in a big house in Miami where Pat Riley was now part of the Miami Heat organization. They were coming to Atlanta to play the Hawks and I made the call, "How about a couple of tickets to the game?" "Let me see what I can do." Steve called back a week or so later and said to go down to the will call window and the tickets will be there. My older son Marcus and I went down to see the game. We got to the will call window and told them our name, the man there told me he didn't have any tickets in my name, I assured him there must be a mistake. He looked again as the people behind me began to get angry as they waited. He again said "no luck" when I finally said, "Pat Riley was supposed to leave two tickets for me." That's when I heard the guy behind tell his friend, "This idiot thinks Pat Riley left him tickets." The man in the booth then said, "Oh, you pick those up at the VIP window." I thought "Yes I do" and Marcus and I walked toward the VIP window and I had to give the guy behind me a little snarl just for the heck of it. We got the tickets and yes they were great seats right behind the Miami Heat's bench. This was years before Shaq and Dwayne Wade got there but we had a blast.

Interestingly enough, during my sales career I've been lucky enough to see some great speakers at our sales conferences, like former Miami Dolphin running star back Larry Csonka. He was Sal's favorite football player of all time; he was a battering ram that just ran over people, you give him the ball and he would not be denied. I also had the chance to see former Pittsburg Steelers running back Rocky Blier speak. His story was amazing; he was injured while serving in Vietnam and was told he would never walk again. All he does is come back and help his team win a few Super Bowls.

Another great speaker was General Colin Powell; here's guy who was told his whole life he would never make it but that never stopped his success.

I have to say one of the best speakers was indeed Pat Riley; he spoke at a sales conference a few years ago. As he walked out the music was cranking to Bruce Springsteen's "The Rising." When he got to the stage he continued to let the music play and began to dance. He was up there with his vintage slicked back hair just having a good time. His speech was how they just came off a tough season, the press was saying it may be time for him to give it up but he would not go out that way. He wanted to come back and prove he could still win. Sure enough a few years later he, Dwayne Wade and Shaquille O'Neal won the NBA Championship.

One thing all this great leaders had in common, they all had adversity in their life and where most people would have just given up they fought on. "Never give up, just never give up" was the common theme. I recently read one of Donald Trump's books, some people may not be crazy about him, I happen to like him a lot. I believe he is a great success story and another testimony of never giving up. He had some hard times as well, actually in huge debt, but never gave up and came back stronger than ever. One quote from his book is something I try to live by and teach to my two sons, "To be successful just do something you like and never give up." Great advice.

A couple more interesting stories, Steve had this great house on one of those islands close to Miami Beach, it sat right on the water with great views looking toward Miami. One day Steve got a call on his cell phone, it was a real estate agent asking him if he wanted to rent his house for a few months. He quickly replied, "No" and hung up the phone thinking it was some kind of scam. A couple weeks later he gets a call again, it's the same real estate agent asking the same question. Steve responds the same way, "No" and just before he hangs up she said, "It's for Cindy Crawford, the super model." Steve hesitated for a moment but stuck to his original answer. He told the woman, "This is my only house; I'm not super wealthy and have several houses." The realtor quickly threw out a dollar figure that was large enough get Steve's attention but again said, "No, not interested."

A few weeks passed and Steve was in Europe on business when his phone rings and this time instead of the real estate agent calling it was Cindy Crawford. She introduced herself and said she would really appreciate it if he would at least consider renting his house to her. She said she would be in New York in a couple of days and conveniently that's where Steve was going to be. They agreed to meet for dinner to discuss the rental agreement. I spoke with Steve after his initial conversation and he said he just was going to have dinner and had no intentions of renting his house to her. He called me a few days later and told me about the dinner and how nice Cindy was, before he could continue I asked "So how much is she paying to rent the house?" He told me the figure and we laughed for a moment. I know my brother very well, being very single at the time and Cindy Crawford being very beautiful there was no way he would say no to her, who could?

She was going to Miami to film the movie *Fair Game* with one of the Baldwin brothers. She didn't want to stay at a hotel because of the lack of privacy, a house would be much better; this was when where she had just separated from Richard Gere. Steve made the agreement where he could come by once a week to pick up his mail, convenient, I know. They met at the house on move in day and Steve showed her where everything was. He had two jet skis which were docked on the water right behind the house. Cindy wanted to be able to use them during the rental period so Steve took her out for a ride on one of them to show her how use them. Cindy enjoyed the house; she and Steve became friendly and went out with a group of people a couple of times, not a date or anything just a friend thing.

One night they went out and met up with Pat Riley, it was Steve, Cindy, her assistant and Pat Riley. They were just hanging out at a little piano bar in Miami with about four other people there. Within minutes the place was packed when the word got out that Cindy and Pat were there, the four of them quickly left there and found a quieter spot to have their dinner. Once Cindy finished up the movie and the rental agreement was up she moved back to California. They kept in contact for little while but that was about it.

A few weeks later I get a call from Steve asking if I had a copy of the current Redbook Magazine. First of all I had never heard of it so the answer was obviously no. He said I needed to get a copy because he just got a call from a buddy of his saying there was an article in there about him and Cindy Crawford. Carol knew the magazine and grabbed one that afternoon. Sure enough there it was, the article talked about how Cindy was dating this real estate millionaire. A good looking man in his 40's they were seen together cruising around on a jet ski and so on and so on. I called Steve and told him about it, his first reaction was "A man in his 40's!" He was still in his 30's at the time. We all got a kick out of it knowing it was being blown way out of proportion but it was entertaining.

While Steve was still living at that house he got another rental offer, this time it was from Al Pacino's people. He was down there to film "Any Given Sunday". Steve was now an old pro at this and negotiated a pretty sweet deal, Al Pacino stayed at the house for three or four months. Steve said he was a nice guy, pretty quite but nice. At least this time Steve knew there would be no rumors of him frolicking on a jet ski.

Another celebrity story, Steve and a good friend were partners in a great apartment in New York City. This place was beautiful, overlooking Central Park on the West Side of Manhattan. Steve's friend lived in Europe for the most part and gets to New York a few times a year, so he rarely used the place. Steve used it when he was in the city for business and the rest of the time the place was vacant. We would try to schedule a yearly trip to New York for a mini vacation and stay at the apartment.

One of the residents in this building is one of my favorite TV personalities, Regis Philbin. Unfortunately all the times we have been there I have yet to run into him, I did get one of the doormen to have Regis sign his Christmas CD for me. To no surprise all the doormen say Regis is a great guy and a normal Joe just like the rest of us. Another one of the residents of the building we have run into is Howard Stern, the great shock jock. I know he would hate for someone to say this but he is a very quiet and reserved guy when you see him in the elevator.

Chapter 45:

Daisy and Sal Can't Live Alone

Back to the more important issues of life. It was getting to the point where we were not comfortable with Daisy and Sal living alone. The problem was what do we do? They did not want to leave Florida, they loved their little house, they had their doctors and friends, it just wasn't going to happen. And none of us could move there.

I flew down for a visit as Sal's health started to quickly decline and the doctors told him he may not make it to the New Year, this was in November. All four of Sal's kids came to visit; this was a shock because not all of them were really that close to Sal, Denise was, she had become part of our family from Day One. Pam was close with us as well but she also liked her space. She became pretty close with Michele only living a few miles apart when Michele went back to New Jersey. As for Lenore and Bruce, that was a different story. They always felt like Sal owed them something, believe it or not I think they were mad that he didn't have more money, maybe even that he was hiding it from them. Luckily none of that was issue during their visit and Sal was overjoyed to have all four of his kids visiting him.

Sal was not the kind of guy that showed a lot of emotion but you could tell by the look on his face, he loved that they were there. Bruce, being the first born and only son was his favorite; unfortunately Bruce didn't embrace that relationship, quite honestly I was shocked that he was there. Over the years I became real close to Sal, as far as I was concerned he was my father, he raised me. Sal was close with all of us kids but because he really raised me the bond was different, he was my father, he was there for me when I was growing up and I loved him for it.

Rob loved Sal too. More than any of us, Rob needed a father figure growing up and Sal would have made a big difference in his life if he showed up sooner. By the time he and Daisy got together Rob was well on his way into trouble. Steve and Sal had a mutual respect and Steve loved him because he was good to Daisy and because of that he would do anything for him. Michele and Sal were close but in different way as well, even though Sal had three daughters he was not a daughter's dad, he was a tough, hard core guy, that didn't go hand in hand with raising a girl.

For me, he was everything my real father wasn't, my play catch partner, any trip we would take the ball and gloves would come with us. In a hotel parking lot, a campground field, anywhere and anytime he would play catch with me. He had arthritis in his shoulder and even though he had a high tolerance for pain he would throw with me until it hurt so much he had to stop, the next day we'd be out there again throwing some more. As I mentioned earlier he was my disciplinarian also, he would give me a shot in the arm or kick in the butt when I needed it.

As for Sal's health, Daisy was concerned what to do; the doctors were ready to send Sal home from the hospital. They said he's not sick, he's dying and we can't do anything for him, but he's not sick. That's a crazy way to look at it but that was the hospital's approach.

His heart was just giving out on him. The real question was if any of his kids were willing to move and help take care of them. We all knew that meant nothing to Bruce, he was not doing it. He was never a big fan of Daisy, I'm not sure why, she never tried to replace their mother; she was Sal's second life time friend. I think he was a little jealous of their relationship in some strange way. Bottom line was he wasn't going to help in any way. He did say with him living on the west coast of Florida he would come visit more often. That would mean more to Sal then anything. Lenore, forget it, if it didn't benefit Lenore she was not interested. She was too busy trying to scam workman's comp and other government programs so she wouldn't have to work. I know that sounds ugly but it's the truth. Pam was a single mom trying to raise her two boys and was not in a position to help. She and Daisy had an up and down relationship over the years but had since mended fences. That left Denise, her two girls were grown and on their own, she was living out in Las Vegas working in the casinos, she loved it out there but knew it was time to jump in to help. She said she would go back to Las Vegas; tie up some lose ends and make the move to Florida to live with Sal and Daisy.

My side of the family was very grateful, Pam was happy too, Bruce and Lenore were glad it didn't involve them. I believe Bruce was there due to years of guilt for ignoring his father. Knowing Sal would light up the few times a year he would hear from Bruce, why he wouldn't just pick up the phone for 30 seconds even if he didn't mean it was something I didn't understand.

That was something I did every couple of weeks with my real father Sam. Growing up I had very few feelings for him but knowing it would make his day and take very little effort on my part, why not? I kept hearing the words Daisy said to us ever since we were kids, "It doesn't matter what happened between me and him, he's still your father." Hold a door open for a stranger, help someone pick up something they dropped, give the money back when you get too much change, say hi to a stranger (I do that all the time, living in the south for so many years it just comes natural), it freaks some people out.

One time Steve, my brother-in-law Ed and I were on a hike outside the Washington DC area. It was a lengthy hike, probably about three miles up and down a rocky terrain. I tend to be a people watcher, that's a nice way of saying I stare at people. I don't realize I'm doing it, I just do it. Well on this hike I kept making eye contact with the hikers going the other way and I would say hi to every one of them. I didn't pay much attention to it but we stopped for a break to catch our breath and Steve looked at me as said "Are you running for mayor or something?" I said "What do you mean?" He replied "You said hi to every person we came across." I just laughed.

Don't get the wrong idea, I don't claim to be perfect, I come up way short and I don't have a halo over my head. I've said it before, I was born a sinner and will die a sinner, we all will. I just try to mix some good things in with all the not so good things I've done through the years. If I get cut off in traffic I don't yell out the window, "I'm praying for you, brother." It's more like, "Hey, you jerk where did you get your license, K-Mart?" Christians are human too, that's the whole point I'm trying to make, you don't have to be perfect, because you can't. Christ was the only one who was perfect. Now there are some Christians that strive for that perfection and live a life much cleaner than mine, I think it's great. I've run into many people that claimed to live this perfect clean life, and then the next time I see them they are right in front of me at the liquor store. Does that make them bad people? I don't think so, but for me I just don't believe in hiding the fact that I like to have a Martini or a glass of wine with my cigar, as Sal always said "To each his own."

After Denise volunteered to make the move, we all said goodbye and stated what we would do moving forward. Again, Bruce would make more visits, Lenore would do what she could from out west (I think she was living in New Mexico), Pam would do the same and my side of the family would make sure they would be taken care of financially. Things didn't turn out like we had hoped. For Sal it was good news, he bounced back and was doing better, not great but better, he was home with mom and taking it easy. The bad news was while Denise was back in Las Vegas getting ready to make the move she was in a horrible car accident that left her permanently paralyzed from the waist down. This news was devastating to us all, I had always loved Denise, she and I were as close growing up as I was with my own siblings. Unfortunately there was nothing anybody could do. Obviously she could not make the move and we still were concerned about Daisy and Sal. Denise had a long recovery and had to adapt to life in a wheelchair. Her positive attitude got her through some dark days and I am happy to say some 14 years later she is doing really well. I talk to her all the time and we laugh as we share some old stories. One of the reasons I love her so much is she very much like Rob was. A product of the 60's, she is a free spirit and really doesn't let things get her down. Yes, she's had some tough times since the accident, she loved the outdoors, biking and hiking; now she goes for a spin in her wheelchair for exercise. Another big reason she and I have always been close, she loved Daisy from day one with no agenda and Daisy loved her.

For several months we had some scares with Sal and Daisy both bouncing in and out of the hospital. The worst one was when Daisy had gone up to visit Michele in Boston. She actually flew up for that visit; Sal could no longer travel so she decided to fly instead of making the long drive herself. While there she was not feeling good and told Michele that she wanted to go see her doctor in New Jersey, she got to trust this one doctor while Michele was living there. His name was Dr. Chin, he was a brilliant heart doctor that loved my mother and the funny thing was his accent was so heavy we understood very little of what he said.

Michele took some time off work from work so she could drive mom to New Jersey and see Dr. Chin. Luckily Michele was very well liked and respected at her job because taking time off became a regular occurrence with Daisy's needs. She kept popping in and out of the hospital and Michele was there every time. This is no exaggeration, Michele would ask questions of the nurses and doctors and they would ask her "What hospital do you work for?" They assumed she was a doctor or nurse; she became an expert at whatever aliment Daisy would have.

They began their journey to New Jersey but didn't get very far when Daisy started to have trouble breathing, Michele tried to calm her down but it was getting worse so she picked up her cell phone and called 911. They told her to pull over but she didn't want to do that, she asked where the closest hospital was, luckily it wasn't too far away and she drove like a crazy woman to get there. As she pulled up they were outside waiting to get Daisy in right away. It was a good thing because Daisy had congestive heart failure. Her heart was too weak to pump out the fluids and her heart began to drown, if they hadn't arrived there when they did Daisy would have died in the car.

The good news was they made it on time; the bad news was it worse than anybody realized. Michele called me and told me what happened; I asked if I should jump on a plane to be there, she told me to wait to see what would be needed. I had a problem, I had a bad ear infection and was told by the doctor I could not fly, the air pressure would most likely puncture my ear drum. I suffered bad ear infections my entire youth but I didn't have one for many years until now and the timing couldn't have been worse. I waited a few days while staying in constant contact with Michele. Steve flew in as he wanted to be there for Daisy and support Michele. Michele tried to fill me in on the phone; she said it was not good. I couldn't wait any longer so I jumped on a plane and made my way to the hospital. When I got there I couldn't believe my eyes. Michele and Steve tried to prepare me before I went in to see my mom but nothing could describe what I was about to see. When I walked in I almost passed out, she was hooked to all kinds of tubes and had a pipe going down her throat to help her breathe. I was devastated; the tears began flow as I reached down to kiss her knowing this was the end. She could not speak but the look on her face said it all, she knew it was not good but she was happy all her children were there.

She loved Steve in a way that is hard to describe and she was so proud of his success. Her relationship with Michele had evolved from her helping Michele through very difficult times in her younger years, helping her raise her young children as a single parent and through the awful situation with her husband being crippled. Now the roles had reversed to where Michele was her everything. Not only is a mother daughter bond in a Jewish family very unique but Michele took it to whole new level doing anything she could for mom. But my relationship with my mother was special. Being the youngest child and living with them when everyone else had moved out, working with her side by side for several months, this allowed us to grow a bond that I wouldn't have traded for the world. The funny thing was for my entire life she always introduced me as her "Baby," no matter what age; I was always her "Baby." For many years I didn't like that title, as years passed I grew to cherish it.

The problem now her condition was such where the doctors were not sure if she was going to make it. After a brief visit I went out to speak with Michele and Steve, that's when the tears really came out. I was not ready to lose my mother, she was always the rock of the family, losing her was not something I could handle, not now. I stayed for a few days and after what looked to be a pretty grim situation Daisy began to stabilize although she would never be the same. Her heart had been severely damaged and was in need of surgery. But again, the problem was her diabetes had progressed to a point where nobody would operate on her. The fear now was, the heart was too weak to survive any surgery and even if she did survive her circulation was so bad that her incisions might never heal, she would have to live with a heart that was a time bomb.

After a few weeks she was finally released from the hospital and stayed with Michele as she slowly regained her strength. I would call every day to talk with her and I would never end a conversation without saying "I love you." I knew it was the love of her children, grandchildren and the love for us that kept her fighting to get better, something she would admit years later. She said "There were many times where I just thought it was my time and wanted to stop the fight, then I would think about you kids, my grandchildren and thought, I still have a lot to live for and I'm not giving up that easy."

Recovery was a painful and slow process but she was committed to it. Michele completely changed Daisy's diet, everything was fat free. Over time she ended up losing a bunch of weight, I'm guessing it must have been close to 100 pounds; she looked great and felt so much better. Daisy was far from perfect, but she eventually went back to Florida and to her life with Sal.

Sal hated the new fat free lifestyle but he also lost weight. All things considered, from what they both survived they were doing pretty good, it wasn't an exciting life but they were happy. Daisy went back to her routine of going to auctions with her friends, playing bingo and other fun stuff. Sal didn't care much for that, he would stay home and watch old war movies on cable. We all knew they were both were not in the greatest of health but there was nothing we could do, just show them and tell them how much we loved them.

Daisy had rekindled something from her youth that her mother had taught her, knitting, she used to knit all the time but just gave it up many years earlier. The doctor told her it would help with the circulation in her hands so she knitted and knitted and knitted. We would get a box every so often with sweaters, mittens, blankets, and scarves and other things for the boys, Carol and me. During our daily conversations she would ask me what I wanted her make. I would always ask for scarves for Carol me and they would show up at the door a few weeks later. If I ever mentioned that one of my friends had a baby she would ask if it was a boy a girl, not too long after a box would show up with a blanket and sweater with the appropriate color for a boy or girl, my friends loved it. They all loved Daisy, everybody did.

Chapter 46:

My Pal Sal Part 2

Back in New Jersey everyone had a nickname and Sal was not left out even though he didn't know it. His was "My Pal Sal"; Daisy's was "Crazy Daisy." This was now a year and a half after they told us Sal had 30 days or so to live when his health did take a turn for the worse again. He was always such a strong son of a gun but his heart was just about to give out; Daisy called 911 and had him rushed to the hospital. She called and said she thought this was it; I was ready to get on a plane when a few hours later she called back and said she just left the hospital and Sal was doing great; we thought the doctors were over reacting again. The next day I went to work and then got the call that I was not expecting, Sal had died. Mom went to the hospital and said he had a certain glow about him, he was feeling great. They were talking, he was really happy, which he hadn't been in a long time. He had just had a snack and while he was telling Daisy how good he was feeling in mid conversation he gasped for a second, mom leaned over the bed to see if he was ok and that was it, he was gone. He died with Daisy's hands holding his head. She yelled for a doctor but there was nothing they could do, he was gone.

Daisy was crushed but knew it was his time, the fact that he was so peaceful just before passing put her at ease, she knew Sal was with God. The news hit me hard, this was the man who was my real father, he was there for me and I didn't want him to go. Mom and I shared some crying on the phone and I told her I was on my way down. When I got there I helped her with the final preparations, Sal wanted to be cremated, he didn't want anything fancy. We went to the funeral home to finalize everything and that was it, no big ceremony, just as he asked, Sal was gone but surely not forgotten.

Daisy would have good days and bad, we all called her on a regular basis as always to check on her. In the middle of a conversation she would start crying and say "I miss Sal so much." He was such a big part of her life for over 30 years and now there was a big vacancy in our world. When I say they would argue constantly this is no exaggeration, they really loved each other but had different opinions on most subjects. Sal would always tell Daisy "I'm packing my sh– and heading back to Jersey" which Daisy would reply "Go, who gives a sh–." Ten minutes later Sal would ask "What's for dinner? I'm starving." Daisy would whip something up in about 15 minutes and all was good again. One of Sal's favorite lines to me was about his arguments with Daisy, "Ron, I'm still batting a thousand, I haven't been right yet." I would just laugh which would make him crack a smile as well. He was a great man, he didn't show much emotion but he had a kind heart, a very typical old school Italian man from his generation, tough exterior but soft on the inside. This many years later and I still miss him. It's hard to put in words what it means to a young boy who was starving for a male role model in his life. Sal was far from perfect but he was perfect to me.

Chapter 47:

Death and Rage

Sal had been gone about a year and Daisy was getting lonely and bored. She went to stay with Michele for a while and made a visit to see us but she still had way too much time on her hands. We suggested that she get a computer and get on the Internet, with all the information out there surely that would keep her entertained. She bought a little computer and she went to the local college with one of her girlfriends to take a beginners computer course. It was a hit right off the bat, first of all she loved being at the college and being around people much younger than her. When she finally did get on the Internet she found this new world for her called "Chat rooms."

She was in all different types of chat rooms, for seniors, for people that speak French, people who speak German, Jewish chat rooms, singles and a few others. The fact that Daisy spoke several languages opened up the possibilities to many different audiences. She actually helped English speaking students learn French in one of the chat rooms. She was a little shocked at first because of what she found out there. Not that she was old fashioned and it took a lot to make Daisy blush but she said there was a good bit of obscene stuff out there, she would quickly get out of those chat rooms and find new ones.

She would tell me about all the great people she met online. I warned her not to be too trusting, the Internet is a great place for people to hide who they really are. Her response was always "But they are all so nice." We all warned her not to share any personal information like real name, address or phone numbers but Daisy trusted everyone and would give out her number to talk to some people. The curiosity was too much for her she had to know more about some of the people. A few times things seem to be getting a little too advanced with some men and she asked our opinion about meeting them face to face. We all would scream "NO WAY" but again Daisy was a trusting soul. She met one man who happened to be local, it was just a few lunch dates and that was it. He was a much younger man somewhere in his late forties while Daisy was in her late 60's. Daisy said he was very lonely and wanted someone to talk to, that lasted a little while and then faded away.

After numerous "almost connections" with some people but only that one local face to face meeting, Daisy started get real close with a man from New Mexico. The same line "He is so nice, it would be great to meet him." We continued to warn her about all the crazies out there and to be very careful. This Internet relationship graduated to a phone relationship. One day Daisy called me and said she really wanted to meet this man and asked me, "How would you feel if I invited him here to Florida for a visit?" I didn't know what to say, I wanted to be supportive but cautious as well. I said, "If you really think it will be OK I support whatever you want to do." She told me to hold on for a minute and the next thing I know I hear a man's voice on the phone saying, "Hi Ronnie, my name is Bob." I almost fell out of my chair but I didn't want to let him know that. We talked for a moment and then he handed the phone back to my mom. When she got back on she wanted to know what I thought. Her voice was so upbeat and happy the only thing I could say was, "Have fun but be careful."

The story doesn't end there. He is there about a week or so when Daisy and I talked again, I called every day but it took a week for things to take a turn for the strange. She said they were having a good time, going to lunch, sitting on the beach, watching movies at home and just enjoying each other's company. I asked her to tell me more about him and she went on to tell me that he was a Native American Indian. I thought that was interesting, Daisy didn't care one way or the other; she was very open minded and didn't have any prejudices toward anyone. She wanted to share another interesting fact, his Indian name. She asked me to guess, I didn't know where to start when she just blurted it out "Death and Rage." I said "What about it?" She said "That's his name, Death and Rage." I was speechless, I didn't know anything about American Indians and how they got their names but that one seemed to be self explanatory.

Daisy knew I was upset, she was all alone with this man and I was not happy. She assured me he was a nice man and had been nothing but a gentleman. That made me feel a little better but not much, Steve and Michele were not crazy about the situation either but what could we do. A few more days passed when during our conversation she said they had just got back from seeing the dentist for Bob, aka "Death and Rage." I guess he needed some dental work and wanted to get new upper and lower dentures. She told me it was going to be around five thousand dollars. I told her, "Wow, at least Bob is not a poor man."

The phone rang again a couple days later and the story had changed completely. She told me they were going back for Bob's follow up visit to the dentist when he told Daisy "Don't forget your checkbook." Mom quickly replied "What for?" He thought Daisy was a rich widow and she was going to fork over the money for his new teeth. I loved this part; she told him "Are you out of your mind? You think I'm paying for your teeth? I'm sorry mister but you are way off, you need to pack your sh– and get the hell out of my house." That is exactly what he did. That was the end of that relationship, Death and Rage went back out west and was never heard from again.

Mom cooled it on the computer for a little while but eventually got back into the chat rooms. She was a little more careful about which ones to get in and played it more conservative about giving out too much information. She told us about all these nice people but no in-person visits this time. That is until one man caught her attention. Again, "He is so nice." One problem, he was married. Daisy assured us he was in the middle of a separation. He had been married many years and they were still living together but it was just for convenience. That didn't sound too good to us; our thoughts were he needed to make a decision. Mom told me he was coming down to meet her in person, I told her "This time I'm coming down too." The timing was right were Carol and I could get off work and our boys were on spring break from school.

When we got there he was already there, and it turned out he actually was a very nice guy. Very quiet, he didn't say much, almost shy. You could tell they were getting along very well, he would jump any time Daisy needed anything, take out the trash, do the dishes and all other chores. At this point the circulation in her legs was very bad and walking any distance was a big challenge. He didn't mind, she cooked and he cleaned up. We stayed for a few days and I have to admit we really liked the guy.

During that visit a funny thing happened, a story that I have told friends over the years. When we first got there Daisy gave us four coupons for a free meal at a local fast food fish restaurant. She said they were there a couple of days ago and "Loved it." We told her we might go before we left but she was really pushing these coupons and urged us to go. Daisy's theory was, "if it's free it's for me." We took the coupons and went to get our free meal.

The food was all fried which the boys and I loved but Carol was not a big fan, we gobbled it all up then headed back to Daisy's house. As soon as we walked in Daisy eagerly asked, "How was it?" By this time the greasy food had Carol's stomach a little upset and I wasn't feeling so great either, while the kids were fine. I didn't want to hurt her feelings because she was so high on the place but I couldn't lie, I said, "The food was too greasy and quite honestly I need to go to the bathroom." She replied, "That's the same thing that happened to us, we've had diarrhea for two days after eating there, and I just wanted to see if it would happen to you or it was just us." I couldn't help but laugh and then quickly ran to the bathroom.

We went back home to Atlanta, I filled Michele and Steve in on our visit and assured them mom's new friend seemed to be a nice guy. He lived in the Boston area so when Daisy went to visit Michele in Massachusetts he came over so they could all meet. Michele approved of him as well and their long distant relationship was in full swing. He went to Florida for some more visits and took Daisy on a nice cruise. She couldn't walk much at all so he pushed her around in the wheelchair for the entire cruise. She didn't pay for anything; he picked up the tab for the whole trip. Daisy was being wined and dined (really just dined, she didn't drink) and she loved every minute of it. After a while he decided he was going to make the move, retire from his job of thirty plus years and move to Florida.

His move to Florida would not last long; Daisy said he couldn't sit still. He was used to working very hard as a welder and the problem was if he sat down for too long he would just fall asleep. That drove him crazy; he would get up and go for a walk or starting cleaning the house. He also was feeling guilty about leaving his family; his children relied on him for moral and financial support. Daisy knew he was not happy and suggested it would be best if he went back to Boston. He hated to leave her but after a few weeks he did go back. He thought about going back to work, his doctors advised him against it. Due to years of welding in some hazardous areas he had a respiratory problem which scarred his lungs and gave him an incurable cough.

They would stay in touch on line and with phone conversations but it wasn't the same, Daisy missed him. She would not beg him to come back; if he did it would be his decision. He continued to say he would come back he just needed more time. This went on for several months, we just kept telling mom she needed to move on, he was a nice man but he had family commitments which we understood and respected. The calls kept coming and he would throw out a date that he would arrive, the date would pass and he would set another date. This frustrated Daisy to no end but there was nothing she could do about it.

In the meantime Daisy's health continued to be a challenge. The diabetes was stable but the effect of having it for so many years was taking its toll on her. She had to have a few more toes cut off due to infections that would not heal. There was no choice, you cut the toe off or potentially lose a foot or maybe even the leg. Daisy took it all in stride she would say "10 toes, eight toes, six toes, what's the difference I can't feel them anyway." She was a trooper, she would go in to the doctor's office and within an hour she was on her way out less one toe. She was leaving toes all over the country; she had one taken off in Florida, one in Boston while visiting Michele and one more taken off while visiting me in North Carolina where we moved when I had a job transfer after 11 years of living in Atlanta. Even though these things didn't seem to faze her we all knew it was not a good sign for her long term health.

By now Steve and his long time girlfriend were engaged and ready to get married. The big question was where? They loved California so Steve started looking for the perfect place to have the wedding. It took weeks and weeks as they looked at all kinds of different locations, hotels, bed and breakfast spots, private homes and several other choices. Steve found the ideal spot; it was a private house overlooking Malibu beach in Southern California. We all flew out to California for the big affair; they had invited about 200 people. We all stayed in Santa Monica for a couple days prior to the wedding. There was the rehearsal dinner; we also had to rent tuxedos for me, our boys as well as my nephew Johnboy.

When the big day arrived we all drove out to the house in limousines. Daisy, Michele, Johnboy, Carol, Marcus, Lucas and I were all part of the wedding; I was privileged to be the best man. That also meant a speech in front of a lot of people, but for Steve I would do anything. We all arrived at the house a few hours before the big event and couldn't believe our eyes. This place was huge, probably 15,000 square feet overlooking the Pacific Ocean; it was breath taking to say the least. It turned out that the owners rented the house out on a fairly regular basis but not usually for one day, Steve paid dearly for that. The house was used during the filming of TV shows and several movies including *Last Action Hero* starring the Govenator himself, Arnold Schwarzenegger. The wedding was amazing, it was a Jewish ceremony and following tradition all the males wore Yamakas. The catering was actually done by the famous chef Wolfgang Puck who Daisy thoroughly enjoyed talking to. My boys were still pretty young but got a big kick out of the whole thing.

When it came time to deliver the best man speech I stepped up in front of all those people and poured my heart out in a heartfelt poem I wrote. It basically was about how he was such a special person in my life as well as the rest of our family and I loved him very much. The tears came flowing down and I choked up, the hard part was seeing my mom sitting out there, she starting crying before I even walked up. Over all it went well, my message came out loud and clear and the wedding was a smashing success.

As the years rolled on and our very small family got smaller with the loss of Rob and Sal, Michele wanted to be closer in distance to me than several hundred miles. Michele and I had always been close; being a little over a year apart we were inseparable as kids. The only thing she didn't like was when we were younger and I got to close to her girlfriends but she put up with it. Michele was also my protector growing up, I mentioned it before, not many people wanted to mess with her, myself included.

She had left her job to raise her two young boys and was living in a nice house in Connecticut. Her husband, Gene, commuted into New York City every day for his job, which made for a very long day and not much time for family. Michele figured she and the boys didn't see Gene much now so why not move to North Carolina and he could commute back and forth on weekends. He wasn't crazy about the idea but similar to Daisy, once Michele made up her mind to do something it was done.

Daisy was visiting Michele at the time, believe it or not, at her age, in her condition; she still drove by herself from Florida to Connecticut just stopping in rest areas for a little sleep. We tried to talk her out of it, saying she should fly instead, she didn't like being somewhere and not have her car with her, and she wanted to be able to come and go whenever she wanted. The plan was for Michele to come down and stay with us for a weekend and do some house hunting. They would drive Daisy's van to North Carolina, look at some houses then Michele would fly back home and mom would continue on and drive herself home to Florida. The night before they left Daisy took a shower so she they could get up early in the morning, just jump in the van and go. One problem, she let the shower heat up before stepping in, the water was just hitting her from the lower leg down for a moment, when she went to get the rest of her body wet she realized the water was scolding hot and quickly turned it down. Remember she had no feeling in her feet so cold or hot, it didn't matter. After finishing her shower she stepped out and saw that her feet were very red and quickly called Michele to come in. When she got there she saw that Daisy had burned all the skin off the bottom of her feet but didn't feel a thing. Michele hurried to get Daisy off her feet and called the doctor to see what was best to do. There really wasn't much to do other than put some antibiotic cream on her feet and rap them in gauze. Needless to say Daisy was in no shape to drive which was OK for the first leg of the trip because Michele drove. The second leg to Florida was the issue. Daisy really wanted to get home and did not want to wait around for her feet to heal so I told her I would drive her to Florida and fly back home.

The timing wasn't best to be flying; this was October of 2001, one month after 9/11. I wasn't crazy about the idea but I didn't want to take the train or bus. When I thought about it I always said, "When the good Lord is ready for you He'll come get you." Michele did her house shopping, saw what she needed to and knew she was ready to make the move. She then flew back home to tell her husband and finalize their plans.

The next day Daisy and I jumped in her van and started our long drive to Florida. We took off early; Daisy always liked leaving at the crack of dawn if not earlier. The first couple of hours went pretty smooth, no traffic or anything to slow us down. We were getting hungry and decided it was time for a food break. Daisy and I were always big fans of buffets. We saw a sign for a Shoney's, that caught Daisy's eye and that would be our lunch stop. After we both had our fair share to eat we wanted to get back on the road, as mom went to the rest room, I went to pay and pull the van around front so she wouldn't have to walk very far.

A few minutes later Daisy came out and got in the van. She told me she had a bit of a stomach issue and that's what took her so long but that she felt better. I started to pull out of the parking lot when Daisy yelled, "You need to find a bathroom, I've got to go." I was surprised and said "But you just went." Her reply was, "I know, but I have to go again."

Before I go on you have to know some of the history with Daisy and having to go to the bathroom when none are around. Bashful she isn't, when she has to go she has to go, it doesn't matter where, when or who is looking, she could care less. I don't think it was a medical condition when she was younger but I know the diabetes begins to take a toll on the body's organs and as Daisy got older I believe that was the case.

The first story I remember was when we first moved to south Florida in the mid 1970's. We used to love to go and pick fresh fruit and vegetables in the fields down there. Coming from northern New Jersey this was something completely new to us. We would go as a family, Daisy, Sal, Rob, Michele and I. Sal would go for around five minutes and that was enough for him. Rob would examine every piece looking for the perfect one. Mom, Michele and I were the workers, we got the volume. While Rob was hunting for the perfect strawberry or green bean he stumbled across Daisy squatting in the field. He let out a big yell, luckily we were the only people picking at that time, we all went running to him to see what the problem was and laughed our behinds off when we got there.

Another story is when Michele and Daisy were shopping up in Connecticut at a boutique knitting store. Unfortunately the urge hit Daisy and she went running to the bathroom, by this time in her life her running was a fast walk for most people. When she got in the bathroom she didn't quite make it to the toilet and what was left was a mess on the floor. She took off her underwear and used it to clean up the best she could then run out to Michele. That was her calling card, she would use her underwear to clean up and leave them behind. She told Michele, "We need to get out of here before someone goes into the bathroom." She didn't need to say another word, Michele knew exactly what that meant and they ran out the door. There is story after story like this, with her and Sal doing so much cross country driving we always joked, rest rooms across the US are littered with mom's underwear. The good news was every year we knew what to get her for Christmas, new underwear.

Back to our trip, I pulled out onto the road that lead to the highway entrance but Daisy pointed to a small gas station across the way and told me to quickly pull in there. As I got close I realized it was one of those small places that typically won't let you use the rest room. I saw another gas station that was bigger and sped over to it. As I was getting ready to drop her off in front, I saw her rocking back and forth in her seat I couldn't help but start to laugh. She tried to hold back her laugh and told me, "Don't make me laugh I'll crap right in the van." That shut me up pretty quick. She jumped out of the van and went as fast as she could to the restroom in the back. I decided I would get some gas; it's only fair for the use of the facilities. I finished filling up and continued to wait in the van. I waited and waited until she finally came out. She was moving rather quickly even for her condition when she jumped in the van and told me, "Hurry, take off." I asked, "What's wrong?" She said, "All I can say I don't have any underwear on." I have to tell you I have had some good laughs in my life but that one took the prize. I was laughing so hard I was having hard time breathing never mind driving. Daisy was laughing right along with me as she told me what happened. Of course she didn't make it to the toilet and you can figure out the rest.

We were back on the highway for about five minutes when she looked at me and said, "Oh no, I've got to go again." The only thing I could do after hearing those words and seeing the look on her face was start hysterically laughing again. She told me to get off the next exit which was nowhere in sight. I stepped on the gas to get there quicker realizing I didn't want this to happen in the car, we still had several hundred miles to go, that would make a very long drive even longer. I got off the next exit and found a gas station and the same routine. I dropped her off in front and waited for a few minutes when I decided I needed to go check on her. I tapped on the bathroom door and asked if she was alright, I heard her voice back say, "Get me some underwear." I almost fell over laughing again but did as I was instructed. I delivered her the underwear and we were back on our way. That was the last of those issues on that trip and after a very long journey we made it to her house.

The final note on that trip was my flight back. I had a 6:00 a.m. flight the next morning, with 9/11 just happening the security was insanely tight. I knew I had to be there by 4:00 AM to give enough time to get through security. It was around 11:00 PM and I figured we would get a few hours sleep and then go to the airport which was about an hour away. I tried to lie down for about 10 minutes and got back up. I told Daisy we need to go now, I was afraid we would over sleep and I didn't want to miss my plane. We drove down to West Palm Beach airport in the middle of the night figuring I would go inside and sleep at the gate, wrong.

The airport doors were locked, I couldn't even get in. We sat out in the van for a few minutes when a police officer shined his light in my face and said "What are you doing?" I told him the whole story about being afraid to over sleep and all. He looked at me like I was a nut but figured we were not the terrorist type. He told me the doors would unlock soon and even though he shouldn't do it he'll let me go in a sleep on one of the chairs. I gave mom a hug and kiss good bye and went in for a little snooze. There were police and police dogs all over the place with guns in hand. I got a couple hours sleep and after a long wait finally got on the plane. All was good until we are starting toward the runway, when I hear the pilot say we are cleared for takeoff, that's when I felt this draft in front of me. I reached my hand out to see where it is coming from and the exit door was actually cracked open a little bit. I was sitting in the row behind the exit door and was the only one that could see it. I quickly hit the service button and waved my hand, this did not go over real well with the other passengers. People were tense enough about flying post 9/11 without people waving their hand in the air minutes before takeoff. The flight attendant came over to see what was wrong and quickly called the cockpit to have the pilot wait a moment. At that point she asked me to stand up so she could see what I was looking at. She then reached over and opened the door and that's when you could see the faces of the other passengers, it was pure panic. They thought something was going way wrong, the attendant slammed the door shut, I sat back down and all was fine. I did get a few dirty looks but that was about it.

Chapter 48:

New York We Have a Proble

We were trying to convince Daisy it was time to move in with one of us, with Michele being the obvious choice. She was the best caregiver and the best prepared to handle her. Michele and her family made the move to North Carolina and had bought a house one mile from us. It was good having her close again, it had been many years since Carol and I had lived close to any family.

My real father, Sam, was starting to decline with his health as well, both mentally and physically. When he would be off his medicine it was just crazy. I would call him and urge him to go to the VA to get his prescription renewed but he would tell me he was too busy working. I knew what he was doing; he was back to writing letters to the President of the United States, he would stay up all hours of the night writing that nonsense. He wouldn't take his medicine because it made him drowsy and also took away all his madness which kept from writing. He would tell me, "I'm protecting Mom and the family. I'm almost done, and then everyone will be protected. I won't be pushed around by those anti-Semites in Washington."

I have to admit it was an entertaining conversations and he was very convincing. If you didn't know him you would think he was telling the truth. I kept trying to get him to go to the VA but he just wouldn't go. He would tell me, "They're trying to poison me; I know what they're up to." I asked him his doctors name and finally called the VA myself to see what I could do. When I reached his doctor he said, "I was wondering where Mr. Craig was." I asked, "Don't you follow up with patients with mental illness like that, knowing they are out in the public?" His reply was, "If they don't come for help we can't do anything about it." I pleaded with him to at least mail the medicine to him which he finally agreed to do. I called Sam to tell him the medicine was coming and he promised me he would take it when it got there, it took several days but it did finally get there. When I called to confirm he got it and indeed took the medicine Sam said, "Yeah, I got it....I threw them out!"

I couldn't believe it, I screamed at him and asked why he would do that, he replied, "They had my name on it I had to throw them out to protect the family." How do you argue with that logic, I was speechless. I also knew what was coming in the near future, I was going to have to go up to New York and see what I could do with him and his twin brother, Uncle Gabe, who wasn't doing much better.

In the meantime Michele, Steve and I all continued to try to convince mom it was time to move in with Michele. She spent several months a year with her anyway, what would be the difference? She knew what the difference would be, she would be admitting she was no longer independent, a day that would be tough for anyone to face. For Daisy, a survivor of so much adversity in her life and always being able to bounce back, this was especially difficult. She had another health episode where if one of her neighbors didn't come to see her she may have died and nobody would have known. Michele had to fly down to Florida again to be with her and finally told her she needed to come to North Carolina. Michele put a spin on it to make Daisy feel better, she told her with having the young boys it was too difficult to leave on short notice and it would be best for Michele if she could move in. Daisy gave in and said she would come up for a few months to see how it would work. The truth was it would be no different than the million other times she stayed with Michele except there would be no going back.

She packed a bunch of her stuff and Michele drove her back to North Carolina. Mom didn't know it but we had already decided she was not going back to Florida, this move was permanent. Michele decided in order to make her feel more at home she built a huge addition on her house so she could have her own bedroom, bathroom and a living room; it took a few months to complete but it was beautiful. Daisy was feeling right at home and our plan was working to perfection. She would say, "I don't know if I could go back to living alone, I love it here with the kids running around, dinner with family, birthdays with the grandkids, it's great." It was great having her close, she loved Carol and Marcus and Lucas enjoyed having their nanny around.

Meanwhile things were getting worse in New York so I made a trip up there to see my dad and my uncle. They lived in the same building in Queens, NY. Sam lived on the first floor and Gabe on the third. They were in the same apartments for 33 years, it was rent control and they paid $350 a month to live in a nice building in a great part of Queens. During my visit it didn't take long to realize both of these guys were in trouble. How they survived day to day was a surprise to me. Neither of the apartments had been updated for the entire 33 years they lived there. Both of them would freak out if anyone other than each other would step foot in their apartments so they didn't even think about asking the landlord to update the place. The apartments did not have a working stove, they each had a small dorm room type refrigerator, the walls were old and cracking everywhere, black mold in the bathrooms, it wasn't great but they were just fine with it.

I met the landlord and his wife, they were very nice people. They lived in an apartment on the first floor for free as part of the pay for running the place for the owner of the building. The wife, who was from Russia or Romania, I can't remember but she was a sweetheart. She knew both my dad and uncle for years and would look after them the best she could. I gave her my phone number so in case anything ever happened she could call me.

There was no one else for them; my dad and uncle were the only siblings left that we knew of. There was an estranged sister down in Florida but nobody had heard from her in a while. My uncle was never married and never had children so he was really alone. He was a gentle quite man, he didn't say much but when he did he was pretty funny. He would complain about Sam and always say "He's a pain in the ass, he's always bothering me, I just want to be left alone." He kind of knew he was slipping and asked if I would help him out with his day to day stuff, bills, medicines and such. I told him I was there to help him as well as Sam in any way I could but also told him I had to go back to my family in North Carolina. I tried to get their bills and their medicines straightened before I left but within a day or two of being home both were a mess again. I flew back a few weeks later to try again; it was a short term fix and again didn't last.

I talked with Michele and Steve, I told them I didn't know how much longer they would make it by themselves, and we would have to do something. We realized none of us were real close to Sam due to our history, but we also knew we couldn't just let him sit there and die. I started to think about potentially bringing them down to North Carolina, when I mentioned it to Sam he jumped at the offer and had a bag packed before I hung up the phone.

I had to slow him down and told him it was something I was thinking about but have not concluded yet. Gabe initially liked the idea but went back and forth between yes and no.

A couple of weeks passed and I had tried calling Gabe for a few hours with no luck. It was late at night and it wasn't like him not to be home. I called Sam and talked to him a bit and then asked him if he heard from Gabe, he said "No I haven't, not for a couple of days." When I asked him the last time he saw him he told me "I haven't seen him since he got in the ambulance the other night." "WHAT?" Was my first reaction, just a small detail that Sam kind of threw in there.

I called some local hospitals until I found him, what happened was a police officer found him lying on the sidewalk unable to get up. He was barely coherent so they rushed to the hospital; he was severally dehydrated on top of not being on his proper psyche drugs. They kept him for a few days and then he went back to his apartment.

Sam was still acting crazy because he wouldn't take his medicine either; this was becoming a real challenge, one that I wasn't sure I was up for. I still had a full time job, a wife and two young boys. There were a few more episodes both nothing to prepare me for what was coming. This was a real bummer because our everyday life was great, Carol and I were strong in our relationship, jobs were good, Marcus and Lucas were great kids, Marcus totally involved and excelling in sports and Lucas becoming a pretty good musician but this black cloud was hovering over me.

Back home in North Carolina, I'm in a deep sleep when about 2:00 a.m. the phone rings. When you have elderly parents in failing health the last thing you want is the phone ringing in the middle of the night. I jumped up and grabbed the phone, the voice on the other end said, "Mr. Craig?" I said, "Yes." "This is Sergeant so and so from the New York City Police Department, are you related to a Mr. Gabriel Craig?" While he was talking I couldn't help but notice some yelling in the background, I did acknowledge he was my uncle. The officer then said, "I'm sure you can hear the screaming, that is your uncle. He was running up and down the hallway on the third floor completely naked yelling." I could now hear him shouting, "Jesus Christ, Jesus Christ, Jesus Christ." Quite honestly, at the time that is exactly what I was saying, "Jesus Christ please give me the strength to handle this."

The officer went on to tell me they were going to take him the hospital for medical treatment, I explained his mental condition and was sure he was not on his medicine. He gave me the name of the hospital where I could follow up on him. Just as it sounded like he was ready to hang up he asked "By the way are you any relation to Sam Craig on the first floor?" I confirmed that he was my father, he said "Oh yeah, we're taking him too." He went on to tell me the neighbors have been complaining about him for weeks and when they went to handcuff Gabe Sam went crazy. I've heard of two for one specials but never like this.

With Sam, this wasn't much of a surprise; it was just a matter of time. During one of my previous visits we went to a local pizza place for lunch. When we walked in the guy behind the counter greeted us "Hey Sam, how you doing today, is that your son?" Sam yelled back, "Don't talk to me like that." He looked at me and said something like "He works for the government, be careful what you say." While we were walking down the street a man walked by and Sam quickly turned around and said "Did you hear what he said about your mother, I'm going after that son of a b....?" I quickly stopped him and told him it was a mistake. We then walked past a woman's clothing store and Sam stopped, he was looking in the window talking and smiling. I went back to see what he was doing when he told me "Can't you see I'm talking to Michele."

There was a mannequin in the window with a wedding dress on, he was commenting how good Michele looked with that dress on. We walked a little further and he stopped again, it was another woman's clothing store. He stood there, waived to a mannequin and said "Hi Daisy, how are you today?" As we were getting ready to walk away a woman came out of the store and said hi to Sam. I asked her if she knew my dad a long time, she told me he'd been coming by the store for years saying hi to Daisy. People always say how cold and tough New Yorkers are, yet in Sam's little neighborhood the locals were very caring for a man who quite frankly was a real pain in the ass.

Back to the situation at hand, I really had to think about what I was going to do, it was now clear neither one could be left alone. I called the hospital to check and see how they were doing. They had them both calmed down and were evaluating their medical condition. Gabe was medically doing OK, but he was requesting to go to the VA hospital. He was comfortable in that environment; he spent many months over the years in and out of there due to his psychiatric condition. After a couple of days I arranged for the hospital to transfer him over to the VA hospital in downtown Manhattan.

As for Sam, that was a different problem. He had some physical issues, he was having difficulty urinating, which he failed to tell me that had been a problem for quite some time. They made me aware that his insurance would cover him for a certain amount of time and then he would be sent to a state run facility which didn't sound good at all.

Gabe was doing much better with the VA knowing what medicines to give him. In talking with his doctors they confirmed he would not be going home alone again, he needed someone around full time, even though I knew that, it was tough to hear it. Sam was indeed transferred to another hospital, a local nursing home that would take Medicare and Medicaid, neither which I was sure he had. I knew one thing; he sure didn't have the money to pay for it himself. I was able to speak to him on the phone and he sounded terrible, afraid and desperate. He told me he had a bag attached to him for urine and the doctors mentioned a surgery to connect it permanently. I tried to calm him down and assured him I would get things worked out, the reality was I didn't know what to do.

After digesting all that for a while I called Michele to discuss our options, plus she knew much more about the medical world than I did. When I mentioned the bag and the surgery she said it was time for us to make a trip. This was not easy for her, she was not a big fan of Sam but she also didn't want to see him suffer. Within a few days we flew to New York to see Sam at the hospital. When we got there you would have thought he just won the lottery, he was thrilled to see us. You could tell for the first time in his life he felt like he was close to dying and he wasn't ready to go. He looked horrible; he lost a good bit of weight in the few weeks since I was there last. I could have stood on my head and whistled Dixie, with Michele in the room he barely noticed me, and I was fine with that, anything to put him at ease. We spoke with him for a while; all he did was plead with us to take him to North Carolina. We told him it would not be that easy, we needed some time to get it all worked out. It was kind of sad, he was crying as he begged us to help him. The reality was he didn't deserve what we were getting ready to do for him but all I could hear in my head was my mom's voice, "No matter what problems I had with him he is still your father."

We talked to the doctor and he confirmed he was going to attach a permanent catheter. The thought of it made me gag a little, Michele didn't flinch that stuff never bothered her. After we finished with the doctor we told him not to do anything without our consent. When he walked away Michele looked at me and said "We need to get him out of this dump before they butcher him." That was good enough for me. I told Sam we had some things to work but I would be back for him soon and make the move the North Carolina, even though I knew that was easier said than done.

Chapter 49:

I'm Leaving on a Jet Plane

Michele and I went back home and starting looking for a place for Sam to live. Taking him in with one of us was not an option, we wanted to help but that was more than we could handle. After searching a bit, asking around and making some phone calls we decided on place a few miles from us. We wanted him close in case anything ever happened. We decided Sam would be pretty much my responsibility to take care of, she had Daisy, which was plenty for her to handle. We wanted a place that would make sure he would get his medicine ever day, eat well and be kept clean. He didn't have any real special needs as long as he was on his medicine. We also needed to get an appointment with an urologist as soon as he got here to get him off that bag.

Within a week I was back on a plane to New York, I first went to see my uncle in the VA hospital. He was stable but he would have some good days and some bad days. I confirmed with the doctors that he could no longer live alone; I needed to do that before I gave back his apartment. With the rent control they had we would never be able to find a decent place for that price again, so once that decision was made there was no going back. After visiting with my uncle for a while I took the subway up to Queens and began to clean out both apartments. It took several hours to pack everything up in boxes and prepare for the movers to take it to North Carolina. I knew Sam was coming and my plan was to move Gabe there as well.

It was summer time, very hot and my dad did not have air conditioning in his apartment. The air was so stale; he had smoked cigars in there for years. When I took pictures off the wall that had been up for years you see the discoloration from the smoke. By the time I was done I had a brutal headache from breathing that air. I had a hotel room about four miles down the road, instead of taking a cab I decided to walk to get some fresh air. That may have been one of the most interesting walks I have ever taken. In that few miles I started out in the Jewish part of Queens by the time I had made it to my hotel I passed through several different ethnic neighborhoods. I'm guessing but I think it was Spanish, Russian, Italian, African American and Asian, a little slice of the world all within a few miles. This is something you don't see in every city, I'm not saying it is good that things are segregated like that but it was just interesting the differences in each neighborhood. I never felt threatened, I kept to myself although I got a few funny looks like "What is he doing here?" but that was it.

That night it took a couple glasses of wine to wind down but once my head hit the pillow I was out. I got up the next morning and was on my way to get Sam. When I got there I told the nurses I was taking Sam with me, they urged me not to do that because of his pending surgery. I told them there would be no surgery, he was leaving. When Sam saw me he jumped out of his bed and gave me a big hug. Right then I knew I was doing the right thing and living up to how Daisy raised me, help people any way you can. The bad part was he was filthy and smelled of urine; this was not the best thing for me being a confirmed germaphobe.

I told him we were going to North Carolina which brought tears to his eyes; he couldn't believe it was really happening. He would never admit it but deep down he knew what he had done in the past didn't call for this type of love. He was luck because with both Daisy and God whispering in my ear I felt compelled to help. I quickly packed his stuff up, got his medicine chart, grabbed a taxi and headed to the airport. Sam did not look good, he lost a bunch of weight, part from worrying and part from poor health. He had that darn bag hanging off him, it was turning my stomach. I just wanted to get this trip done and get him to his new home without having to empty that thing.

About being a big time "Germaphobe." It started several years earlier when my two boys were toddlers. They kept getting colds, we would take them to the doctor and I would ask "How can we prevent these colds." The doctor said, "Just keep washing their hands. Well, that's all he had to tell me and the obsession started. On top of that I would be watching The Today Show, 20/20, 60 Minutes, at some point every show would cover something about germs, colds, the flu and they would all say the same thing "Keep your hands clean."

Here's a quick funny story about taking my boys to the doctor. Carol and I were both working full time but I had more flexibility with my job so I was the one taking them to the doctors. When you go into the pediatrician's office they always had the well side and the sick side. It didn't matter whether my kids were sick or not I always went in the well side, sorry but I didn't want anyone else's germs. One time I had them in for a cold or maybe just their yearly checkup. Within a few days I started having these red bumps pop up all over my body, I caught the chicken pox. I called Daisy and asked if I had them as a kid, she couldn't remember which told me I probably didn't have them. A few days later both my boys caught it and three of us were laid up for a few days. My doctor had warned me that it could be dangerous to get chicken pox as an adult, among other things if you spent any time in direct sunlight it could cause you to become sterile. I thought about this for a minute and I went right outside and sat in the sun. We knew we were blessed with two healthy children and I was going to get a vasectomy anyway. I figured if I could do it this way it would save me from being cut on. I was out there for a while sweating like crazy when Carol came home, after I told her what I was doing she looked at me like I was nuts. I'm not sure if it really worked or not because I ended up getting a vasectomy a few years later anyway which leads me to another funny story.

Carol had been bugging me about doing it, at the time they said it was not good for woman to stay on the pill for too long. Also, for a woman to have her tubes tide or any other procedure was major surgery. For a man it's outpatient surgery, I figured she went through the pain of childbirth twice it was only fair that I did this. Plus, I've heard some horror stories, one in particular where my friend refused to get it done. So his wife went in, had the procedure and ended up with terrible complications. She had to take estrogen or hormone pills, she gained like 50 pounds and it also completely ruined their relationship. I could never forgive myself if that happened to Carol so it was an easy decision.

Carol came home from work one day and I told her I made the appointment and she freaked out. She said "What, we haven't talked about it, are you sure?" In the back of her mind she wanted to try for a girl but for me my two boys were plenty good for me. We went for the initial consultation; I always try to make fun of situations that may be a little uncomfortable so I started joking with the doctor. I asked him "Do you have a steady hand doc, you don't drink, do you?" This guy had the personality of a toaster, he never cracked a smile. Carol asked the question women are most likely ask "Will everything work the same?" He assured us he was a pro and everything would be fine.

A few days later I went in for the big cut. He told me he would need to shave down there to limit the risk of infection and asked if I wanted him to do it prior to the surgery, I told him I would handle that part. Carol asked if I wanted her to do it, I told her the same thing. Remember I'm a germaphobe, so I made sure there was no hair in sight of where they would be cutting. They gave me a little pill to take prior to coming in to kind of relax me, I was feeling pretty good, I could have used a couple more but one had to do. When they called me to go in Carol grabbed me and wished me good luck, she was more nervous than I was. I kind of have the same outlook as my mom for stuff like that, "Whatever will be, will be."

I went in to get prepped for the procedure; two nurses greeted me and said they would be getting me ready for the doctor. I was hoping for two "Hooters Girls" but got two ladies that defected from the Russian heavyweight wrestling team, oh well. They gave me a cover to put on, they told me they would step out while I got undressed. I threw it on and jumped on the table. They came back in and asked me if I was ready so they could sterilize the area, I assured them I was ready to go. When they lifted the cover they looked at each other, smiled and simultaneously said "Nice shave job." I had shaved every hair from my knees to the middle of my chest. They kind of laughed but I was not going to get an infection from any hair that's for sure. The procedure went fine; it was not a big deal. I went home, covered myself with ice for about eight hours like they told me to and I was back to work in two days.

The real funny part was when I went back for the re-check. In order to see if the surgery worked you had to bring back a sample of you know what for them to test. They would check the first time after a few weeks and then again in a few more weeks. I went back with my sample, I walked in with my paper bag looking like I'm carrying my lunch to school. I went up to the desk, where an elderly woman was sitting. I whispered what I was there for but she didn't hear me. I didn't want to scream it out; the waiting room was full of people and that's not something you want to share with the world. She asked me again to repeat what I said, I spoke a little louder. She grabbed the bag from me turned in her chair and yelled to one of nurses "SPERM SAMPLE." I didn't look but I imagined the entire waiting room laughing their head off, I just ran out the door. As for the second sample, it never happened; I told Carol I would rather risk having another child before I get humiliated like that again.

The last part of the story was telling Carol's sister about the procedure. She and her husband Ed were considering the same thing. Brenda and Carol are as close as two sisters could ever be. We all became very close, vacationed every summer together and always talked on the phone. I always teased Ed, "You have no choice but to like me because our wives are going to spend a lot of time together so you better make the best of it." As for the vasectomy, I got on the phone with Brenda and told her the whole story, except for one small, itty bitty detail, the part about getting the sample. I told her the nurses actually helped to gather the sample to make sure the test was accurate. I played it up, I told her "It's not a big deal, I just went in and they assisted me in getting the sample." She said "WHAT?" Brenda was always easy to convince so I really exaggerated it. "Brenda, do I have to spell it out? They helped me, you know, get the sample." She was shocked but told Ed "If that's what they do so be it, you're getting it done." We let her believe that for a few weeks until we finally let her off the hook. We had a good laugh over that one.

Back to the airport with Sam, we were pretty early for our flight, we sat and talked for a while, I told him about his new home, how nice it was and how he was going to love it. He only cared that he was finally going to be close to his children and grandchildren, the rest was irrelevant. I happened to look down at his urine bag and it was almost full, I hated it but I had to take him to the restroom and empty it. I tried not to make a mess but it didn't work; I got pee all over my hands but finally got it emptied; I bet I washed my hands six times and still felt a little queasy.

Chapter 50:

Nothing Could Be Finer

We finally got on the flight and headed to Sam's new home in North Carolina, luckily it was a pretty short flight with no problems. We exited the airport and headed to the assisted living home, a place I would later call "The Ritz Carlton." It was a little expensive but we didn't want to go to one of those places you read about or see on TV where they abuse the elderly. As soon as we got there they greeted him with a welcome basket and helped us carry his things to his room, Sam loved it already. This place was a million times better than his old apartment and 10 million times better than the rat trap state hospital he was in. We weren't there five minutes and they offered him a nice lunch. Like the rest of the family, Sam loved to eat; he just never had enough money to eat well. When he was living alone, his VA retirement was enough for him to pay his rent, phone, electricity and one, maybe two meals a day. He would make up for every lost meal very quickly. They would offer him two different choices for breakfast; he just said "Yes" and had both. Same for lunch and dinner, within six months Sam gained 65 pounds. He was happy to say the least, he settled right in and I felt good about what we had done for him.

Sam was in a spot where he had never been before; he had all his bills taken care of, all the food he could eat and a clean living environment. This was a guy who never had anything, being raised in an orphanage, due to mental illness he retired early and lived in poverty for 40 years. The problem now was he was eating too much and at his age to gain that much weight was a strain on the heart and he began to have medical complications. My feeling was he had never had anything his whole life, how much longer would he live, he was in his late 70's, let him enjoy it. His doctor didn't see it the same way and wanted him to lose weight.

Before I forget, within a couple of weeks of being there I took him to the urologist, he needed a procedure where the prostate takes pressure off the bladder and the bag was gone. That other doctor in New York wanted to maim him permanently when all he needed was a minor outpatient surgery. Always get a second opinion when the first one seems a little drastic.

Sam was enjoying life, we brought him over to our house for cookouts, and birthdays, Thanksgiving dinner, Christmas, and Michele even gave in and had him at her house several times. The funny thing was Daisy was living there and to see them together was kind of weird. Daisy was fine with it, she always had compassion for him she just couldn't live with him.

It was good for my boys and Michele's kids to get to know their grandfather, good or bad; he was blood and part of their history. He was always interesting to talk to; he's a walking history book, we called him "The Rain Man". Not only that, it was good to teach them compassion, with my family history I may find myself in the same situation and hopefully my boys would do the same for me. Although Carol and I have an agreement, if I go off the deep end I want her to pull the plug. I told her to put me in our little boat, give me a case of wine, a bunch of cigars and point the boat toward Cuba with a sign clearly visible that says "Castro is an idiot" that should end things pretty quick.

The sad thing is even as nice as the place Sam was most of the elderly people that lived there never have any visitors. I guess their children figure "They have everything they need why do I need to visit?" I couldn't do that, regardless of our past history, old age can be very cruel and I got to see it firsthand.

Daisy always pleaded with Michele to never put her in a home. That would never be problem; as long as Michele was still breathing she would take care of mom at her house. The problem was Daisy's health was deteriorating, she lost a couple more toes, she was down to one of her left foot and three on her right, the pain in her leg was getting worse as well. One day she called me screaming in pain; Michele had since gone back to work and was out of town on business. I ran over to get Daisy and took her to the hospital even though we both knew there was nothing they could do. It happened to be during a flu epidemic, there were people getting deathly ill all over the country and when we got in the emergency room there were people coughing, lying on the floor looking like they were minutes from death. They had hand gel and doctors mask for people to wear, I quickly gelled our hands and put a mask on both of us.

While we waited to see the doctor Daisy and I started to get into a pretty deep conversation, she was feeling her time was coming to an end and I had a hard time saying otherwise. I knew it was time to have the faith talk. Before Rob had died he asked me to promise him I would have this talk with Daisy, he wanted assurance our mother would join him in heaven. I figure this was as good a time as any. It's interesting, you can talk about faith with a total stranger but talking with your family is much harder. I knew how Daisy felt when Rob brought it up years earlier, she did not want to abandon her Jewish heritage, she had family members die for it and she almost did as well.

I just blurted it out, "Mom, do you believe that Jesus is the son of God and he died for our sins?" Her answer shocked me. She said "Ronnie, I started praying to Jesus right after Robbie died and I've prayed every day since." Those were the best words I've ever heard, not only did I know I would be with our mom for eternity but I fulfilled my brother's dying wish. She went on to tell me "There's only one God, we all pray to the same One, people can call Him what they want. I also know I will always be a Jew, I was born a Jew and I will die a Jew but that doesn't mean I can't believe in Jesus." All I could say was "AMEN."

I've said it before; I don't know who gets to go to heaven, that's God's decision. I just know what my faith tells me is the guaranteed way to go. The thought of my mom going anywhere but heaven would be hard to believe but there's nothing wrong with a guarantee!

The doctor arrived and told us what we already knew; her circulation was so bad in her leg and that's what was causing the pain. There was nothing he could do; luckily the pain had subsided with some medicine they gave her so I took her home. There was only one reason for us to go to the hospital that day; God wanted me to have that conversation with Daisy. Germs and all, it was one of the best days of my life. It ranked right up there with the day I married Carol and when my two boys were born as the best days of my life.

Chapter 51:

Nothing Could Be Finer Part 2

It was now time to get Uncle Gabe to North Carolina. I had spoken with his VA doctors numerous times and they continued to say the same thing, he cannot live alone, even though some days he was completely lucid and perfectly fine, the next day he would have no idea where he was or what year it was and he could also be violent. With that being the case I figured I would get him a place at the same an assisted living home as Sam, it would be perfect. I talked to Sam about it and he advised me against it. He told me Gabe was very sick and I was getting into something I could not handle. I have to admit, I have never taken any advice from my father and I wasn't starting now, I knew this was the right thing to do.

I made all the arrangements with the VA as well as the nursing home. I bought some new furniture, a TV and had a lot of his belongings from his old apartment to make him feel at home. I spoke with him on the phone and he was very excited about coming to North Carolina, he sounded perfectly normal on the phone, all was a go.

I made the flight plans and flew up to get him. Once I got to the VA, they had him packed up and ready to go. I signed some forms and off to the airport we went. He was almost bouncing up and down he was so excited, I was telling him about how nice the place was, all new furniture, nice people and his brother Sam in the same building. I even got him on the third floor just like his old apartment. We got on the plane and within minutes things started to change, he got a look on his face like something was wrong. When I asked him he mentioned he was having terrible back pains and he kept fidgeting in the seat. I tried to calm him down some but he was getting rather irritated. The flight attendant came over to check on him, I told her his was just a little nervous, I really didn't know what was wrong or what to do. After a few minutes he finally relaxed.

Once we landed in North Carolina I took him to his new home. They did for him just like Sam, greeted him at the door, made him feel right at home and offered him some food. Sam was there waiting as well, when Gabe saw him his only comment was he couldn't believe how fat Sam was. We got him settled in his room, he seemed quite content so I let him get some rest and I headed home. I caught up on some work, had dinner with Carol and the boys and relaxed myself for the rest of the night; it had been a long day.

I put my head on the pillow and I was out cold. That was until another one of those late night phone calls, it was about 1:30 a.m. It was the nurse at the assisted living home, Gabe was very upset and causing some trouble, I jumped out of bed and raced over there. When I got there he had just ran in from the cold, it was about 30 degrees that night and he was running outside with just his underwear yelling "I want to go home, I want to go home." All I could think was, "Oh no, what have I done?" I tried to calm him down but he was not the same man I dropped off several hours ago. He was trying to punch the nurses and even took a swing at me. There was nothing else to do but to try to give him a sedative to calm him down. The VA had given us a prescription just in case he needed it but I didn't figure it would be like this. They tried to give him one but he spit it out, after trying to calm him down for about 30 minutes I was losing my cool. It was now pushing 3:00 a.m. and the fun had long been over. I told the nurse to give me the pill; I grabbed it and literally forced it into his mouth and made him swallow it. We waited for a while for it to kick in and he finally began to relax. We escorted him back to his room and put him to bed. I went home and tried to get some sleep before I had to get up for work.

After putting in a few hours at work I went back to check and see how Gabe was getting along. He had no recollection of what happened the previous night, which was amazing to me. I was starting to learn more about mental illness and I liked it less and less. He and Sam spent most of the day together; Sam was there for most of episode the night before so he wanted to help keep him calm. All seemed to be OK so I went back to work.

A quiet evening at home with Carol and the boys, then we all went to sleep. Until the phone rings again, it was about 12:30 a.m., same thing; Gabe is causing a ruckus, hitting the nurses and screaming down the halls. I raced over there to see if I could calm him down. What had upset him was he was sleeping and had a bowel movement in his pants, when I got to his room the odor almost knocked me over. There were feces all over his bed, on his sheets, blanket, night stand, it was everywhere.

Gabe was so upset, I felt so bad for him he was disorientated from being in a new place. The VA doctors had warned me this might happen for the first few days but then he should be fine. The nurses cleaned him up, cleaned his room and put him back to sleep. I went home, threw up, took a shower and went to bed.

On night number three, another late night phone call, another episode, and same violent issues. This went on for 10 straight nights, it was a nightmare, Uncle Gabe was suffering and I didn't know what to do. They had an Alzheimer's ward there; it was safer for him and safer for the nurses. He stayed there for five more nights and had a few more issues. They told me if he had any more violent outbursts he would have to leave.

Day 14, it was about 10:00 AM, when my phone rang at work, they called and told me this time they were calling the police. I pleaded with them to give me 30 minutes and I would take him with me. I raced over there; while I was driving I knew there was nothing else I could do but bring him to the local VA hospital. It was the only place he felt comfortable, they were familiar with his medical history and knew what it took to keep him stable and safe.

When I got there he was in a rage, kicking and screaming. I told him I would take him out of there and go to the VA, he calmed down immediately. It was the strangest thing, this place was great, a clean new building, wall to wall carpeting, and all the good food you could eat, great nurses and helpers, but he wanted to go back to the dark and dreary VA hospital. Don't get me wrong, for what they have to deal with and the funding they have to work with the VA does a tremendous job. I know recent headlines will tell you differently but my experience with both my father and uncle were nothing but good. They respect the veterans and a lot of the people that work at the VA are veterans themselves. Yeah, most of the facilities need updating, more room for the patients and some other creature comforts but overall they do a pretty good job. Again, this has been my experience which is all I can base it on. I'm sure other people may have a different story.

Chapter 52:

The Longest Day of My Life

Gabe and I made the 30 mile ride to the local VA hospital; luckily he was pretty calm by now, unfortunately it wouldn't last. After numerous visits to the VA for both Gabe and Sam, one thing I did know this would be a very long process. That was my only real complaint about the VA; just a normal visit could take several hours. Going through the emergency room, I knew I needed to go ahead and get comfortable. I needed to have him committed to their psyche ward, before that would happen they would have to do a bunch of tests even though they had his file in the system from New York.

We walked in about 11:30 a.m. and started the process. I told the admission person what had been going on and gave her Gabe's information. The next line would be the phrase of the day "Have a seat; we'll call you when we're ready." We waited and waited and waited. Gabe started to get antsy so I went up to one of the nurses and told her we were heading for trouble. She said "Have a seat; we'll call you when we're ready." Gabe started pacing back and forth; another problem was his balance was off, and I was nervous he would fall. I tried to walk next to him but he pushed me away. I got him a wheelchair to sit in that kept him quiet for a while.

We finally got the first call about 2:00 p.m. I talked to the nurse explaining what had been happening while she was checking him over. A few minutes later we went back out to sit and wait for the next person to see us. Some more pacing, a couple of trips to the bathroom and about 5:15 p.m. we got the next call. This time a doctor checked him out while reviewing his file. He told me he needs to get back to an environment he is more comfortable with, I couldn't have agreed any stronger. But the process was far from over; they wanted to do more tests. It was now approaching 8:00 p.m. and we both were wearing down. Carol kept calling to see how things were going if there was anything she could do. I told her I would get home as soon as I could.

They now wanted to do a CAT scan; they thought he may have had a stroke based on some of his symptoms. I warned the doctor that this was not going to be easy, they didn't seem concerned but I sure was. There was no way he was going to lay in that tube long enough for them to get what they needed. They took us back to the room where the machine was, it was getting late so nobody else was back there other than the one technician. He slowly eased Gabe on to the table and within five seconds Gabe jumped up from the table and on to the technician and began punching him. I then jumped on Gabe to try to get him off the guy but he had a firm grip on him. After a few seconds we wrestled Gabe to the floor and held him until he settled down.

They were finally convinced I was right; he was not going to give in to have this test. The technician said he had an idea; he took some bed sheets and tied them around Gabe in order to keep him still enough to get the CAT scan. It was a little barbaric but it was the only way. After the test was done he took the sheets off and Gabe promptly assaulted him again and for good measure

Gabe then took a few shots at me as well. We got him back in the wheelchair and secured him by tying the sheets around him again.

Back out to the waiting room, it was now about 10:00 p.m. and we were both dragging. Honestly I think Gabe had more energy than I did. I hated it, but he had to sit in the wheelchair while being restrained by the sheets. It was breaking my heart but it was for his safety as well as others. The doctor came out about 10:30 p.m. and told me he was going to start the process to have my uncle committed. I was relieved but very sad at the same time. I really thought I was doing the right thing by moving him to North Carolina, ultimately Sam was right, it was too much for me to handle. They had to have a sheriff sign the papers to make the process legal, which was the last piece of the puzzle to wait for. I saw a police car pull up about 11:30 p.m., the officer went in and spoke with the nurses and doctors and within a few minutes they were coming to get my uncle.

Gabe was still restrained but by now he was wiped out and they since had sedated him, they realized he was no longer a threat so they took the sheets off. The officer came up to me and told me what was going to happen, he would have to go to a state facility, which was affiliated with the VA, then he would be sent to another VA location about two hours away. The local VA hospital did not have the type of personnel that could handle his condition and unfortunately he would not be as close to us as I had hoped for. We spoke for a minute, the officer told me there was nothing else for me to do and I could go home.

All day long all I wanted to do was get out of there and now that the time had come I had a hard time leaving. I saw Gabe, he was now lying on a stretcher, and he looked peaceful for the first time in a while. I went over and said good bye to him then made my way out the door as the tears flowed down my face. I got in the car and the clock showed 12:01 a.m., we had been there over 12 hours and I was physically and mentally wiped out!

I got a few hours sleep that night and then called to make sure Gabe was OK. He was resting comfortably as they did some more tests to see what they could do to help him. Within a few days he was transferred to the new VA location and a couple weeks later Sam and I took the two hour ride to see him, we couldn't believe our eyes, he was a completely different man, calm, smiling and talking normal. What I realized is to never feel bad about putting people in a situation that may be uncomfortable for you but the right environment for them; it was obvious this was the right place for Gabe. We talked about normal stuff, family, work and current events. He said he was feeling much better and wondered when he could go home. That was the tough part, as good as he was doing a relapse could not be far away which the doctors confirmed, his condition would not get better, just worse.

We continued to make visits; Carol and the kids came a few times as well as Sam and Michele. It was not the best environment for kids but I thought it was important for them to see my uncle and it was good for Gabe to be around young people as well. We would bring lunch, eat and talk for a while; he would be fine most of the time. The doctors warned us to be prepared for anything; during one visit with me and Sam we would see that first hand. We were just sitting there having a normal conversation and something triggered him. He spilled some food on his shirt and when he looked down at it he said "This is not my shirt." He stopped eating and then just got a blank look on his face. I called for one of the nurses; I knew it was time for Sam and me to leave.

The nurse came over to help me get Gabe up because he was struggling to get out of his seat. Just as I reached over to him he took a swing at me barely missing my face. The nurse jumped in and secured him, Gabe starting kicking and screaming "This is not my shirt, I'm an invalid, I'm an invalid, I'm an invalid." Sam looked on in shock, the nurse took him away and we knew it was time for us to leave.

The visits became more and more painful as his memory started to fade. He would say "I haven't seen you in years, why don't you visit me?" We had just been there a few weeks earlier but he had no recollection, which was heartbreaking. Soon he became a shell of the man he once was and also causing the nurses big problems. He would hit other patients, not eat his food or take his medicine; he thought they were trying to poison him. It got to the point where they said our visits were not helping him, it would only make him more hostile when we left. They told us we could still come any time we wanted but they wanted us to know what was going on. I would call the doctors and nurses to see how he was doing, and it was a steady decline. The dementia was completely taking over his mind and body.

Sam was not happy about not going to visit Gabe but he also knew there was not much we could do. I became a frequent visitor in Sam's place and after a while some of the other elderly people began to recognize me and would come up to hug me, shake my hand or pat me on the back. They were all very nice but my germ phobia was causing me to get a little crazy. I didn't want to be rude and not shake their hands or give them hugs but it became very tough. As I told these stories to some friends I always said this was all payback for my past sins, nothing could be worse for a germ freak. There were many more germ stories but I won't bore you with them, I'll just give you the all time winner.

Sam had been in and out of the hospital a bunch of times since I moved him south, mild heart attacks, the flu, dehydration and several other issues as he continued to age. I thought he was going to die several times but he had a strong heart. I truly believe the fact that he walked so much living in New York his entire life, his heart was very strong. A life time of psyche drugs, bad diet, and smoking and there he was still kicking in his early 80's, unbelievable.

One of his trips to the emergency room was for some type of virus. They had called an ambulance and then called me at work to let me know. I met him at the hospital and waited with him for the doctor. He was dehydrated but they would have to run more tests to find out what else was wrong. He was admitted to the hospital so I went home and came back the next day to check on him. I found his room; his door was open so I walked in. We talked for a few minutes; he said was feeling much better but he didn't know what was wrong with him so I paged for his nurse. As I looked out the door she came walking up. She said, "I know why you are calling me; you want to know about the sign of the door." I said, "What sign?" She pointed to the sign on the open door which I never noticed. It said something like "To enter this room you must wear protective clothing and gloves." I almost fainted, but had to ask, "What the heck does he have?" I was not ready for her answer: "He has an infection caused by fecal matter, which he has ingested." "WHAT? You need to say that in layman's terms." She said, "He has an infection from swallowing fecal matter, it's common with the elderly, they go to the bathroom and don't wash their hands good enough." I told her to please stop, I was getting sick but I wanted to confirm. "Are you saying he has poop on his hands then he touches his mouth?" "Yes." I quickly turned to look at Sam in his room and said "Dad, I gotta go, you have a very contagious disease, I don't want to catch it and bring it home to my family I'll see you in a few days." That one was the all time winner!!!!

I don't write about these things to gross people out, although that's what is does to me. I write about it because I feel people need to know what happens to some of the elderly, it can be quite cruel. We need to prepare for our advancing years, even though

Carol will pull the plug long before I reach a needy level, if she doesn't I will be very upset. I know it's easy to say now, I don't want to live like that, we'll see how I feel if I get there; maybe my feelings will change. As for dealing with my dad and uncle, I've done the best I could under the circumstances, could I have done better? NO DOUBT. The care my sister was giving to Daisy, we should all be so lucky, she treated her like a queen and Daisy deserved it.

Chapter 53:

The Final Cut

Life had gotten pretty crazy for a while with Sam, Gabe and Daisy, but we were all dealing with it. Unfortunately Daisy's diabetes was starting to really take a toll on her body. The pain in her leg was getting to the point where she could no longer walk. Michele took her to the doctor again even though we all knew what was needed. After doing some tests he said in order to alleviate the pain he would have to cut off part of her leg. He didn't know how high up he would have to go until the actual surgery. Mom had long come to grips with the fact she would eventually lose her leg and gave us her customary response, "What are you gonna do, if he says to cut it off then cut if off." The pain had gotten to the point where it could put a strain on her heart and that could be tragic.

Days leading up to the surgery she tried to joke about it. She actually made a bet with Michele how much weight she would lose once the leg was gone. You hear it all the time, the mind is very strong, and if you remain positive even with very difficult situations you can survive just about anything. I saw how it worked in the opposite way as well with Rob. He was doing great for so long, motivated to help others by educating them about HIV and AIDS, once his mind turned negative he was gone in six months.

Surgery day for Daisy was here. Steve flew in so the three of us were there comforting Daisy as they wheeled her in for the surgery. She was smiling all the way saying "Goodbye, leg" and "This is some Christmas present." It was days before Christmas 2003. We waited for what seemed like a very long time but it was around two hours. The concern the doctors had for Daisy with any kind of sedation was the possibility it could cause a problem with her heart. Like all the surgeries to remove her toes she was also awake for them to cut off her leg, even though she was drowsy, she was still awake.

The doctor came out to give us the news and told us he had to cut to just above the knee but everything went very well. Ultimately it really didn't matter how high they went we knew mom would never walk again. Being elderly, diabetic and not having a lot of upper body strength it would prohibit her from wearing a fake leg; there was also a risk of infection if it caused a blister.

We waited for a while and then went to see her in recovery. She was still smiling although there was a tear mixed in, part of that was she was with her children and the fact that we were there for her. She went back to Michele's house after a couple of days in the hospital and tried to adjust to her new body. It was not easy; she had a hard time moving herself around so Michele had to help her with just about everything. You don't realize how much leverage and balance you lose when a large part of your body is gone.

Daisy was a trooper and put on a good face but deep down I knew she felt differently. She called Denise and they shared stories of life in a wheelchair. Denise always loved Daisy and she tried her best to comfort her, it was bad for mom but even worse for Denise, she didn't have use of either leg.

Michele was trying her best to keep mom upbeat and we did try to have some laughs. I happened to be there when Daisy needed to get back in her bed. Michele went in there to help her; I asked if I could help, they both said they could do it. I was getting ready to leave when I heard a big yell from the room. I went running in and Daisy was on top of Michele. I quickly helped Daisy to the side of the bed and got Michele out. They were laughing, I was scared to death. Michele tried to get Daisy from the wheelchair to the bed and the little throw rug in front the bed slid out from under her and down they went.

There were a few more mishaps, eventually they got into a routine of getting Daisy up in the morning, getting dressed and eating breakfast. All during this Michele still managed to work full time and take care of her family. Like Daisy, Michele is a strong woman; most people would have caved long before. There was a nurse coming in during the day to check on Daisy and help with anything she would need, the rest of the burden was all on my sister. She was struggling with balancing life, two young boys, a teen aged son, husband and full time job and don't forget a 71-year-old woman with one leg. The crazy part of it was Michele doesn't even drink, for sympathy I picked up my intake of red wine hoping it would rub off on her.

During all this Michele's husband, Gene, was a real trooper. He was a big help with caring for Daisy as well and showing so much compassion. His home was being turned upside down with everything going on and he never said a bad word, he just wanted to know how he could help. And it wasn't just this latest chapter, Daisy had been in and out of their house for the past several years and Gene was nothing short of great, he loved Daisy and Daisy loved him.

We tried to include mom in everything we could, I took her to one of my son's basketball games. She loved it, a bunch of 12 year old kids playing their hearts out, they had to I was the head coach. It killed me when after the game Daisy said "Marcus is really a good basketball player, I wish I could have seen more of his games." Mom was never a sports fan, as obsessed as I have been my entire life with playing and watching all kinds of sports, she could take it or leave it. Now that it was her grandchildren and she may have been feeling a bit of her mortality, she was excited to watch them play.

Even though it was a challenge to get around, Daisy did not want to become stale, so she kept moving. The problem which nobody really talked about was Daisy could no longer drive; it was her left leg that was amputated but the fact that she could never get in and out of the car by herself made driving impossible. Of all the issues she faced in losing her leg losing her ability to drive was probably the biggest. Once you take independence and freedom away from someone their life has been altered in a negative way. The fact that Daisy depended on Michele for just about everything before the surgery was never thought of but the surgery made this fact official.

The next few months were a little bumpy; Daisy's spirits were up and down. We tried to go see her and have her surrounded by the grandkids as much as possible, family had always been number one with her and now it meant more than ever.

Carol's sister Brenda and her family were visiting for a weekend and we went to Michele's for a cookout. We were all having a good time, joking around, telling old stories and of course eating. After a while Daisy went to the living room to watch a little TV and do some knitting, she loved her knitting. Brenda's seven-year-old daughter, Sabrina, was mesmerized by Daisy's knitting. She just sat there talking to Daisy, asking her all kinds of questions. Asking questions is what Sabrina was best at; she was so curious about everything. As I said before our family and Brenda's family have always been very close so I got to know her three children very well. By far Sabrina was the most intriguing, entertaining and precious. She was always small for her age, people always thought she was much younger than she was, that was until you spoke with her, then you thought she was 22.

As with most kids, including mine, they all can be a pain in the butt at times and Sabrina was no different. She wanted to be in the middle of all the adult conversations, you would think she wasn't listening, a few minutes later she would ask a question about your conversation. She was so interested in watching Daisy knit she stayed there for quite a while without moving. Mom didn't mind, she treated her like one of her own grandchildren. Most little kids would have been spooked by Daisy's missing leg, not Sabrina; she would ask her questions about that too. "What happened? Where is your leg now? Will it grow back?" Being the patient person she was Daisy answered all of her questions best she could.

The knitting and conversing continued for quite some time, at one point I looked over and saw what may have been the most touching moment of my life. Sabrina was leaning up against my mom's wheelchair while she was knitting. As she watched Daisy knit she was gently rubbing her on the arm with a look of "I'll take care of you" on her face. It was truly a priceless moment I will never forget.

After the marathon talk and knitting session Sabrina went over to Brenda and asked if she could begin knitting lessons as soon as they got back home and within a few weeks Sabrina began her knitting education. She loved it, the only thing she liked more than knitting was dogs, any animal for that matter. We had an old beagle, Bogy, that had passed away a year or so earlier. Sabrina loved that dog so much, when she came to visit she would bring her own leash to walk him and bring treats for him that she kept in her little purse. Brenda and Ed knew that she would be devastated to find out Bogy had died so they told her he went to live on a big farm and run with horses. Every time she came to visit she would confirm with me that Bogy was doing ok on the farm. I always assured her he was very happy and enjoying his new life.

It was now approaching spring and we could all tell Daisy was going through some tough times. She even said a few times to Michele, “I don’t know how much longer I want to live like this, I’m becoming too much of a burden on you.” Michele would never admit it but it was true, not only physically but mentally, Michele was feeling the strain. Daisy would get demanding sometimes just out of frustration. Michele would be in the kitchen cooking and Daisy would want to get in or out of bed, Michele would get there in a few minutes but that was not fast enough.

As much as a burden Sam was on me and Gabe for a while, they did not live with me, and it was completely different. I would get the phone calls when something happened but the nurses would take care of it, or call 911 to get them to the hospital. Michele had 100% of our mom on her shoulders and it was wearing her down.

Chapter 54:

The Late Night Phone Call I Never Wanted

It was April 29th, my younger son Lucas's birthday. Mom had gone into the hospital the night before; she had some trouble breathing, some extra fluid had built up in her system, this had happened numerous times without any real serious repercussions so we didn't make much of it. It was a crazy day at work, when I got home we had dinner and then cake and ice cream for Lucas' birthday. He got all his gifts, we cleaned up the kitchen, and it was 9 p.m. before I knew it. I wanted to go see mom in the hospital but by that time I was tired and figured tomorrow morning before work would be better. We went to bed kind of early, maybe 10:30, that's early for me. I was in a deep sleep when the phone rang at 11:30 p.m. I jumped up and was afraid to answer it but eventually grabbed it. Michele was on the other line telling me the words I knew were coming but never wanted to hear "Mom died."

I was crushed, speechless, numb, hurt, sad, angry, and a several other emotions. The phone had woken Carol up and she saw the look on my face and knew what happened as well. She started to cry and gave me a hug before I went to get Michele and make the drive to the hospital. The crazy thing was I didn't cry, I had all the emotions but no tears and I'm the one who inherited my mom's emotions, we both could shed a tear at the drop of a hat.

Here's a few occasions that brought out a tear or two:

I went to Yankee Stadium in 1983 and saw Dave Righetti pitch a no hitter.

I've watched kids get picked to go after their dream on American Idol.

I've watched people get new houses on Extreme Home Makeover.

I watched Dan Marino give his retirement speech on TV.

I've watched Jerry Lewis sing "Walk On" at the end of every MDA Telethon, which is a yearly cry I can count on.

And I've dried my eyes many times watching Oprah throughout the years. Yes I'm an adult male that watched Oprah.

But the person I loved with all my heart and soul just died and I didn't shed a tear, I couldn't figure it out. I got to Michele's house; she and her husband Gene were waiting for me. Gene was trying to comfort Michele but as much of a loss as it was for me, this was even bigger for Michele it was not only her mother but her best friend.

We drove to the hospital and called Steve on the way there to give him the bad news which he didn't take well either. When we arrived at the hospital we went in the room to see mom, the good news was she looked at peace. They said the heart monitor went off and when they got in the room a few seconds later she was gone. I grabbed her hand, kneeled down next to the bed and did a prayer knowing exactly where she was. She was walking the streets of heaven with my brother Rob, Sal, her mother, her father and many other loved ones. We didn't stay long, there were a few details to take care of and then we went back home. Getting to sleep was another story it took a while, as Carol and I talked for a bit before I passed out from emotional exhaustion.

For Michele, sleeping was not an option. She went in Daisy's room and starting cleaning things, organizing, talking to Daisy before lying down at about 6:00 a.m. for a couple hours of sleep. When Michele woke up she jumped out of bed after having a very vivid dream. She said she came out to the kitchen and Daisy was sitting in her normal spot at the table. After talking for a moment Daisy got up from the table, Michele looked on in shock because Daisy had both of her legs. She started walking toward the garage when Michele asked her "Where are you going?" Daisy replied "It's time for me to go." Michele said "go where?'. To which Daisy said "It's ok, I'll be fine, it's just time for me to go." Michele watched as Daisy walked out into the garage got in her van and drove off. The question I had then and still have today, was it a dream or was Michele getting a message from Daisy telling her she was fine and on her way to heaven? In my mind Daisy was indeed on her way to heaven.

The next morning my boys got up for school, I didn't want them to have this on their mind all day at school so I decided not to tell them until they got home that afternoon. When the time came, that was the first time I shed a few tears. I knew how they felt about their Nanny and how she felt about them, it was not easy. Even tougher was for Lucas, who asked, "What time did she die last night?" I couldn't lie; I told him it was about 11:00 p.m. You could see the look on his face; he hated the fact that it was his birthday and said so.

I did some quick thinking and explained to him "Yes, right now we are sad, but moving forward we will not mourn Nanny's death we will celebrate her life. She had a full life with no regrets; April

29th will always be a day to celebrate your life and Nanny's." I'm not sure where the words came from but they were true and after thinking about it for a while I believe Lucas felt the same way.

That night Marcus has a baseball game and he wasn't sure if he should play. He loved playing but under the circumstances would it be right? I told him it was his choice but also stated "I fully believe if Nanny was here she would tell you should play, life must go on." With that he decided to go ahead and play that night. So the game was going on as normal and it was now Marcus' turn to bat. As he got in the batter's box he was very deliberate in his approach. Just before he stepped in he made a gesture to the sky, I was sure it was for the grandmother he loved. A couple pitches later he launched one deep into the night sky landing well over the fence for a home run. He rounded the bases as his teammates cheered and when he reached home plate he touched his heart and pointed toward the heavens and later he told me he said, "Nanny, this one's for you."

It may not seem like a big deal for a 12-year-old to hit a home run; the interesting part was up until that point Marcus had never hit one. He was one of the best hitters in that league but the home runs had eluded him, not on this night, not with Daisy cheering him on from heaven. The great sportscaster Al Michaels said it best when the US Olympic Hockey team beat the Russians in the 1980 Olympics "Do you believe in miracles? YES!" And I do.

The next few days were tough, making phone calls to friends and family. You're trying to move on and stay positive but its difficult continuing to talk about her death. I got through the calls but there was one more to make and it would be the toughest one, her best friend Toby. Their friendship not only transcended many years but also many life altering experiences, they had been through a lot together. I finally picked up the phone to call Toby and when she answered I didn't know what to say. I tried to find the right words, there just weren't any. I said, "Toby, I've got some bad news", and she automatically replied, "its Mom, is she OK?" and I had to tell her, "No, she passed away last night." Then it finally happened, the tears flowed like Niagara Falls. I was and still am so close to Toby, I love her so much and she meant so much to my mother. She ended up trying to comfort me on the phone instead of the other way around. She always called me the same thing, she said, "Bubala, it will be OK, Mom is done suffering, during my last visit she told she hated losing that leg, she hated being a burden on Michele and she was ready to go." We talked for a bit longer before ending the conversation with telling each other "I love you". Talking to Toby made me feel better as well as getting the tears out but there were more to come.

We had a small, family only funeral for Daisy, nothing big, I feel just how Daisy wanted it. It was good to have the family together, we shared some great Daisy stories and try to laugh through the pain. Daisy wanted to be cremated which she was and still lives on Michele's fireplace mantel.

A few days later I had to make a two hour drive out of town, during the ride I did what I always do in the car, play music. A song came on the radio that talked about "doing anything if I could see you just one more time". The words resonated through me and WOW! The tears starting flowing again like a river and then all of a sudden I got this warm feeling, a comforting feeling. I knew exactly what it was, my mom was with me, she was in the car to comfort me and let me know she was OK and I would be OK too. It's a hard feeling to describe but what a great feeling it was. I know many people will say I'm crazy but to me it was very real, strange but very real.

Chapter 55:

Knitting With Daisy

A couple last stories to share, a few years ago we lost a very dear friend, Elaine. John, her husband and their two children Keith and Lindsey, started out as our neighbors but what has evolved was a great new friendship that we have grown to cherish. Elaine had battled cancer for about two years; it was a very tough situation with having two children under the age of 12. We along with many other friends and neighbors tried to do what we could for emotional support; we continued to vacation together when Elaine would feel up to it. As her journey looked to be coming close to the end Carol had gone over to spend some time with her. That particular day Elaine didn't have the strength to get out of bed so Carol just sat by her bed side and talked about a lot of things. What Carol took away from that lengthy discussion was what a brave and spiritual person Elaine was. Don't get me wrong she did not want to die; she had a loving husband and two wonderful children. With her being a person that had a career in the medical industry she knew the end was near. She told Carol she was in complete comfort of what awaited her when her time was up on this earth and she was ready for the pain to end. God was calling her home and she would be fine, she was worried about her family but she hoped their faith would see them through the difficult times ahead. Carol told me before she left that day Elaine clearly stated "what matters most in life is God, family and friends."

Unfortunately Elaine did pass a few days after that talk with Carol; I was honored and blessed to be one of the pallbearers at the funeral. There were a lot of tears, a lot of love and a lot of faith. We got to meet Elaine's family who came down from Virginia; it was no surprise how nice she was after meeting her loving family.

John and the kids have pulled through unbelievably and I am happy to say they are doing great. We still do our little weekend getaways with them to the beach or lake together and treasure their friendship. For them, life goes on, it's not the same, it never will be, but it does go on and I know their faith has helped them through some tough times.

I will end this book with one more story. A few years back Carol and I were down at the beach for the weekend, we had a house full with the boys and their friends staying with us. Saturday night April 22, 2006 we went to bed when in the middle of the night Carol's cell phone rang, it woke me up but I didn't get it. I looked at the clock; it was 2:00 a.m. I tried to fall back to sleep but the missed call was bothering me so I got up to see who it was. It was my brother-in-law Ed, for him to call at that hour was strange; he was not a late night person. I tried calling back but there was no answer. Now I was really nervous, I knew something was wrong. Was it my in-laws, they were both in their 60's at the time. What could it be?

The phone rang again and I ran to get it, it was Ed. When I heard his voice cracking on the other end my heart sunk into my stomach but I wasn't prepared for what he would tell me. He said, "We're just coming back from the hospital, Sabrina was playing, she hit her head, we're not really sure what happened, she's dead, my little girl is dead!"

As I try to write this I'm still almost speechless, just like that night, I didn't know what to say. They just lost their nine year old daughter. I fumbled through a few words "How, what did, what can I do, I don't know what to say." Ed knew there was nothing I could say, he cried through the phone and said "I know, it's terrible, my Sabrina is gone, I don't know what I'm going to do. Please tell Carol, I know it's late but she has to come up to be with her sister, I'm worried about her and Carol is the only one that can help." I assured him we would head home first thing in the morning and Carol would be on her way there as fast as she can.

Carol woke up after a few minutes of hearing me on the phone and then I tried to tell her, I couldn't say it but she was starting to cry without knowing anything so I told her "Sabrina died, she hit her head or something, I'm not sure." I tried to comfort Carol but that was not going to be possible, we sat there and talked, cried, talked, cried and finally got about 45 minutes sleep before waking up.

Like I said we had a house full of kids, we could not tell our boys, it would be too much for them to deal with having all their friends there. They were very close with their cousin and this was going to hit them hard. We made up a story, we said it was going to storm there so we wanted to head home, we packed up in a flash and drove back home. Carol talked with her mom and sister on the phone in the car, they speak fluent Spanish so the kids didn't know what they were talking about but knew something was wrong because Carol was crying. When we got home all the other kids left, the boys saw Carol crying as she packed another bag and wondered what was wrong, and then we finally told them.

Our boys had always treated Sabrina like a little sister, very protective, very loving; it was awful to tell them. They were 14 and 15 at the time; we had always been a family of faith and felt like we gave them a good foundation of spirituality to build on. That went out the door, when they said, "How could God let this happen, how can there be a God, she never hurt anybody." How do you answer that? Carol had packed in about five minutes and was on the road to DC. I wanted her to wait to calm down a little bit, that was a waste of time she was going. My plan was to stay back with the boys until the funeral arrangements were made. It was during the school year and I thought it would be best to keep them in routine for a few days before going to DC for the funeral.

I tried to comfort my boys but nothing was working. Marcus had completely lost his faith and Lucas was just silent, not a word, not a tear, nothing. I pulled out all my speeches, "These things happen, I don't know why, it's God's plan and His plan is perfect." They replied "I don't believe that, why, what did she do? What good can come out of this?" I kept trying, "I don't know I just know it will." Great speech, yeah right, I was at a loss, they just found out their little cousin died and I was hanging on to them by a thread. Quite honestly I had questions as well, when something like that happens you can't help but ask why. I know what the woman told me many years ago to never question God, but this time I flinched, this one was tough to figure out.

Carol made it up to DC and was comforting Brenda, Ed and the rest of the family. Carol's parents, Oscar and Martha were obviously devastated, they lost their granddaughter. Not surprisingly Carol was able to bring some sense of calmness to the situation, she had always been the rock for her family and they needed her now more than ever. Carol and I spoke several times a day, not that there was anything I or anybody could do. I tried to keep myself and the boys busy knowing the funeral was coming in a few days and that was not going to be easy. Carol told me some of Brenda's friends would be writing some things to be read at the funeral and she asked me to write a poem to represent our family. I was honored to be asked, until I thought about it, then I was clueless on what to write.

I stayed at my desk trying to come up with something for them to read but nothing was coming out. On most occasions I could whip out a poem in just minutes, but not this time. I do my best thinking on a long jog with my headphones listening to my favorite music, The Eagles, Bruce Springsteen, Billy Joel, Elton John and other musical icons from my generation. I figured I'd get the kids off to school in the morning and go for a run; I needed to write something soon the funeral was in three days. That morning Carol called and said there was a change in plans regarding the speeches, instead of the pastor reading them all she told me each person will deliver their own. That changed everything, now I was not only nervous about what to say; now I had to stand up and speak at a very difficult situation and try to do honor to my loving niece. There were so many things I should have said to her when she was alive, now I must try to make up for it in this final tribute. Obviously my nervousness was insignificant compared to what Brenda, Ed and the rest of the family was going through.

After I got the boys to school I put my running shoes on and went to see what words would come out. It wasn't long into the run when the emotions starting pouring out and the words were not far behind. I didn't realize how much I loved my little niece, how much I was going to miss her. Then I thought about how she would not have her teenage years, no prom, no graduation, no college, no marriage and no kids, pure devastation.

While running through my neighborhood I was speaking out loud some potential words to the poem as the music pumped through my headphones all the while crying my eyes out. I didn't notice anybody, I was in a trance, and if anyone saw me that day they must have thought I was some crazed person.

Like most things in life, you take people for granted until they are gone. I started thinking about all the crazy stories; we would get a call from Brenda or Ed around once a week with "A Sabrina story." She was just so full of life with no inhibitions. It would be nothing for us to all be at the beach and we look up, there is Sabrina sitting with a bunch of teenagers. You could see she was leading the conversation, Brenda or Ed would go over to rescue the teenagers but they didn't want her to leave, they loved her. She would be asking them about their boyfriends, "Do you hold hands"? "Do you kiss"? "How often"? All kinds of crazy questions.

One time it was one of our boy's birthdays, Carol and Brenda took all the kids to Hooters, my boys love that place, imagine that. Sabrina was there for the first time and she was having a great time. All good looking young ladies with cool outfits, this was too much for her to believe. The waitress came by to fill up their drinks and when she asked Sabrina if she needed a refill she replied, "Yeah, babe." From that day on if you asked Sabrina what she wanted to be when she grew up the answer was "A Hooters waitress." Coming from a little girl it was hilarious. No doubt, Sabrina was one of kind.

The time now came to take Marcus and Lucas up to DC and prepare for the funeral. My boys were still not doing well and I had long run out of explanations. When we got to their house we all hugged and try to say the proper words but nothing seemed to come out right. The boys were both being very quiet until they saw their two cousins, Derek who was 11 at the time and Daniel who was six, that seemed to break the ice. Like younger siblings those boys looked up to Marcus and Lucas and I believe they found a little comfort with their cousins being there.

The next 24 hours were spent reminiscing about Sabrina in between a lot of tears. People were knocking on the door all day; Carol said that had been going on all week. As to what happened, they were all at a friend's house and a bunch of kids were playing in the basement when Derek heard a noise in the other room. He went in and saw Sabrina lying of the floor struggling to breathe, he quickly ran to get his father. Ed, followed by the other adults came running down to see what happened. They found Sabrina on the floor gasping for air, 911 was called as they tried to get Sabrina to breathe. Nobody knew what happened, the assumption was she was playing, doing a hand stand or something and hit her head. There was a small spot of blood on the back of her head which led them to that conclusion. I'm sure it seemed to be way too long waiting on the ambulance so Ed grabbed Sabrina and was going to take her to the hospital himself. The ambulance finally showed up and hurried Sabrina into the vehicle. I don't know much more about the rest, I was not there and it's not something you ask about. I don't know when she actually died, it may have been in the ambulance or at the hospital, it didn't matter, she was gone but surely not forgotten.

There were rumors around the DC media circuit that there may have been foul play. For someone to actually print that not knowing any of the facts was horrible. You have parents suffering more than anyone could ever imagine and this crap is being discussed. Police were involved, they have to do their job and everyone understood that,

Ed stayed in touch with the detectives for weeks. It didn't take long for them to realize whatever happened foul play was not involved. Another small child that lived in the DC area died shortly after Sabrina and media turned their attention to that tragedy and no longer wrote about her.

The detectives were very understanding of the situation but continued to tell Ed they had a job to do. Ed wanted to know what happened as much as anybody, the doctors at the hospital could not figure it out. There were no wounds, injuries, other than the small spot on her head but that was not big enough to give them any clues. This would go on for weeks until the autopsy results finally came in: Sabrina died of a heart attack. They found scarring in her heart; apparently she had a virus years earlier, a normal virus all kids get. The difference was it attacked her heart but there was no way of knowing that. There were no symptoms, nothing that could tell you something was wrong. After reviewing the autopsy the doctors told them it was only a matter of time before this was going to happen, even if a doctor was there when it happened it wouldn't have changed anything, she died immediately. There was no one to blame and nothing to prevent it. There was some comfort there realizing Ed and Brenda did all they could to save her.

As for the funeral, the immediate family got to the church early to go over some of the details. The casket was closed, there would be young children there and they thought it would be best that way. As the time got closer for the start of the funeral people started pouring in. People were coming up to meet Brenda and Ed, they were mostly parents of Sabrina's classmates; they spoke of how special Sabrina was to their child and shared quick little stories. Interestingly Sabrina never spoke of most of these kids, they knew she had a few friends but not this many. The people were coming in by the dozens, before long this large church was full; they had to set up monitors in an auxiliary building to video the funeral for the overflow of guests. Nobody ever took a firm count but the guess was between 600 and 800 people.

You would never think a nine year old little girl would have this type of impact on that many people, it was now becoming evident to everyone this was not your normal nine year old girl. She made an impression on so many people, the stories before the funeral and after was more than anybody had realized. The few people that were blessed to be asked to present eulogies shared similar stories. One of Brenda's dear friends, Laura and her young daughter wrote an amazing dedication to Sabrina. It was a struggle to for them to get through it but they did. Brenda's oldest friend, Kelly, also delivered stories that allowed people who may have not known Sabrina; get a clearer picture of this wonderful little girl. Another close friend, Jane, did little Sabrina justice from her point of view. It was interesting how people, young and old, were changed just by knowing my little niece. Ed also went up and suffered through his words, it was tough to watch a father say goodbye to his daughter at such a young age.

In the middle of these eulogies it was my turn to see if I could do Sabrina proud. Luckily everybody shared lighter stories as well as heartwarming ones; this allowed me to attempt to reduce my tension by telling a funny story. I explained I had something to read but I wanted to lighten up the moment. I knew it would be the only way for me to get through it. The story I told was one that was shared to us by Brenda and Ed during one of the weekly calls for a "Sabrina story."

Ed and Brenda had hired a babysitter one evening so they could go out to dinner. The young female babysitter was about 17. She had sat for them numerous times; Sabrina and her two brothers really liked her. During that evening the sitter's cell phone rang while she was in the bathroom. One thing we all knew about Sabrina if a phone was ringing, regardless of whose it was, she was going to answer it. This time was no exception.

This is how it went:

Sabrina: "Hello."

Young Man: "Hi, is so in so there?"

Sabrina: "She's busy right now."

Young Man: "Can you please get her; I want to talk to her."

Sabrina: "I told you, she is busy."

Young Man: "It's important, where is she?"

Sabrina: "I told you, she's busy."

Young Man: "I really need to talk to her."

Sabrina: "Well, if you must know, she's in the bathroom."

Young Man: "Can you get her out?"

Sabrina: "No."

Young Man: "What's taking so long?"

Sabrina: "OK, if you must know, she's in the bathroom kissing another boy, goodbye."

Sabrina hung up the phone and that was the end of the conversation. Until the young girl got home that evening and she called her boyfriend. He was very upset about what happened and asked "Who were you kissing?" She was stunned, "What are you talking about?" He said, "The girl told me, you were in the bathroom kissing someone." The babysitter started to laugh and explained she was just kidding and said, "She's nine years old." The boy said, "But, she was so convincing." That was Sabrina. It did lighten the moment and allowed me to begin my poem which I share with you below.

TODAY WE CELEBRATE THE LIFE OF SABRINA

Today we celebrate the life of Sabrina
Not so easy to do as we fight through the pain
We're left wondering what might have been
One thing for sure her life was not in vain

I urge you to look around

All these people were touched by my little niece
From this day on
In our heart she will always own a little piece

Just seeing her you couldn't help but feel happy
Young, old, girl or boy
Sabrina was loved
And brought us so much joy

She had a special spirit
Losing her feels so wrong
The Angels in heaven needed her so badly
When she got there they said what took you so long

Sabrina I ask you a favor
As I write you this goodbye
Tell little Bogey, my brother and my mom
We all said hi

Today we celebrate the life of Sabrina
For on this earth she is gone
I say until we meet again, we all love you
Marcus, Lucas, Aunt Carol and Uncle Ron

I cried most of the way through it, although I did feel I was able communicate just how I felt about my dear little niece.

After the service everybody made their way to the cemetery which was just behind the church. The immediate family stayed in the church for a few minutes, Brenda and Ed wanted to open the casket and say their final good bye. When we got to see her she looked just like an angel, she was beautiful. We all went up to say our final words; Marcus and Lucas had long since shared their emotions and had let out many tears.

Brenda wanted something to remember Sabrina so she cut a lock of her hair for her keepsake. Before closing the casket Brenda tried to comfort her two young sons and she spoke words that said it all "Don't worry boys, she's fine, she's up in heaven, Sabrina is knitting with Daisy." For the first time in my life I actually felt my knees buckle, Brenda was right, there was no pain, no suffering, no sorrow, just knitting with Daisy.

Lucas, Marcus, me and a few others carried the casket out to the cemetery, a few more prayers were said and the ceremony was over. We stayed for a while, talked with family and friends before heading back to their house for some more family gathering. When we got back in the car I experienced something that I wouldn't trade anything in this world for. Both my boys were proud of my speech and more importantly they both felt the power of God in there. Quite honestly you would have had to been numb not to feel it, it was truly a blessed event. They now knew yes, Sabrina was gone but she will not be forgotten and surely did not die in vain. Personally, it was the most powerful spiritual experience of my life. I did share with my boys my belief that there were many people that day that began their walk with Jesus Christ. I could see it, feel it, the Holy Spirit was so strong. It was the only way that a totally horrible situation could turn into a truly monumental day; it was God Himself blessing every person there. Regardless of belief, faith, religion, every person walked out of that church a different person than when they walked in. For my two teenage boys, who had every reason to question their faith, they walked out of there feeling the power of God, it truly was a miracle.

While back at the house with family and friends piling in, a woman came and introduced herself to me. She went on to introduce her beautiful young daughter as well, I wasn't sure why they made a point to seek me out, and then she told me. "My daughter is the babysitter, the story you told about her being in the bathroom, it was her." The young girl turned a little red in the face, I asked her not to be mad at me but the story had to be told. She was cute as a button and said she felt honored to be part of the ceremony. The rest of the day there were many tears as well as a few smiles but we all knew we just lost someone very special.

Chapter 56:

We Are Blessed

The years have passed and so have many of our loved ones including Uncle Gabe a few years ago. It was a merciful death, old age, Alzheimer's, dementia, bipolar disorder and other ailments became very difficult to watch and the good Lord took him home. Gabriel had a tough life, a lonely life but we were able to introduce some quality family time in his later years and I think he appreciated it.

For Uncle Gabe's funeral I took Sam on the two hour ride to the VA cemetery. We had him buried at a Veteran's cemetery with full honors; the honor guards gave him a 21 gun salute and presented Sam with an American flag. The interesting part was when they presented Sam with the flag they said "On behalf of the President of The United States." Well that's all they had to say, the entire two hour ride home I heard how the U.S. government had been part of Gabe and Sam's life and it just confirmed all his conspiracy thoughts. A few days later Sam told me he and Gabe were part of the Kennedy assassination. As I said, Sam is Sam, never a dull moment. I thank God for the invention of red wine and cigars, they help keep me sane, for now.

Unfortunately Sam also passed away almost two years ago. He got an infection that just overtook his body. I was at work when they called and told me Sam was very sick. They found him in his room almost unresponsive and rushed him to the hospital. I quickly jumped in my car and actually beat the ambulance there. I asked the receptionist for an update and she told me the ambulance was only a minute away. They did get there a couple minutes later and told me to wait for them to get Sam checked out and then I could go back to see him.

Really not knowing how serious it was because I really started to think Sam was going to outlive me, he had so many issues over the years since I moved him to NC but just seemed to fight them all off. After a short wait a doctor came out to meet me and escorted me back to the ER where Sam was. She went on to tell me it was a very serious and Sam was fighting for his life. She suspected he had sepses, which is a total infection of the blood and stated a man at his age (84) it would be rare for him to come back from that. They could not get him to respond to verbal commands and thought he may be in a vegetative state. She started asking me how far they should take the treatment, meaning if he is not mentally there do I want them to keep him alive. She told me they hit him with the life paddles already in the ambulance to bring him back once and needed to know what my feelings were. I had medical proxy for Sam ever since I moved him to NC but now realizing I was making life and death decisions was not what I had expected.

There was not much time to think about it so my concern was how far gone was he? I did not want him to live just for the sake of living if there was no quality of life, just a body laying there on a breathing machine. I feel the same way about me, let me go meet my maker, PLEASE let me go meet the Lord.

She tried to tell me she wasn't really sure about his condition. Then my concern turned to make him comfortable, was he in pain? I continued to hear the nurses in the background calling him "Mr. Craig, Mr. Craig, can you hear me"? After a short time they asked me to come over and talk with him. When I finally saw Sam up close it was not a pretty sight, he looked gone to me. The nurses continued to work on him and then asked me to talk to him to see if I could get a reply. I just blurted out, "Hi, Dad, it's me" and within two seconds his eyes opened and said, "Ron, is that you"? WOW! I was shocked he was now completely lucid and the nurses and I smiled as Sam was getting color back in his face and I thought everything was fine. A moment later Sam seemed to drift off again and this time when I called for him again he replied "Dad? Hi dad." I said, "No, it's me, Ron." Then I realized he was crossing over, he was seeing his father. A relationship he longed for his entire life and that's who he was seeking and seeing but just a moment later he was back with us and said my name again. After a few minutes of the nurses working on he that had him stabilized but still very ill.

I called my sister to get some moral support and medical advice as well. She told me she was on her way and showed up a short time later. While I waited I did some reflecting and I also started to recount Sam's life. He had a tough one no doubt, being abandoned as a child, living in an orphanage and not really having any family for his prime youth years. He also made some choices as an adult along the way that he probably wished he hadn't. He left his family, but was he sane enough to make the right choice, maybe, maybe not. I had long forgiven him and made peace with my childhood and upbringing, after all I had many good years with Sal being my father so no regrets for me.

Some days were tough as I didn't like being the gopher but in a weird way I had grown to appreciate how much he needed me. When he would see me walk in to the nursing home he would light up and run up to hug me. We would then sit and talk about the past, which was his favorite subject. He still brings up the murderous one legged prostitute who tried to kill him back in the early

60's and even how he thought he saw her recently in the nursing home dining hall. I got past trying to argue, I just assured him she couldn't hurt him anymore. Of course the government conspiracies would always come up, very entertaining, crazy but entertaining. After conversing for a while I'd give him a hug and be on my way laughing or shaking my head. I was there once or twice a week to give him his cigarettes and other necessities. From time to time the other residents would run up to me, shake my hand and hug me, I came to realize it gave them some comfort because most of them never had any visitors.

Sam was a man of faith; he never gave up on his Jewish heritage but he also believed that Jesus Christ died for our sins. We had those conversations many times over the years since his move to NC. But make no mistake about it Sam did not want to die and during a moment of consciousness he point blank asked me, "Ron, am I going to die? I don't want to die." I said, "Dad you're going to be fine, just relax." But I did use the moment to ease his fears and asked, "Dad, what happens when you die?" He answered, "You go to heaven." I said, "Exactly. So just relax and don't worry about that." The fact that he didn't want to die made me feel good because that told me he liked his life. He was well taken care of in the nursing home, he was able to know all his grandkids over the past eight years, and was involved for holidays and birthdays. I did feel like I fulfilled my duty as a son to give him the life he longed many years for, a family life. .

Michele showed up and I now had some help as we continued to talk with the doctors and assess the situation. The doctor was still concerned and told us even though he's conscious he's still very ill. If they could not get the infection under control it would take over his body, shut down his organs and he would not make it. They were pumping him full of antibiotics and we hoped for the best. Michele and I stayed there and talked with him as he would stay awake for a bit then just fall back asleep. His breathing labored but he fought on.

Michele and I also used this time to reflect about Sam, both good and bad, the funny stories mom had told us over the years but Daisy also instilled the values to help others if you can. We knew if this was indeed the end we would have made Daisy proud. Actually during the last year of Sam's life Michele had taken on most of the day to day duty for Sam as she saw the years of caring for him and some for Gabe had taken an emotional toll on me. It was a welcome break. Many people would say, "Ron, you really stepped up to take care of your father and uncle," and I would truthfully answer, "If I knew they were going to live this long I may not have signed on."

A lot of people ask me, "How did you make it through some of the tough times, how did you not lose your mind?" First of all, I'm not sure that I didn't lose my mind. Some days were pretty tough, a lot of prayer, strong faith and I have to admit modern medicine helped as well. I go back to what an old friend told me, "If you're not laughing, you're crying, if you're not living, you're dying." So my advice is start laughing and start living, pretty simple but very true.

Michele and I stayed there to late in the evening and Sam was pretty stable. The doctor assured us he was doing better and we should go get some sleep which we did. The next day while trying to catch up on work the hospital called and said we needed to get there right away. I picked Michele up and rushed on over. When we got there we saw a different Sam then we saw the night before, his breathing was really laboring, each breath seemed like it might be his last. We talked with the doctor and they said they could not get control of the sepses, the infection was taking over his vital organs and that was what was making his breathing hard.

Michele asked many questions to see what options we had to help Sam but ultimately it was now in God's hands whether he would live or not. We also asked a real tough question "What quality of life would he have if he survived?" They told us we were looking at it, trouble breathing, bed ridden and unable to do much. We also asked how we could put him at ease because he looked like he was struggling. He was not really coherent as we tried to talk to him. They said some morphine would help settle him down and allow him to rest because he was fighting it and making it worse. Shortly after giving him the morphine he did settle down and it relaxed his breathing. It was now about 11:30 p.m. and Michele and I pretty much decided to spend the night in his room and began to get comfortable. We had been calling Steve all along to keep him up to date, he felt helpless because he was in Europe on business.

Michele and I talked and reminisced about many things as we kept an eye on Sam. In mid conversation we looked over and saw that Sam was very still, we walked over to check on him and he indeed had peacefully and quietly passed away. I would be lying if I said we sat there and balled our eyes out, we had mixed emotions but ultimately we were at peace because after a very tough life Sam was at peace.

Steve flew in and we had the same military funeral that we had for Uncle Gabe and it was again well done by the VA. His final resting site was only a few feet from where his brother was buried so again I feel we did the best we could.

Surprisingly I periodically do miss Sam, I really didn't think I would. Nothing like I miss Daisy but I do miss him. Regardless of what happened years earlier he ultimately loved his children and to lose someone that cares about you that much you can't help but feel like something is missing.

I continue to move forward in my life and try live it to the fullest (something I need to get better at). This life on earth is not a dry run; this is it, so make the most of it. Try doing what you can for others (another thing I need do more of). Some may ask why the book is filled with people dying. The book is not about dying, just the opposite, it's about living, more specifically, it's about trying to live right (another daily struggle for me). We are not here forever, what happens after here is forever, that's why I plead with you to, pursue your dreams whatever they may be, do what makes you happy and get right with God. There is a spiritual life after this life on earth and you must prepare for that as well. I often go back to what my brother Rob said: "No one gets out alive."

I know I've written about many tough situations me and my family have been through but I truly know we have been and continue to be very blessed. Carol and I both have great family support, wonderful lifelong friends, I have two brother-in-laws that I consider close friends, how many guys can say that? We are blessed with good health and continue to try to grow spiritually.

Carol and I have two amazing sons who are doing great in college and keeping out of trouble, as far as we know. It's a fun time as Carol and I recently became empty nesters. Marcus is in his Junior year in college studying business and Lucas is a Sophomore studying music. Praise God the boys are happy and healthy and completely different in many ways. Lucas is a very talented composer and musician with hopes of career in that arena while Marcus is a smart kid with a great personality that everyone says makes him a natural for a career in sales, we tend to agree. My message to them has always been, "The world is there for the taking, do or be whatever it is that you desire as long as it makes you happy, you just have to have the guts to go for it." I wish I would have pursued my dream of being a writer a long time ago, but ultimately my mom and niece supplied me with the motivation and guts to finally do it.

As for my loving wife Carol, as Daisy and Sal always said "She deserves a medal for putting up with you." To say I'm a little difficult to live with is a bit of an understatement. Carol has been there with me through the thick and the thin and there has been plenty of thin. I have just enough of the crazy DNA from my dad's side of the family to keep things interesting around the house. Luckily our love for each other has been strong enough to overcome those issues. Carol and the kids both know I'm a bit of a nut but the love I have for my wife and children far outweighs the amount of craziness I have. They are the reason I get up in the morning.

The rest of family is doing well also. Michele and Gene are doing great, a happy marriage and growing boys. She still misses mom almost on a daily basis, we continue to remind each other of a funny Daisy story and that seems to ease the pain. Michele and I have always been close, since mom passed our relationship has taken on a new definition, she really looks after her younger brother and I love her for it.

I've gotten really close to my nephew John (formerly Johnboy). He reminds me how much of an influence I was on him when he was younger; with Michele working and trying to make ends meet, he would spend many a day at our house where Daisy was supposed to be watching him. The truth was I was using him as my own little tackling dummy. I worked him over pretty good; he was the little brother I never had. I would wrestle with him all the time trying to toughen him up for the real world that awaited him. He recently told me I even taught him how to shave, which I don't remember but more importantly he does. For all the abuse I gave him he still thinks pretty highly of his uncle Ron so I guess I did something right.

Steve is doing great in his life; he is and will always be successful. With his schedule we don't see him as much as we would like, although when we do get together it's a special time. Through the years Steve has been there for me and the entire family for that matter, he was always the rock of the family and I love him for it. He has had his hard times like everyone else; the difference for him is he never gives up. My relationship with Steve changed the day we became roommates back in 1984. Before that I have to say I didn't know him, what I found was a loving generous brother with a big heart, and we remain close brothers and best friends.

My in-laws, Martha and Oscar are doing well. They struggle with the loss of their granddaughter but have coped the best they can. They are great in-laws as well as grandparents and worship their grandchildren.

For Brenda, Ed and their two sons life has been challenging, losing a child at the age of nine is something I can't relate to, unfortunately their life will never be the same. They do take comfort in knowing Sabrina is with God. We see them often and vacation together at least once a year, we always have fun but now there is a piece missing.

On the one year mark of Sabrina's passing Brenda wanted to do something to make it a special day. She had heard about how another family filled a bunch of balloons with helium, attached a pre-address stamped postcard memorializing their child and requested who ever found the card to mail it back. She decided to do the same thing.

Brenda asked friends and family to join her family in this memorial of Sabrina's life. Carol, me and the boys did a smaller version of the same from our home in North Carolina. Brenda and her group sent up 300 balloons from the metro Washington DC area and we launched another 50 from North Carolina. None of us knew what to expect, how far would they go? Would anybody return them?

The card Brenda and Ed wrote and attached to the balloons read as follows:
Sabrina,
We see your beauty in the snow covered trees
We feel your warmth in the kind words of strangers
We experience your joy in seeing the playfulness of our puppies
We feel your presence as we watch the dolphins jump and dive near us in the ocean water
We see your smile in the stars at night
We feel your love through the laughter and closeness of family and friends
We find your peace in the sound of the river
May the wind carry this message to heaven so she knows that we love her and that she is always with us.

May you who find this postcard celebrate the beauty, warmth, kindness, joy, laughter, love and peace that Sabrina brought us during her lifetime and continues to bring us during our lifetime.

Please join in the celebration of Sabrina by mailing this postcard back to her two brothers (ours said "her two cousins") so they can see how far she flew.

What followed was nothing short of amazing. Brenda received about 70 post cards back and we got another 10 or so. Most were just the cards saying something to the effect of "We are not sure what happed to Sabrina but we wish you well," or "We are praying for you."

A few took the time and wrote some beautiful notes which I will share with you below. Most of them shared directions to their home in case Brenda wanted to visit, some had numbers and names; I will leave out that information to protect the privacy of these very special people

"Hello,
Our son Chris (18) found your card and balloons (which were all popped) while they were out in the cornfield picking up some of last fall's broken down corn. They found it in the woods by our creek, for they'd ridden down on horseback before hitching the horses to the wagon. We are an Amish family on a farm and also have a sawmill. We have 11 children, 8 boys and 3 girls ranging from 21 to 1 ½. If you ever come to the —area hunt us up. We are off Route –. We would like to know the story of Sabrina and what happened to her. We express our sympathy."

Another one read:
May the God of all comfort be near you in this time of grief. As you look to Him, He can heal the bleeding hearts. Sunday evening some of our family and visiting friends were taking a walk in our big woods. While back there they found a balloon with this postcard attached. Even though we don't know you we have been thinking of you and praying for you since we found the postcard. God commands in the Bible to "Weep with them that weep" in Romans 12:15. So we will keep thinking of you and if we never meet on earth may we each strive to meet Sabrina in heaven.
With love and prayers.

A gentleman sent this wonderful note I copied below.
Hello,
My name is John --- and I live in ---, Maryland. Today, April 22nd my friend Marilyn and I were canoeing in a small river that flows through the marshes and empties into Jug Bay on the Patuxent River. It was about 2:30 in the afternoon when Marilyn saw something falling from the sky. It landed in the river and we retrieved it.

It was your postcard. I have always loved the marshes. They are full of life and beauty. The cycle of life is very strong among the rushes and reeds, the birds and dragon, and damselflies, the fish and turtles, the otter and muskrat. To quietly sit in a canoe in the spring in a marsh is to experience the birth and continuation of life at its fullest.
When I read your postcard I thought that it was appropriate that it would land in the shallows of a marsh, the boundary between land and water where life is created and nurtured. I hope that your postcard project brings you happiness and satisfaction. The card was beautifully written and a beautiful tribute to your daughter.
In Peace,
John —

This next one is short and sweet.
Just a little note letting you know that we found the balloon @ Taylor's Island white fishing for rock.
Thanks for letting us be a part or your lives.
May hope, guidance and love always lead you in the right direction.

This particular letter just blew me away.

Dear Family,
My husband found this in (I won't say exactly where they said, let's just say a very rough part of Washington DC).
Sabrina flew into this area to bring hope where there is hopelessness and beauty where there is pain and brokenness. She flew into an area of violence and abuse.
I pray that you will continue to carry her in your heart and you deal with what seems like a senseless act, a life taken before time. I thank God for the lives that your family will touch in the future because you have touched both sorrow and joy, grief and happiness, anger and peace. Thank you for sharing Sabrina with my family. I will remember her smile always.

And this final note sums it up completely.
I wanted to write you a short follow up letter after mailing Sabrina's postcard back from — Maryland where I found her on April 28 while wild turkey hunting deep in the forests of Charles County Maryland.
It seems miraculous to me that she was on my route out of the woods as if looking up at me. I feel she did land in heaven… as I feel the solitude of the forests are heaven to me. The card (poem) was beautiful and truly touched me and all I shared it with. I truly believe I was "touched" by and Angel.
My Sincere Condolences.

So I conclude this portion of Sabrina's life by saying after being part of a spirit filled, emotionally charged, Godly ceremony at Sabrina's funeral, seeing all the people she touched, how my two boys went from questioning God on many levels to truly feeling Gods presence, reading letters from total strangers and knowing lives were changed with more people going from non-believers to beginning a journey with God, I know my little niece did not die in vain. My challenge is can I have the same effect on that many people? I've started by writing this book, what will you do?

Yes my life, like yours, has had some ups and downs but that's live. What I realized from losing loved ones, you never stop missing them, over time the sadness of loss goes away and the memories are of the good times.

I end this long journey letting you know it's there for all of us, young, old, male, female, black white, green or blue, God has open arms for you. Yes, I have a LONG way to go before I consider myself to be a good Christian, if you rank it from a 1 to 10 with 10 being the highest, I would say I'm about a 3 so I ask you to start your journey with me, one step at a time. The good news is if God can forgive a street kid from New Jersey for all my sins, and they are plentiful, He can forgive you, He loves you and is waiting for you to call on Him, it's never too late.

My prayer is this book in some small way can help in making this world a better place by turning more people toward God. I want to live in a society that is determined to help one another. I, like many, struggle with the "love thy neighbor" challenge the Bible puts before us.

Someone shared a great little story about helping others and I want to share it with you.
A mouse looked through the crack in the wall to see the farmer and his wife open a package. The mouse wondered, "What food might this contain?" He was devastated to discover it was a mousetrap. Retreating to the farmyard, the mouse proclaimed the warning: "There is a mousetrap in the house, there is a mousetrap in the house". The chicken clucked and scratched, raised her head and said, "Mr. Mouse, I can tell this is a grave concern to you, but it is of no consequence to me. I cannot be bothered by it."
The mouse turned to the pig and told him, "There is a mousetrap in the house, there is a mousetrap in the house." The pig sympathized, but said, "I am very sorry, Mr. Mouse but there is nothing I can do about it but pray. Be as you are in my prayers."
The mouse turned to the cow and repeated the same statements. The cow said, "Wow, Mr. Mouse. I'm sorry, but it's no skin off my nose."
So the mouse returned to the house, head down and dejected, to face the farmer's mousetrap....alone.

That very night a sound was heard throughout the house, like the sound of a mousetrap catching its prey. The farmer's wife rushed to see what was caught. In the darkness, she did not see it was a venomous snake whose tail the trap had caught.

The snake bit the farmer's wife, the farmer rushed her to the hospital, and she returned home with a fever. Everyone knows you treat a fever with fresh chicken soup, so the farmer took his hatchet to the farmyard for the soup's main ingredient. But his wife's sickness continued, so friends and neighbors came to sit with her around the clock. To feed them, the farmer butchered the pig.

The farmer's wife did not get well and she died. So many people came for her funeral the farmer had the cow slaughtered to provide enough meat for all of them. The mouse looked upon it all from his crack in the wall with great sadness.

So the next time you hear someone is facing a problem and you think it doesn't concern you, remember when one of us is threatened we are all at risk. We are all involved in this journey called life. We must keep an eye out for one another and make an extra effort to encourage one another. Each of us is a vital thread in another person's tapestry; our lives are woven together for a reason. One of the best things to hold onto in this world is a FRIEND!!

So please join me on my long journey of faith, if my prayers are answered more people will be living, laughing, smiling and becoming one with God, then when this life runs out we can all be like my beautiful niece Sabrina in heaven, "Knitting with Daisy"!

God Bless and Amen.

The End

8993766R0

Made in the USA
Charleston, SC
02 August 2011